Thomas Binney

Lights and Shadows of Church-Life in Australia

Including Thoughts on some Things at Home...

Thomas Binney

Lights and Shadows of Church-Life in Australia
Including Thoughts on some Things at Home...

ISBN/EAN: 9783337162504

Printed in Europe, USA, Canada, Australia, Japan

Cover: Foto ©Lupo / pixelio.de

More available books at **www.hansebooks.com**

LIGHTS AND SHADOWS

OF

Church-Life in Australia:

INCLUDING

THOUGHTS ON SOME THINGS AT HOME.

BY T. BINNEY.

TO WHICH IS ADDED,

TWO HUNDRED YEARS AGO:

THEN AND NOW.

SECOND EDITION.

London:

JACKSON & WALFORD, 18, ST. PAUL'S CHURCHYARD.

MDCCCLX.

CONTENTS.

Preliminary Chapter.

NOTES.

ON THE UNION OF PROTESTANT EVANGELICAL CHURCHES.

ADDITIONAL.

TWO HUNDRED YEARS AGO!

THEN AND NOW.

POSTSCRIPT TO THE SECOND EDITION.

LIGHTS AND SHADOWS

OF

CHURCH-LIFE IN AUSTRALIA.

Preliminary Chapter.

I. The Break-down—The Voyage—Inter-colonial travel—Materials for a book on Australia—Never intended—" Stop." II. A word to the Reader—Accidental authorship—Adelaide—Tasmania— The " Charge"—Perplexing questions. III. Special Services— Co-operative action—Theatres—The Bishop of Melbourne— Sunday morning on board a Ship—Present movements—What may come of them—An earnest Laity—The two Pictures—Convocation and the House of Lords. IV. Liturgical revision— Religious nonconformity—Historical—Relative—Clerical subscription—Going to Church—The beam and the mote. V. Church publications—Taylor and Gell—Dr. Robinson's scheme—Not much hope—Why so Warlike?—" A more excellent way." VI. Conclusion.

I.

In the spring of 1857, when out on a journey, preaching and lecturing in different places, I was suddenly prostrated, as by a blow;—utterly deprived of power to think or write, to contemplate or to undertake any public service. It was as if a bolt had been withdrawn, or a wheel broken, in some whirling piece of machinery, and the entire apparatus had at once come to a dead stop! After trying in vain home and continental travel, a long voyage was recommended; circumstances and interests connected with Australia led to the determination to proceed thither.

We left Liverpool on Christmas Eve, 1857, and arrived at Melbourne on the 31st of March, 1858. We never saw land of any sort, island or continent, from the time we lost sight of the English coast till we neared Australia; nor had we any great changes of wind or weather. A voyage of three months, without a break, is usually a somewhat monotonous affair. I amused myself by keeping a journal. By making a daily entry of any occurrence, no matter how minute, which caused a ripple on the surface of our ocean-life, a manuscript volume, I may say, was produced, which, on its being looked through as a whole, I was surprised to observe was really by no means devoid of variety of incident. If, after getting on shore, I had continued to keep such a daily record of what I saw, heard, and thought, I might have been able to listen to one or other of the London or Edinburgh booksellers, who have expressed their wish to negotiate with me for any work on Australia I might be intending to publish.

Melbourne was the centre to which I returned, again and again, from the other colonies; but Sydney was the place where I remained the longest, and where, after a time, I was first conscious of improved health, and felt the return of ability for labour. I saw something of the four colonies—now five;—New South Wales, Victoria, South Australia, Tasmania, Queensland. In New South

Wales I went up to the north as far as Brisbane and Ipswich. The people were then [June 1858] full of the idea of becoming independent. The question of "separation" was constantly coming up, as was that, also, of what town ought to be the capital of the new colony. We went southwards in New South Wales only as far as Camden. On the east coast we enjoyed a visit to the beautiful localities of Woolingong and Kiama. In Victoria there was Melbourne, with its surrounding suburbs, Collingwood, Richmond, South Yarra, Prahran, and three or four others, each in itself a considerable town; Geelong, a city noteworthy for many things; the diggings of Castlemaine, Forest Creek, Bendigo, Ballarat, all of which we explored. In South Australia, settling in the neighbourhood of Adelaide, we took journeys, more or less extended, in almost every direction:—to the north, by Gawler to Angaston and Kapunda; south, to Port Elliott—the one-half of the way through valleys and over hills singularly beautiful, the other through sand and bush, wild but interesting; east, across the Murray—the finest river in Australia, and to the Lakes Alexandrina and Albert. In Tasmania, we visited Launceston and Hobart Town, passing through the places on the splendid road between them, crossing, by the bye, *the Jordan*, twice or thrice, and catching a sight of *Jericho, Jerusalem*, and *Bagdad!* From Hobart (as it is often familiarly called) I took a trip up the Huon river as far as Franklin. It was in July, the Tasmanian winter; magnificent hills, or rather mountains, rose on all sides, their tops white with snow. Franklin, it may be observed, is a settlement which takes its name from the distinguished navigator (once the Governor of Tasmania), whose recently ascertained fate has stirred so many hearts with tender regret, and filled them with a mournful satisfaction,—the felt relief which flows from certainty.

If I had thought it my vocation, I dare say I could have written a book about Australia. In the course of my journeys, and during my residence in various places, there was much to observe; much which it would have been a pleasure to describe. Many things occurred highly worthy of record and remembrance; not a few were noticed that might have been discussed with some hope of interesting, perhaps of benefiting, parties on both sides of the world. Like others, I might have written about "People I have met with." I could have noticed the leading men, and have attempted sketches of the Governors of the different colonies! I might have referred to the experiments which our friends are making in political matters,—entering into "the Land Question," and other peculiar Australian problems; it would have been natural to have described, possible to have become eloquent in describing, Sydney harbour, with its innumerable bays and marvellous beauty; Melbourne, with its crowded waters, noble streets, public buildings, and a hundred other things, on all of which one looks with perfect amazement, when reflecting that a very few years ago the site of the city was uncleared bush, and that on the very spot on which now stands some superb erection, in which thousands can congregate for instruction or song, there might have been witnessed a battle or a Corrobory of naked barbarians. Then, the gold fields might have furnished matter for remark ; or the Chinese, and the questions and controversies respecting them ; or a comparison of the colonies,—their special character-istics and common properties ; prospects of literature, colonial authors, the newspaper press ; educational sys-tems ; material resources ; railways ; telegraphs—sur-face and sub-marine ; English habits—how far preserved, lowered, exaggerated, or likely to be modified by foreign admixtures ;—all these, and a thousand-and-one other things, of which I could not be unobservant, and which were constantly coming up in my intercourse with men of different ranks, views, and parties, might have been turned into the topics of a book, which might possibly have breathed its little day,—of which Mr. Mudie might have taken so many copies, and for which the author might have received so many pounds.

But I never for a moment entertained the thought. I left England with no expectation of accomplishing any-thing. I might possibly attempt to minister, to some limited extent, among the Churches of my own denomi-nation—beyond that I had no hope ; as to publishing an account of my voyage and visit, with observations on the men and things of Australia, I no more thought of that than of my finding a manuscript among the aborigines, the relic and proof of former civilization,—learning the language,—doing the work into English, and sending it forth to interest the public and employ the reviewers ! *From the applications which have been made to me by publishers,* I am very much afraid that I am expected to produce a book of Australian travel, perhaps of adventure ! and that somewhere disappointment will be the consequence of my not doing so.   I can only say, that never, on one side of the world or the other, have I myself done or said a single thing to encourage any such expectation.   Why should I ?   I could have said nothing, given no information, expressed no opinion, indulged in no comments, uttered no prophecy, but what has been better said, more fully and more accurately given, by others;—persons, whose opinions or strictures —especially on general, commercial, and political matters—from their position, habits, period of residence, and so on, are far more entitled to confidence and consideration than anything I could advance would be. But the simple truth is, a book on Australia was never in my intention.   I had no thought of that in going thither at first; and, when health returned to me there, I still thought of nothing but of using my recovered strength in such work as properly belonged to me,—in preaching as much as I could whencesoever the call came, and in giving in the central cities occasional lectures to young men.   If any one has taken up this book under the unauthorized and gratuitous expectation to which I have referred, hoping for entertainment, or looking for information respecting Australian matters *in general,* I trust that as soon as he gets to this page, he will at once lay it down.   It will not interest him; it was not meant for him.   I regret that he should be disappointed, but for that disappointment I am not to blame. Let him not avenge himself on the innocent.   There is great danger of this; that is, of his being severe and unjust towards this unoffending volume, because it does not happen to be what *he* wished for, but what its author never intended. There is no necessity in such a case for deciding on one of " three courses," or even between *two ;* the obvious and only course is a matter of intuition —" STOP ;" " *don't go on.*"

II.

To those who advance further,—venturing, from interest or curiosity into this second section,—the author has a word or two to say, that a proper understanding may be established between himself and them. It so happened, then, that although I never contemplated writing anything about Australia on my return home, I was yet led, unexpectedly to myself, to write a good deal while there, which, in one form or another, came before the public. My visit, too, still more unexpectedly, called into exercise the pens of others. Out of these two things springs, as by accident, the present volume. In South Australia, all denominations are more completely on a level than in the other colonies, in consequence of *State-aid* having entirely ceased for some years. This religious equality has not been without its influence on the thinkings and sentiments of several in the Episcopal Church ;—on the Bishop himself, some of the clergy, many of the members. Singularly enough—very much to my surprise at first, somewhat afterwards to my annoyance—the cogitations of others found utterance in what connected my name with *two* subjects of public discussion. They were started—the one by the Bishop, the other by laymen. I have reason to know that, in both cases, my presence was merely the occasion of bringing out what had long been revolving in the minds of the respective parties. It called into articulate utterance (and by no intentional or conscious agency on my part) thoughts and feelings which, for some considerable period, had been rising and simmering, and slowly taking definite shape, or trying to do so, in his Lordship on the one hand, and the Laymen on the other.

In respect to both questions, my position was somewhat difficult. The laymen only wanted, they said, the recognition of a *principle ;* but they sought for this *in my person.* It was not easy, so circumstanced, to engage in the discussion of the question; nor was it comfortable to witness its discussion by others. It necessarily provoked allusions and remarks, more or less personal, which unnecessarily encumbered the argument, or conveniently confused it, by obscuring the distinction between a principle and a man. The Bishop's question, on the other hand, though directly proposed to me with a request to examine it, was set forth in a letter so carefully written and of such length, that it could not be treated with becoming respect, or receive adequate attention, without more quiet than my constant removals from place to place allowed me to secure. At length, while enjoying something like rest in Tasmania, the annual meeting of the Congregational Union of the colony occurred; and by the courtesy of the Committee I was invited to preside over it. I availed myself of the occasion to discuss the subject submitted to me by the Bishop of Adelaide. This was the origin of the " Address" which constitutes the substance of the present volume; an Address which the newspapers persisted in calling a

" Charge !" They had, perhaps, some ground for that ; for it not only took two hours in the delivery (a frequent Episcopal requirement of time), but I *sat* while I read it to the members of the Assembly,—the presbyter-bishops and lay delegates of the Churches,—to use high-sounding terms, which may be quite as appropriate when so applied as in some other cases.

The Address was requested to be published, and a promise given that the request should be complied with. A sudden call, however, from Tasmania to Sydney, and many subsequent interruptions and migrations, prevented the immediate fulfilment of the promise. While the work was being thus necessarily intermitted or delayed, things were constantly occurring and coming to my notice—things spoken, written, done,—touching, more or less, myself, my brethren, or the principles and institutions with which we are identified. I was drawn on to advert to matters which all this suggested, (perhaps in some instances provoked,) and thus, in more ways than one, something came to be aimed at in the publication *beyond* the first projected reply to the Bishop of Adelaide. This explanation was given in the preface to the colonial edition of the Address; which preface, after a reference to some other points, concluded thus :—" The movements to which this volume refers may, it is believed, turn out to be *the beginning* of events which will furnish matter for a chapter in the Ecclesiastical History of the Australian colonies. Whenever that chapter is composed, these pages, it is hoped, will contribute something towards its being fully and correctly written." In this way I looked upon the book as published in Australia;—a spade-full of rubble thrown in among the first rude layers of the Colonial Ecclesiastical structure, which might not be without its use. This, not so much from anything it contained of mine, as from its being a memorial of the facts on which it was based, and a repository of letters and documents to which they had given rise, and which were included in it under the title of "The Adelaide Correspondence."

But why re-publish such a book in England? Especially why, when it will only disappoint, perhaps vex and annoy, those who are looking for something else; many of whom are not interested in the topics discussed; or who are tired of them; or who will not be bored with what, in their opinion, can only seem important when viewed through the peculiar medium of "the clerical mind," or as exaggerated by the action of sectarian prejudice? I have put these questions to myself once and again, and have as often thought only of the obvious practical answer—*doing nothing*. For many weeks past nothing *has* been done, from this and other obstructing causes. Nevertheless, I have at length decided to send forth a home-edition of the work. Many considerations, spontaneous or suggested, have led to this. The reader does not wish to be troubled with these;—the fact in which they have terminated is, of course, sufficient for him. I have strong reasons, however, for wishing to refer to *two* of the considerations which have weighed with me in deciding as I have done. The exposition of these will not be a mere matter of personal interest,—of defence or apology,—but will consist of something far more important, involving allusions to facts and occurrences of some moment in themselves, and which will not probably be without results.

III.

The first consideration arises from the singular forms of religious action which have been going on during the last two years, and which, within the last three months, have rapidly developed into something still more remarkable. Just as I was leaving for Australia, one of the Metropolitan Cathedrals was about to be opened for evening service. Preaching to the masses went on at an increasing ratio, till there has come to be the extraordinary forms which it has now taken,—not only in the fact of the use of Theatres for the purpose, but in that of the Episcopal clergy uniting with the ministers of other bodies in instruction and worship. In addition to this, both in the Metropolis and in other places, special services of various kinds have been extensively multiplied, in which clergymen have often been prominent;— services for prayer, addresses, communion, sometimes on neutral, sometimes on denominational, ground. The result of this has been, if not the springing up of a large-hearted catholic sentiment, at least the practical oblivion of sectional differences. Now, without, of course, knowing that any such thing was about to occur, I referred, in the following Address, to the opinion which, in common with many Dissenters, I had long held, that far more might be expected from something of this sort,—men and ministers being brought together in friendly and co-operative religious action,—than from anything else. Better this, than either an attempt to bring others to " join with *us* " on certain defined " indispensable conditions," or to argue, from a distance, on their deficiencies or faults. Something, of course, must be wrong somewhere, as the root of the religious divisions which distract the Church. No wise or candid man can think that the sin is all on one side. I have intimated my belief that much is not to be expected from parties merely attempting to prove each other in the wrong, but that perhaps something might come, of change and benefit to all, if there was more of united action in Church-life. Love and sympathy, practically manifested, might do more to open the eye to perceive, to dispose the tongue to acknowledge, and the hand to rectify, denominational evils, than any controversial logic, however demonstrative. We cannot preach in one another's pulpits ; well,—be it so ; in one aspect of the matter this is a singular and startling fact. Singular, as the Bishop of Adelaide puts it, " that a mid-wall of par- tition should so have separated kindred souls ; pledged to the same cause, rejoicing in the same hope, and devoted to the same duty of preaching Christ and Him crucified to a dark and fallen world." But whatever may be our respective idealisms, it so happens that we are all living among very imperfect and rude realities ; old, hard, complicated systems, intolerant of innovation, which cannot easily be touched or handled, and which must be accepted and worked with all their conditions. If, however, we cannot do one thing, we may do another. If there are forms of religious recognition and action, by which the representatives of different Churches can come before the world,—a world which, while understanding nothing of their ecclesiastical niceties, *needs to be saved,* and may be won to wisdom by the very sight of men who differ among themselves uniting in their solicitude to serve and bless it,—let us hope that this will be beneficial to both parties. To those without, who are to be acted *upon;* and to those within, —the different sections of the visible Church,—whose members and ministers are agents in the work, and who " strive together" with cordial sympathy and mutual good-will.

Some of our friends are not at liberty to go into any place of worship different from those of their own communion; to take part there in religious services; to appear to unite with the Society, or Church, assembling in it, as such, though they may feel no difficulty in devotional engagements with the ministers and members of various bodies, as individual Christians, and on some neutral platform. On all hands the question seems to be,—how to express brotherly love, and to manifest spiritual union in Christ, without appearing to countenance or sanction the supposed defects of one or other ecclesiastical *system?* There are those who think that they can interchange pulpits without meaning more by that act than to express their oneness in respect to the central truth or truths whence emanates " the common salvation." But if this cannot be done in Church or Chapel, it may be well to do it in Music Halls, or Theatres, or anywhere else. My friend, the Bishop of Melbourne, when applied to on the subject, withheld his sanction from clergymen attending special religious services, or social meetings in Non-episcopal places of worship; their uniting with the ministers and congregations of other bodies, as such. But when he and I were passengers together from Sydney to Melbourne, his lordship himself proposed, on the Sunday morning when a service was to be held, that he should read prayers, and that I should preach. I would much rather have listened to him; but I gave in. After his lordship had gone through the English service, I took his place, and addressed the congregation. After I had offered, at the close of the sermon, a short prayer, the Bishop pronounced the benediction. This need not have been,—but I preferred it, and paused on purpose that it might be, deeming it becoming as an act, if I may so speak, of ministerial courtesy. But a service like this could not have taken place on shore;—in an Episcopal Church, or a Congregational;—or with the congregation of either, as such,—or with both united. But in the cabin of a ship, and with a promiscuous collection of individuals, it did not involve what it would have seemed to do in an ecclesiastical edifice, with its customary attendants. Since I left Australia, I observe that special religious services have been held in different places, over one of which the Bishop of Melbourne presided. It was held in the Athenæum, or Mechanics' Institute, at Geelong, and was conducted by ministers of different denominations.

Any thing that leads to united religious action,—to co-operative effort,—aggressive, missionary, or whatever form it may take,—any thing that leads to this, among men who, while adhering to different forms of Church organization, are one in faith, must be good. The present extraordinary movement may not do much, or not at first, or not all that its originators anticipate; and care may even be taken by some engaged in it that it shall not appear to *say* too much. Still, something may be expected to come out of it in the way of re-action, as well as of direct result. Preaching in Theatres, *special* services, denominational or united, cannot be expected to become fixed and permanent. From the very nature of the case, the extraordinary is exceptional, and must give way to or grow into something else. Popular preachers addressing the masses will cease to be a novelty; the movement may probably lose its power when it has lost its freshness; it will need to be intermitted, and may then be resumed again with new vigour; and thus it may perhaps take something of the form of the great preaching seasons in the Romish Church. In the mean time, it may be casting light on the problem which has never been met by either Church or Chapel, the Establishment or the Sects, namely, the *accommodation* of the masses in places of worship. That the Churches, as buildings, belong to the poor, is as much a myth, as their flowing into and taking possession of the pews of the Conventicle would be a practical difficulty. When either Churches or Meeting-houses have offered sermons to working men, they have been specially set apart for them at particular times. If all the Non-church-going population, respecting the classes and numbers of which we often hear such startling statistics, was to rise *en masse* and pour like an inundation into all the places of metropolitan worship, it would very much embarrass many a respectable congregation, and perhaps rather annoy a fashionable audience. The idea of a number of persons meeting together, sitting in something like private boxes, listening Sunday after Sunday to the same individual, who for years and years, with little variation, goes through the customary service,—this is not, I should think, very much like what a Christian assembly was in apostolic times! It may be all very proper and right as things are, and according to modern notions and habits. But it is no matter for lamentation if, now and then, something occurs to break in upon our stereotyped traditions and pharisaic respectabilities. It is well when unwonted audiences can be collected together, assembled under exciting circumstances, and spoken to without conventional formalities. If in Cathedral,—Church,—Chapel, well; if not,—*anywhere*. The present singular spectacle of turning Theatres to account, looks at first very startling; almost as if it betrayed that the cause of religion was becoming desperate. I confess I shrank from the idea myself, when it was first mooted,—shrank, with a sort of instinctive recoil, the revulsion of the sense of professional decorum! The same thing was felt by many; but the palpable and manifest success of the measure,—success in the highest and best sense,—has greatly modified or altogether removed this. Of course, the procedure in question is not itself an end; but it may be used as something towards higher results and ultimate objects. It is a sort of sudden development of the missionary character of the Church,—its actual and designed relation to the world. It will give freedom, boldness, glow, power, to its speech and action. While it

will operate spiritually in many ways, leading to simpler
and more forcible forms of preaching the Gospel, properly
speaking; promoting the conversion of the rude and
godless, " delivering them from the power of darkness
and translating them into the kingdom of God's dear Son;"
it may operate ecclesiastically so as to help to the
solution of vexed questions, or to break up traditionary
abuses. Men, saved by their being gathered together
where there is the free proclamation of the truth, may
be changed from being the gratuitous recipients of the
Gospel to being its eager and willing supporters; and
instead of refusing to go into a Church because of its
supposed expense or exactions, may esteem it their
privilege to have a place there, and to help to sustain
it for themselves and others. Settled congregations
may receive benefit; ministers and people may get
new views of their respective duties. On the one hand,
there may be the ready abandonment, for frequent or
occasional special service, of what many would seem
to think it their right to monopolise; and, on the other,
a more efficient fulfilment of " the work of the ministry,"
by the energetic " doing of that of the Evangelist."
Different denominations, engaged together in the same
high service, because, with all their diversities of order,
they stand together round what is central and therefore
catholic truth, will learn, in the discharge of such combined
action, better than in making complimentary speeches at
public meetings, the true meaning of Church, Churches,
Ministry, Sacraments, " One Lord," " One baptism,"
" Diversities of Administration," "The same Spirit," and a
hundred other things, which, *in time*, will operate bene-

ficially on all sides.   Having long entertained such
thoughts, and having been led to give utterance to some of
them in the following Address, I am willing to hope that,
though the circle to which its interest must necessarily
be confined here will be very limited, its publication
may not be altogether inopportune or useless.   As the
new movements to which I have referred, originated
with, and have principally been sustained by, earnest
laymen,—as high ecclesiastics have looked on, neither
blessing nor cursing, approving or disapproving, willing
to let things take their course since they have begun
to move, but acknowledging that they must have
forbidden action had they been consulted,—I shall be
pardoned, I hope, if, on this account, I yield to the
temptation of troubling the reader with the following
extract.   It is taken from a paper which I had occasion
to publish in Adelaide, but which it did not appear
necessary to include in the present volume.

" The probability is, that any general agreement
among Christians, any new order of things, will spring
out of our acting together as far as we can, and not
from the discussions of ecclesiastics.   The inward life of
the Church itself, the spiritual longings of the flock
of Christ, may become so strong, active, and irresistible,
that, without breaking down the form of the folds peculiar
to particular portions of the whole, they shall yet one
day so overpass them as to reach and realise, through an
accomplished fact, what never would have been secured
by ecclesiastical negotiations.   As women, by a quick
unreasoning instinct, often arrive at the best and wisest
practical decisions, while men are thinking and hesitating

on the subject, and getting more and more hopelessly perplexed, so a religious, zealous, and active laity will often be found ready for an advance, and will be prepared to settle some knotty question by positive acts, before the clerical mind can see its way. We divines, especially in relation to ecclesiastical matters, are apt to forge strong iron bolts with which to bar our doors against each other; the laity have not skill to draw these bolts, and we dare not or will not; but every now and then a time comes when the force of the confined and crowded mass presses against the limits which enclose it—the doors suddenly open—the bolts are broken or fly off, being found, after all, to have no better fastening than tin-tacks. Thus will it be, most likely, with practical measures of Christian co-operation between different Churches. Instead of everything being settled and arranged first, by our all agreeing in certain specified ecclesiastical traditions, something will be done —somebody will act—arguments will afterwards be found to justify it; and then out of this may emerge at length " the Church of the Future."

The correctness of what I have been saying, and of what was said before in the above extract, has, while I write, been illustrated by facts singularly significant. I refer to two pictures—worthy of being painted and preserved—which have recently been placed before the wondering eyes of the English people. On the one hand, the scene in Convocation, where the clergy met to talk, and to do *nothing;* where they protested against the slightest symptom of progress,—proclaimed that no step could be taken for fifty years to come,—would not recognize the propriety of altering, in the least, old forms,—and professed their utter inability to make a new prayer! On the other, the scene in the House of Lords, when Lord Dungannon introduced his motion against preaching in Theatres,—where the sole manifestation of thorough earnestness appeared in Lord Shaftesbury, as the representative of the active *Laity* of the Church. I try all I can not to use strong language, but it is difficult to avoid it when looking on the contrast between words and work,—sham and reality,—fettered traditionalism and free zeal,—muttering shadows, the ghosts of the past, and living men of flesh and blood, with arms and hands to do something!

IV.

The second consideration which has induced me to consent to the present issue of this book, arises from the advance which seems to have been made, during the last two years, in the matter of Liturgical Revision. On this subject I have always felt a deep interest, not only although I am a Dissenter, but *because* I am one. The question necessarily came before me in the following Address. One or two of the things referred to in connexion with it will be new to some. I shall be glad if any thing I have said comes to be of service. My reasons for being interested in the subject are manifold; —two or three of them I should like to mention. They are such as these:—

In the first place; because the religious grounds of Nonconformity to the Church of the Prayer-Book are, as I think, far more intelligible and convincing to the common mind, and, perhaps I might say, far more serious in themselves, than the grounds, theoretic or practical, of Dissent properly so called; that is, Dissent regarded simply as a protest against an *Establishment*, irrespective of the tenets of the Church established,—although these are by no means inconsiderable, especially in an advanced state of society, and in a nation like our own, in which liberty of thought and action is secured.

Secondly; because of the effects of the exacted subscription of the Church of England on personal character, private feeling, and public morality. I go by what I have read of the acknowledgments of clergymen, by what I have seen and heard in my intercourse with the world, and by the very nature of the case.

Thirdly; because, whatever may be the right or wrong in theories of Church Government and systems of doctrine;—however we may profess to take our stand on Scripture itself, as if we were living on an island, and the Book had dropped down upon us from the clouds, and we had to do the best we could with it for ourselves;—however this may be, the fact is, that the *historical* position of Nonconformity is *a relative one.* It is that of protest against the system which caused and created it. It has a message, therefore, to deliver, a mission to fulfil, in respect to those whose former conduct compelled it to part company with them; who, by what they then retained, adopted, or enforced, in spite of representation, remonstrance, and appeal, occasioned the disruption. Cast out,—reluctantly departing,—obliged by conscience to submit to be reduced to so many separate units, our fathers had to do the best they could to recover anything like a corporate existence. If we have found reasons for preferring the form which their societies assumed, and being satisfied with it, that does not forbid (perhaps it demands) that we should utter our protest against those things from which they fled, and which, being still retained, are not without a palpable relation to ourselves. We have not only a right to complain of what wronged us; it is our privilege to seek the improvement of an institution which, with all its imperfections, has mighty capabilities for good;—an institution, whose moral power would be incalculably enhanced, if, listening to entreaty within and accusation without, it put away what cripples and defiles it;—a result this, which Nonconformity ought to rejoice in as the attainment of one of the ends for which it lives and speaks, whether or not it led to the termination of a long and originally an enforced estrangement.

Fourthly, and as the other side of this same thought; because, in England, and as an Englishman, I regard the Church as a national institution. In the colonies, the Episcopal community is one denomination among many —I heard a Catholic priest, in a large assembly at Melbourne, employ the term in speaking of his own Church—but in England it professes to be national, to belong to and to exist for the nation at large. It does so. We endow it with property and give it the use of edifices which belong to us;—property and buildings in which we cannot cease to retain an interest; for the proper employment of which we hold the Church to be responsible, and to be liable, therefore, to be called to account. Many of the clergy complain that, in their opinion, the Church, from its need of and its resistance to improvement, either operates injuriously to a large extent on spiritual religion, or is not so beneficial as it ought to be, and might be. It is not for us (the people) to suffer such a state of things to continue. It is our duty to prevent this,—to exercise our undoubted constitutional privilege of advancing the interests of the community, serving our own generation and the generations that are to come, by seeking to render a great power in the midst of us—which belongs to us, which is ours, and ours to influence and affect—efficient for good rather than evil. As an Englishman, I claim it as my privilege to interfere with everything that is national, and therefore with the Church. And in respect to *it*,—not merely to touch, alter, modify its external and money-relations to the State, but, by all fair and legitimate means, to seek to influence it as a religious institution,—to promote reformation, revision, improvement, or any thing else, by which it may more fully discharge that spiritual service which, so long as it professes to be national, *the nation* is not only justified in expecting, but in seeing that it is rendered, and rendered in the best possible form.*

Fifthly; because, in consequence of the known terms of subscription, and the popularly-understood meaning of the Prayer-Book, there springs up between the clergy and the laity a state of things injurious to both. This is touched upon in the following Address, and is illustrated by a fact, just brought to light, which

* Note A, at the end of the Chapter.

will surprise some, and which, in itself, is singularly suggestive. I may here add, that the state of things to which I allude—the disbelief in the pew of what has been solemnly accepted by the pulpit, and has on certain occasions to be vocally declared—especially affects many Dissenters who, from various causes, become attendants on Anglican worship. I do not speak of those who practically conform from low motives; who take up with the Church in the hope that the world will take up *them;* who become ashamed of the Conventicle when they rise in circumstances, and leave it for the sake of the countenance of society or the opinion of a neighbourhood. Such people are neither loss nor gain to any Church. I refer, rather, to thoughtful, intelligent, good men;—Nonconformists, who fully understand the religious grounds and reasons of Nonconformity, and who personally believe that the Offices of the Church are designedly built upon, and consecutively evolve, serious error. I am perfectly aware of the many inducements which may lead such men to give up practical Dissent; to prefer going quietly to Church, and sitting down in the enjoyment of what they find there. They may like the ordinary public service, in which there is little to offend; comparatively unobserved, without remark, they can obey or not, as they feel disposed at the time, their inward impulses in respect to communion; they can be religious without saying, or appearing to say, any thing about it; they make less profession; have more freedom; and are less in danger, or think they are, of mistaking sectional reputation for ascertained safety, and of putting the feeling called forth by denominational interests in the place of a wide and comprehensive catholic sentiment. I can understand all that. Nevertheless, with the known views and serious convictions of the men referred to, it is a question whether what they do, considered in its *influence*, is not a great price to pay for what they avoid or what they enjoy. By regular, acquiescent, *silent* conformity, they give their support to the whole of a system,—a system which, *they* think, tempts numbers to say what makes their public position intolerable and false. They perpetuate this. They help to rivet on the necks of many a heavy burden which they should rather endeavour to lessen or remove. In these remarks I am neither calling men from the Church, nor back to Dissent. I am only illustrating the duty, which is that of Churchman and Dissenter alike, of a man's not " condemning himself in the thing which he alloweth." The hope of seeing less of this, in particular directions, is a reason with me for being interested in the progress of liturgical reform.*

Lastly; I am interested in the subject, because the evil combated is only a part, in my opinion, of a general one,—one which, more or less, is to be met with everywhere. The agitation of it, and reference to it, therefore, where it is most patent, and is continually obtruding itself on public attention, may, it is hoped, *re-act* on other spheres and other communities where it is less obvious but as real. With all their professions, and in spite of their repudiation of human authority, there are modes of virtual subscription among the sects, and of legally uniting income and office to

* Note B, at the end of the Chapter.

questionable opinions, which are not without results on the mental uprightness, the freedom, happiness, and self-respect of Nonconformists themselves. In some other bodies, the demand on the young candidate for the ministry of solemn signature and expressed adherence to all and every thing in a volume or volumes of Church standards, is enough to burden both mind and heart,—ever after to repress thought or to make it a torment. I do not say there should be no ministerial confession of faith, or acceptance of order and ceremony, on taking office in a Church; but I do say, that every thing should be as general as possible to avoid its becoming a snare, and that men should rather look to spiritual life than to mechanical appliances. I should like to see, *on all sides*, more simplicity, less exaction. Many can see the mote in their brother's eye, and taunt him with it, who need to be told that " a beam is in their own." Or, we may reverse the case, and, for the sake of argument, assume *that* to be the right way of putting it. My point would then stand thus:—the sacramental and sacerdotal elements in the Offices of the Church, are, to some people, as obvious and offensive as a beam in the eye in the sense of " rafter!" It is well, therefore, to keep their attention awake to such an enormity, since that, by a reflex action, may benefit themselves. In some thoughtful hour, they may be led to the discovery of what they little suspect,—they may find out that a mote is unconsciously interfering with their own vision! and that, too, with disastrous effect— as any small object *close to the eye* will darken the earth and hide the sun.

V.

Such are some of the thoughts which have overcome my repugnance to publish here what necessity compelled me to write when abroad,—to write, after I had hoped that I was done for ever with ecclesiastical questions. Not that I deem such matters insignificant; quite the contrary; only one gets tired of "doubtful disputations," especially when we can be silent without sin, and may leave speech and writing to younger men. I may have mistaken my own motives in past times, but so far as I know them, I never put pen to paper in the way of controversy, but with the hope and desire of promoting ultimately unity and love, through the establishment or discovery of the right and true. Since I came home, several publications have been sent to me by their respective authors, or by unknown friends, bearing upon the questions which are handled in this work. These publications show that CHURCH UNION, LITURGICAL REVISION, HISTORICAL NONCONFORMITY, and kindred subjects, are occupying the minds and moving the pens of clergymen in a way worthy of note. It seemed, therefore, not inappropriate to show how the state of things on this side of the world gets transferred to, and reproduced in the other. I see no help for it; because I see no prospect of Presbyterians, Wesleyans, Independents, and other Non-episcopal bodies, becoming convinced that they are all schismatics, acknowledging their sin, giving up their practical freedom of action, and submitting themselves to the control of the English Bishops. This is what is required, both in England

and Australia, as necessary to Christian union. It may be very proper; but it is not a likely thing in itself, nor likely to be of speedy attainment. Our friends, however, begin with that demand; and it becomes necessary to state to them the difficulties in the way of its being complied with.

Among the pamphlets which have been recently published, there are two which I think specially remarkable. The one is entitled, "THE LITURGY AND THE DISSENTERS." By the Rev. Isaac Taylor, M.A. The other, "THOUGHTS ON THE LITURGY. *The difficulties of an honest and conscientious use of the Book of Common Prayer considered, as a loud and reasonable call for the only remedy,* REVISION." By the Rev. Philip Gell, M.A. Some of the points on which, in self-defence, I had to insist in Australia, are handled in these two works with a fulness and power which far exceeds any thing we Dissenters have ever said for ourselves. In the first, Mr. Taylor shows, by historical facts, what a repelling and schismatical spirit animated the Church in 1661-2; how it not only resisted every approach to conciliation in revising the Prayer-Book, but designedly increased and multiplied difficulties by the introduction of new and objectionable matter; how it culminated at last in the Act of Uniformity, and inevitably, and of purpose, compelled the secession of the ejected ministers. In the second, Mr. Gell enters into the consideration of those expressions and statements in the Offices of the Church, which, in their natural and obvious sense, constitute the ground of our enforced " dichostasy;" which sense he demonstrates to be that in which alone they can ,be understood.   This he does, in opposition to all attempts, by charitable hope theories, hypothetical senses, understood conditions, to make them mean what they do *not* say.   As some of my readers will attach more importance to what comes from within the Church itself, than to what is said by us that are without, I shall give, at the end of this volume, a few extracts from these two pamphlets.   As the second centenary of 1661–2 is close at hand, when it will not be improper for Dissenters to commemorate what their fathers did, and to explain to their children *why* they did it, the proposed extracts may be of use to some in directing or stimulating inquiry. I may possibly also connect with them a glance at one or two illustrative Australian facts.

To the appearance, in England, sometime last year, of portions of " The Adelaide Correspondence," I suppose I am indebted for some of the publications which have recently been sent to me.   Among these may be reckoned one on " Church Questions," by the Rev. C. Robinson, LL.D.   The "questions" discussed are many, but the two in which personally I feel most interest are those on " a revision of the Liturgy," and on the " restoration of Dissenters to the Church."   I cannot afford either time or space for a minute exposition of Dr. Robinson's views.   As, however, he makes " an earnest appeal to all pious Dissenters, to examine deliberately and dispassionately the terms which he proposes for their restoration to the communion of the National Church," it may not be improper to offer one or two brief remarks upon his scheme.   I do not feel that I need attempt more than this, because his terms and conditions so coincide, in many respects, with those suggested by the Bishop of Adelaide, that they are met by anticipation in the following pages. I don't at all pretend that either his views or Dr. Short's are *adequately* met, and by no means so in the sense of being answered; but only that I have explained, as far as I am able, how it appears to me that some in the Non-episcopal bodies will regard them. These men may be right or wrong, moderate or unreasonable,—that is matter of opinion; I can only take the fact and say, that, thinking thus and thus, the probability is, that such and such would be their reply.

As to the question of "revision," Dr. Robinson gives up the form of absolution in the "Visitation of the Sick." He adheres, indeed, to an explanation of it which makes it simply declaratory, not sacerdotal, but he is willing, nevertheless, to let it go. He says, "No alteration, I am sure, would be hailed with greater delight by thousands and tens of thousands of earnest Churchmen than the complete expunging of this objectionable form from our Book of Common Prayer." Looking, however, at his alterations in the Baptismal Service, it may be enough to say, that Dissenters would not; I suspect, regard them as sufficient. I speak more especially for Independents. If I understand their theory, they occupy a middle point between Episcopalians and Baptists. Both these bodies connect baptism with a fact ;—the one uses the rite as the instrument of effecting it, the other as recognizing that it *is* effected. Independents associate the rite with *truth*—a profession of belief in what is exhibited in symbol, with the recognition of consequent relative duty. Dr. Robinson is liberal to the Baptists, telling them that the Church admits of immersion, and, that as she fixes no time for children to be baptized, they might delay the ordinance as long as they pleased. Still, I think both Baptists and Independents would object to his Baptismal Service, and to the words he proposes to insert in the Catechism. He omits the term "regeneration," but he teaches that "*in* baptism we are made members of Christ, children of God, and inheritors of the kingdom of heaven." Now, while one class of Dissenters regards the ordinance as a solemn and significant exhibition of *spiritual truth*, and another regards it, in addition to that, as a profession that the objective has become *subjective*, (to use a modern, or rather revived, dialect,) I doubt whether either would say that *in* baptism *the thing was done*. I am not advocating either the one theory or the other. I merely say that, Independents and Baptists thinking thus, (even though both may be wrong,) I doubt whether they could accept what Dr. Robinson wishes them to receive.

With respect to the union of all other denominations with the Episcopal,—or rather the restoration of the sects to the Church,—I have little to say, Dr. Robinson's views being, as I have intimated, substantially the same as Dr. Short's. Neither of our clerical friends can be satisfied with anything in the shape of union that shall not bring all the existing religious bodies into organic confederation under one recognized ecclesiastical "Rule." Dr. Robinson, indeed, goes so far as to say, that if any Church system, other than his own, can establish a fair claim to become predominant, he would be disposed to say, let it be so; but, as that, he thinks, is quite out of question, the only alternative remains that Episcopacy must be universally accepted. He submits this, therefore, to the Church of Scotland, the Wesleyan Methodists, and other bodies. How far "Moderators" in Scotland, and "Presidents" in England, are likely to agree to be consecrated Bishops, and all the ministers and all the congregations of the two bodies represented by them, to become identified with the English Church, I must leave it for some of themselves to say. It will be enough, so far as I am concerned, to put before the reader a few passages from Dr. Robinson's work, the favourable acceptance of which, by the body of Dissenters to which I belong, appears to me to be at least *doubtful.*

The passages, which thus strike me, are of two kinds; —the one class consists of what Dr. Robinson says *to* Dissenters, as to what he thinks they might do; the other of what he says *of* them, if they won't do it. An example or two of each must suffice. The following belong to the first class :—

"1. Let each denomination prepare a service for themselves out of the Book of Common Prayer, omitting such prayers, canticles, &c., as they object to, and arranging the rest in any order they please; with this exception only, that they alter not a single clause or word in the formularies themselves. This I conceive to be absolutely necessary to prevent unpleasant disputes, and to preserve unity.

"2. When any such service is approved by their own body, then let it be submitted to the Bishops of the Church, that so it may be authoritatively licensed for the use of the particular society in question.

"3. Such services to be used in the Chapels of the society at a different hour from the Church service, except where the Bishop may see fit to sanction otherwise." (P. 43.)

" If a Dissenting minister be willing to place himself and congregation under Episcopal control, but object to re-ordination, the Bishop shall then license him to offer up prayers and preach to that congregation, on condition that he and his people receive the sacraments in the Church, and a pledge be given that, after his death or removal, the Bishop shall ordain a minister to such congregation." (P. 44.)

" If [Non-episcopal] ordinations be only of *doubtful* validity, and *possibly* schismatical, it will be wise in Dissenting ministers to leave the conferring of orders to the Bishops for the future, whilst their renunciation of the office will, in time, absorb Dissent in the unity of the Apostolic Church." . . . . " Without the sacrifice of scarcely a scruple, they would be at once relieved from the odium of schism, and enjoy the inestimable privilege of full communion with the Apostolic Church." (Pp. 45, 47.)

Of the second class, the following may be given :—

" Let us make every allowable concession, and then, if the Dissenters prefer division, and continue in unjustifiable separation from the Church, when she earnestly entreats their return, and is willing to receive them almost on their own terms, upon themselves be the sin of schism, and its inevitable consequences." (P. 38.)

" Of course I contemplate the possibility that, after all, the Dissenters may not be willing to accept the concessions which the Church shall make; that, in spite of every overture, they may prefer open hostility to peaceful communion; whence the question immediately occurs, What then? Shall we establish Defence Societies, and Church-rate Associations, and institutions for protecting the Church from the assaults of her enemies, which some have recommended? Certainly not. I am disposed to say that, if she be not able, in virtue of her inherent powers and Divine authority, to repel with majestic dignity the clamorous agitation of wilful and irreconcileable schismatics, without the lath-and-plaster props of any such temporary expedients, it is time for her to suffer persecution, it is time for her indolent shepherds to be aroused from an inglorious truce with her foes by the trumpet-call to battle, and the sooner the conflict begins the better." (P. 69.)

" Supposing, however, that they [the Dissenters] still refuse to meet us in a conciliatory spirit, and are determined to continue an agitation which is disastrous to the highest interests of the nation, 'then,' as said Napoleon, 'it is a maxim in military art that the army which remains in its entrenchments is beaten.' However painful the duty, there must be no more fraternization with Dissent; we must proclaim from every pulpit the sin of unnecessary divisions, and wage a vigorous and aggressive warfare against sectarianism in all its forms, and make terrible havoc with the strongholds of schism, &c." (P. 72.)

I do not think it necessary to comment upon these extracts; I merely give them as containing matter to which I think Dissenters will object; which is not calculated to meet their views, to alter their convictions, to justify to themselves conformity to the Church, or to conciliate and persuade them to listen to the proposed overtures. Besides, something will be met with in the following pages which will be found to bear on many of the points which are here raised. Dr. Robinson is evidently a zealous, warm-hearted, good man, but I am disposed to think that he is unacquainted with the principles and spirit of religious Dissent,—at least if I conceive of it rightly. For myself, I admire and accede to the views which he expresses, in common with the Bishop of Adelaide, of what should be the comprehensive constitution of the Church; that it might include great variety of association and action, be characterized by a noble breadth, admit of all sorts of societies, lay-preaching, out-of-door services, private meetings for the edification of a few, sober splendour and choral pomp for the impression of the many, if kept in subordination to the exhibition of the Truth; but it is not possible now to make it a condition for this that all must be connected with a universal subjection to one "Rule." It might have been well, if what is called the Church had been loving and wise, and had kept within herself all varieties of action, by allowing free scope to the different manifestations of her own inward life, instead of alienating and driving away whatever overpassed her prescriptions and traditions; but the Church, now, is all God's people in the nation at large (to speak only of our own country), whether united together under one form of discipline or another; and the only way by which it can be felt to be *one*, is by the culture everywhere of a Catholic sentiment, and a readiness among Christians and Christian communities to recognize and rejoice in their mutual brotherhood, and as far as possible to co-operate in action. It is too late for any particular Church to seek to "absorb" all others into itself. Distinct organizations are not necessarily schismatical,—separation in form, if the spirit be right, is not schism. It is beginning at the wrong end to demand of others conformity to *us*, and then, if they should prefer to retain what Christ has blessed to their spiritual sustenance, their solace and their joy, to give them bad names, to deny their brotherhood, to determine to wage with them aggressive warfare, to make terrible havoc upon their strongholds,—perhaps " silencing their ministers " and " breaking up their establishments against their will." Religious Nonconformity has " not so learned Christ." It can recognize His Church under all forms; rejoices in the truth for the truth's sake, wherever it is found in its purity and power; and is ready to fraternize in any way and to any extent with those who hold it, leaving secondary agreements, as to order and rule, to come as a result out of such and so brotherly a beginning. "*As far as ye have attained* walk by the same rule, mind the same thing; and [then] if in anything ye be *differently* minded, God will reveal even that unto you."

VI.

I had once intended to advert to several other things in this chapter, but I have, already, not only made the porch too large for the building, but have placed in it, I fear, some of the furniture of the inner rooms. I shall here close, therefore, these preliminary explanations. In doing so, I must just allow myself two words more.

The first is, to request the reader distinctly to understand, that "Lights and Shadows of Church-Life in Australia," means, not *all* of either, but only *some* of each,— those, which I have occasion to describe. It would be a large book indeed, and might be a deeply suggestive one, which should take up the whole subject, and depict the rise and progress, the condition and action of all the religious bodies in all the colonies, with their excellences and defects, their relations to each other, their prosperity or decline, their degrees of adaption to the state of society, their future prospects, and a hundred other things. I aim at nothing of the sort, and have therefore to request the recollection and application of the rule of the poet—" In every work regard the writer's end."

The second word is, that I cannot present to the English reader what was originated in Australia, without expressing my lively and grateful remembrance of the unlooked-for kindnesses I met with there. No

one was half so surprised as myself by the attention
I received from all classes of the community; from
the different Governors of the several colonies; from
men of all parties of politics and religion; from the
inhabitants of cities and dwellers in the bush! Welcome,
hospitality, outstretched hands and warm hearts met us
everywhere. Green spots live in the memory; forms
and friendships, pleasant to recall, fill the mind with
felicitous recollections. It was good to see crowded
assemblies eagerly listening to the word of life; better
to know that to some souls the message was not without
spiritual results. To the masses of young men who
crowded to lectures especially addressed to them, and
looked and listened with far more than average intelligence, I owe much for their hearty sympathy, and am
willing to hope that some of the seeds, literary or
religious, which I endeavoured to sow, will not be without fruit some future day. For leading men in all
departments,—for those who are the rising hope of the
land,—especially for the ministers of every Church, I
offer my constant supplications to God. With the glow
and earnestness of an undying interest in a country
whose very infancy has about it the prophetic intimations
of future greatness, I utter the wish of its favourite motto
—" ADVANCE AUSTRALIA !"

NOTES.

A.

An unexpected blank space offers room here for a note or two. The following observations of my friend Dr. S——, may interest some. Taking up, in my study, the proof of p. xxxi., and reading it, he sat for some time afterwards looking at the fire, and then said :—

"The ground you take justifies, in my view, agitation on a subject, which it was not, perhaps, within your province to notice, but which is at present occupying public attention;—I mean Church-rates. The strong, obvious, and felt objection to Church-rates is a *religious* one ; the injustice of men being compelled to contribute to the current expenses of the worship of a Church from which they conscientiously dissent,—they themselves providing, in every respect, for the support of their own forms, and even giving largely to many benevolent agencies for promoting the spiritual good of the masses at home, and of the world at large. The *right* of the aggrieved to seek, through Parliament, such a change in the relations of the Episcopal Church to the State as shall relieve them from the felt injustice, is *constitutional.*

"But it may be supposed that if Dissenters are exempted from the payment of Church-rates, it will involve their surrender of the right to interfere with the Church. *Not so,* as I think. The removal of the religious grievance will not affect the political privilege. Dissenters, as Christians, may cease to pay for the religion of others, but, by that, they would not, as Englishmen, make over the property of the nation to a portion of the people, to become the private and absolute possession of that portion, irrespective of the rest. National property would still remain the property of the nation, including Dissenters. *They,* as thus included, would have the same right as ever to see after their own, and to interfere with it. The Episcopal Church, like any other religious community, may possess much which privately and denominationally belongs to it; but there is far more, in the form both of edifices and income, which is the property of the nation, with which, through its Parliament, the nation can deal. With the Church, in its present numerical relation to the people, the matter might fairly be put thus:—those who use the ecclesiastical edifices of the country are its tenants,—tenants-at-will, it may be said, for the nation might determine to have none at all, or might prefer a different class. By the ceasing of Church-rates, the terms of *occupation* would be altered, but the *ownership* of the property would not change hands. Those who used the Churches would do so on a new and more equitable condition,—the condition of keeping them in repair, and paying the expenses of their own worship, instead of, as heretofore, compelling the landlord to do this in addition to his letting them have the buildings without rent. It is not necessary to pay rates, for us to retain, as Englishmen, our interest in the property. If it were, we should do this, so far as keeping up the buildings is concerned, rather than relinquish them,—for the time *may* come, I trust it will, when, by some new and just arrangement, the nation, as a whole, may have the use and benefit of what, as a whole, it possesses.

" Parliament may settle the pecuniary matter by force of law, in spite of the Church; religious reform should be the Church's own act, but it may be urged upon it by remonstrance and argument from without. If the demands of the people come to be such, and to be so seconded by legislative interference, that the *conscience* of the Church must of necessity withstand them, it could protect itself, preserve its integrity, and retain whatever doctrines, claims, and ceremonies it pleased, by ceasing to be an endowed and established nationality."

B.

Page xxxiii.

All that is meant is, that Evangelical Churchmen and Dissenting Conformists should not content themselves with *privately* objecting to the Church formularies. Many a time, in the parlour, I have heard some of both classes condemn the clergy who preached consistently with the meaning of the Prayer-Book, and at the same time wonder how others who did not, and whose preaching they approved, managed to reconcile their position with their opinions. Now, such people, it is thought, instead of so acting as to give the impression that they regard every thing as quite right, should, occasionally at least, in some public way, speak and act with those who are honestly and openly seeking liturgical reform. They would thus be preserved from merely doing what misrepresents themselves and misleads others.

It may be said, that the observations in the text and those just made might, in spirit, be quite fairly used in an opposite direction to that in which I employ them. Admitted. I have no objection. In all Churches there are things felt by some to be erroneous or wrong. Without deeming it necessary, in any given case, to separate, such persons not only *may* speak, but, *if the things be serious*, they *ought* to speak,—express their convictions, and seek improvement. " Christian men shrink from independent investigation, chiefly because they think it *inexpedient.* Certain forms of thought, right or wrong, have, it is said, for generations been regarded as 'worthy of all acceptation;' under these forms men have received spiritual blessings of the highest value; in the belief of them they have lived well and died happily. Why unsettle such landmarks? . . . [Answer :] The forms of thought [in question] are either true or false. . . . If suspicion has arisen that they are, after all, only partially true,—at the best, one-sided exhibitions of the truth ; that they involve fallacies, produce exaggerated, and therefore inaccurate, impressions, they must on no account be shielded from examination, for, whatever may be the supposed value of any form of thought, if it involve error, *the support of it*, or, which is the same thing, *the determination not to undeceive those who hold it, is in the eye of God an immoral procedure.*"*

---

* "The Interpreter." No. I., pp. 5, 6. This is too strongly expressed, unless the above-mentioned condition " if the things be serious" is understood ; for there really are matters, which it *would* be "inexpedient" to do anything with, but quietly to leave to time, the great innovator and rectifier.

LIGHTS AND SHADOWS.

ON THE UNION

OF

PROTESTANT EVANGELICAL CHURCHES,

AND A POSSIBLE

Church of the Future.

BY THE

RIGHT REV. THE BISHOP OF ADELAIDE,
SOUTH AUSTRALIA.

IN A LETTER TO

THE REV. T. BINNEY.

INTRODUCTORY NOTE.

Bishop's Court, October 4, 1858.

DEAR SIR,

I send you some thoughts which have occurred to me on a subject which has often occupied my mind, but more especially since I had the pleasure of forming your acquaintance. Such as they are, and expressed in the words pretty nearly that first came to hand, I lay them before you in the hope that they will not widen, if they do not bridge, the gap that separates us ecclesiastically, though I trust not spiritually, nor for ever.

I remain, Reverend Sir, yours faithfully,

AUGUSTUS ADELAIDE.

Rev. T. Binney.

P.S.—I leave Adelaide to-morrow morning on a five weeks' tour, and fear that I shall not have an opportunity of bidding you farewell.

ON THE UNION

OF

PROTESTANT EVANGELICAL CHURCHES,

&c., &c.

Bishop's Court, September 23, 1858.

1. REV. SIR,—During our social intercourse yesterday, at the house of a common friend, you were pleased to take notice of a remark which fell from me to this effect—that we in this colony had the advantage of occupying " an historic stand-point," so to speak, from which we might look back upon our past social, political, and Church-life in England, and, removed from the smoke and noise of the great mother-city, might discern through all its greatness somewhat of folly and meanness, of defect and vice, in its habits and institutions. The survey would not be unprofitable if it should lead us to perceive how we had been blinded by its attractions, so as to become unconscious of its faults ; and so hurried away by its feelings and associations as to be insensible

of the conventional bondage in which we then lived and moved.

2. It must, I think, be admitted that the clerical mind is peculiarly swayed by party principles and sectarian prejudices. Withdrawn very much from practical into contemplative life, and valuing abstract truth as the basis of all moral obligation and excellence, clergymen are too apt to exaggerate the importance of certain truths which they conscientiously hold, and to treat as essential principles of the doctrines of Christ matters of inferential or traditional authority. I do not suppose that Nonconformist ministers are exempt from this failing, though it may be fostered in the Establishment at home by the alliance of Church and State.

3. Be this, however, as it may, both clergymen and ministers may look back with some degree of regret that a mid-wall of partition should so have separated kindred souls; pledged to the same cause, rejoicing in the same hope, and devoted to the same duty of preaching Christ and Him crucified to a dark and fallen world. By the very discomfort, however, of thus "standing apart," we are thrust rudely back upon the principles in which we have been brought up, and are constrained to put the question to our consciences, "Are you as sure of your ground as true to your convictions? Are your views so authoritatively scriptural as to put you exclusively in the right?" And if, after careful review and earnest prayer, we still feel unable to quit the "old paths," yet does not this very inquiry dispose us to place a more liberal construction on the conduct of others, and to respect their equally stiff adherence to their conscientious con-

victions? A candid mind will not fail to see that much is to be urged on the other side of the question; and if with our present lights we had lived in the time of our fathers, we should not perhaps have been disposed to break up the fellowship of the Reformed Evangelical Catholic Church for non-essential points, or narrow its communion on matters of Christian expediency rather than Christian obligation.

4. I have thrown these remarks together by way of preface, in order to show the course of thought into which an Episcopate of ten years in this colony has gradually led me. You yourself have given a fresh impetus to such reflections. Your fame as a preacher had preceded you. I knew that you would be welcomed by all who in your own immediate section of the Evangelical Church take an interest in religion, and by all in our own who are admirers of genius and piety, even though the echoes of your King's Weigh-house sermon had not quite died away. Hundreds I knew would ask themselves, " Why should I not go and listen to the powerful preaching of Mr. Binney?" And when they had heard you reason of righteousness, temperance, and judgment to come; of Christ, who He was, and what He did; how He died for our sins, and rose again for our justification,—I felt assured that they would ask again, " Why is he not invited to preach to us in our Churches? What is the barrier which prevents him and other ministers from joining with our clergy at the Lord's table, and interchanging the ministry of the Word in their respective pulpits? Was it any real difference with respect to the person, office, and work

of the Redeemer, the power of the Spirit of God, or the lost condition of man without Christ and the Comforter?"

5. I am truly glad that so considerable a person as yourself should by your presence in this colony have forced me to consider again the question, "Why I could not invite you to preach to our congregations?" to review my position, principles, beliefs, and prepossessions; more especially as the absence of sectarian prejudice on your part, and the presence of all that in social life can conciliate esteem and admiration, reduced the question to its simple ecclesiastical dimensions.

6. Again and again the thought recurred to me, *Talis cum sis utinam noster esses!* Still I felt that neither the power of your intellect, nor vigour of your reasoning, nor mighty eloquence, nor purity of life, nor suavity of manners, nor soundness in the faith, would justify me in departing from the rule of the Church of England; a tradition of eighteen centuries which declares your orders irregular, your mission the offspring of division, and your Church system—I will not say schism—but *dichostasy.**

7. But while adhering to this conclusion, I am free to confess that my feelings kick against my judgment; and I am compelled to ask myself, Is this " standing apart " to continue for ever? Is division to pass from functional disease into the structural type of Church organization? Are the Lutheran and Reformed, the Presbyterian and

---

* Gal. v. 20, " seditions," literally " standing apart."

Congregationalist, the Baptist and Wesleyan bodies, to continue separate from the Episcopal communion so long as the world endureth? Is there no possibility of accommodation, no hope of sympathy, no yearning for union? Will no one even ask the question? None make the first move? Must we be content with that poor substitute for apostolic fellowship in the Gospel, " Let us agree to differ;" or an evangelical alliance, which, transient and incomplete, betrays a sense of want without satisfying the craving? Or are we reduced to the sad conclusion that as there can be no peace with Rome so long as she obscures the truth in Jesus and lords it over God's heritage, so there are no common terms on which the Evangelical Protestant Churches can agree after eliminating errors and evils against which each has felt itself constrained to protest? Are not Churchmen, for example, at this day, just as ready as you, Rev. Sir, can be, to condemn the treatment of Baxter, Bunyan, and Defoe, by a High Church Government? And do not Independents and Presbyterians readily allow that a Leighton or Ken relieves Episcopacy from the odium brought upon it by the severities of a Laud or a Sharp?

8. It appears to me that in this colony we are placed in a peculiarly favourable position for considering our Church relations, because one great rock of offence has been taken out of the way—I mean the connexion between Church and State. We can approach the matters in dispute simply as questions of Evangelical truth and Christian expediency. Neither social, nor civil, nor ecclesiastical distinctions, interfere to distract our view or irritate our feelings. There is no Church-

rate conflict here! I have accordingly seized the opportunity of laying before you a few thoughts on the possibility of an outward fellowship as well as inward union of the Evangelical Churches, with the hope that they may suggest inquiry, if they lead to no immediate practical results.

9. The questions I would propose for consideration are—

First.—Whether an outward union, supposing no essential truth of the Gospel to be compromised, is desirable amongst the Protestant Evangelical Churches?

Secondly.—What are the principles and conditions on which such union should be effected?

I submit my ideas to you with great diffidence, but from the desire to show that there is no unwillingness on my part to consider how we might possibly serve at one and the same altar, walk by the same rule, and preach from the same pulpits the words of this salvation.

10. With regard to the first point, I conceive outward union to be desirable, because it appears to me to be scriptural and apostolic. That all the congregations of the Universal Church were subject, under Christ, to the Twelve Apostles, and that the decree directed by the Holy Ghost, but framed by James and Simon Peter, Paul and Barnabas, and assented to by the elders and brethren, was delivered to the Churches to keep, is recorded in the Acts of the Apostles. That the whole Church was viewed as one visible body by St. Paul is evident, when he bids the Corinthians give offence to neither Jews nor Gentiles, nor the Church of God: and whatever be the figure under which the Holy Spirit

characterises the body of true believers in Christ, unity of organized life is the substratum of the idea; be it vine or olive-tree, family or household, city or kingdom, the body or spouse of Christ, the thought is still the same. What, then, should we think of a family, whose several members inhabiting the same house kept each to his own chamber, and though continually jostling on the common stairs, rarely exchanged a friendly salute, and never a visit. Is this family life? And is it true Church life to say, I am of Peter, and I of Paul, and I of Luther, and I of Knox, and I of Wesley, and I of Whitfield, and I of the Fathers? Are we not carnal, and speak as men? In the apostolic age there must have been outward union of the Churches, so far at least as the general order of a common worship, the celebration of common sacraments, the profession of a common creed, and preaching in common the Word of Life! The spirit of Diotrephes we may hope was rare.

11. If the *odium theologicum* be indeed the worst type of that disease, it might be expected that a real union of the Churches, and their publicly acknowledged fellowship in the Gospel, might arrest the progress of that malady. It is the effect of party feeling, jealousy, and suspicion, fostered by rivalry and contention. Thus, Christian sympathy, which is meant for mankind, is too often restricted to a system or a sect. On the other hand :—

12. In what an attitude of strength would such union place the Gospel of Christ before Jew and Gentile; before Brahmin and Mahommedan! No subtle Pundit would then point to the differences of Christian teachers

as indicating error at least in some, and uncertainty in all. No Bossuet could enumerate, and perhaps exaggerate, the variations of Protestants, and, unmindful of the like in his own communion, claim for the Church of Rome the symbol of Unity as the mark of its being the True Church. But now, instead of fighting the Lord's battle as one great army, our resistance to the Powers of Evil is like the death-struggle of Inkermann; a series of hand-to-hand combats, broken regiments fighting in detached parties, never receding indeed, but incapable of combined effort or mutual support.

13. It may, however, be urged on the other side, that the divisions of the Christian Church are helps to its vitality, even as the troubled sea which cannot rest is thereby preserved from stagnancy and corruption; that rivalry promotes exertion, and exertion results in expansion. Yet has not the Bible Society attained its present strength by acting on the opposite principle? Is it not because all Protestants can unite in furthering its object, truly catholic, and because catholic, triumphant?

14. The union I contemplate is not a yoke of subjection—an iron rule suppressive of individual or sectional thought, aspiration, energy, and action; far otherwise. If the great Apostle of the Gentiles would provoke his brethren after the flesh to jealousy, in order to save some—if he stirred up the Churches of Macedonia by the forwardness of Achaia, and reciprocally urged the Achaian Churches to be ready with their contributions lest he should be ashamed of his boasting concerning them—certainly a loving zeal, striving for the mastery, is not to be cast out as unmeet for the Christian com-

monwealth. Unity is compatible with variety, and variety is pregnant of competition. God has created but one vertebrate type of animal organisms; but how infinitely diversified are the specific forms! I know no reason why, in our reformed branch of the Catholic Church, there might not be particular congregations of the Wesleyan rule, or some other method of internal discipline, or usage, or form of worship, even as the Society of Ignatius Loyola, or Dominic, or Francis, exists in the bosom of the Roman obedience. The seamless coat of the Redeemer was woven from the top throughout. The Roman soldiers said, " Let us not rend it !" Why should chronic disunion be the symbol of Evangelical Christianity? I cannot call alliance union: nay, it is founded on stereotyped separations. I pass to the second question :—

Secondly.—What are the principles and conditions on which a union of the Protestant Evangelical Churches should be effected?

15. It must be evident, I should suppose, after an experience of 300 years, that neither the Episcopalian, nor Presbyterian, nor Congregationalist can reasonably hope to force upon the Christian world his own particular system. Is either one or the other entitled by the Word of God to exclude from salvation those believers who do not follow the same rule of Church government? If, however, submission may not be demanded on the ground of its necessity to salvation, then any negotiation for outward union may and must proceed on grounds of what is best and wisest, most likely to unite, as being most in accordance with Scripture and apostolic tradition.

We must lay aside hard words—schism, Church authority, sectarianism. In the comity of nations, *de facto* Governments are recognised and treated with; the question whether they are *de jure* is left in abeyance. So must it be with respect to any union of the Churches. They must meet together like brethren who have been long estranged, yet retaining the strong affection of early youth: resolve to forget the subject of their dispute, and walk together in the house of God as friends. It will be unnecessary to ask, " Which man did sin, this man or his parents?" or to say, " Thou wast altogether born in sin, and dost thou teach us?" or, " We forbade him, because he followeth not us." No; we must meet in the spirit of godly fear, of mutual respect, with the earnest desire by all right concession to promote God's truth, and advance Christ's kingdom. We must receive one another, but not to doubtful disputations.

16. A second principle is, " Whereto we have attained," or shall attain; that some rule must be publicly acknowledged, in that rule we must walk, and by it steadfastly abide. I firmly believe with Mr. Maurice, in his " Kingdom of Christ," that the Church of the apostolic age embraced every principle for which in later times each section of the Christian world has felt it necessary to contend, even to separation from the main body of the brethren. But the Church of the apostolic age, the true visible model Church, does more. It harmonises them all; giving to each its due place, its real proportion. Each portion of the truth, obscured, distorted, or denied in the mediæval Church, each detail of the outward building of God, has been jealously rescued

from corruption or decay by sects or individuals. It remains, perhaps, for this or the coming generation to restore the original fabric, and take away whatever is inappropriate, unsightly, or inconvenient. But is the spirit as yet willing? Alas, I know not. It is certain that the flesh is weak.

17. Let me endeavour to state, as accurately as I can, what seems to be the leading idea, the characteristic principle, of each section of the Christian Church:—

The Church of Rome, then, contends for external unity, founded on one objective creed, in subjection to one visible head of the Church on earth.

The Lutheran for justification by faith, antecedent to and irrespective of works.

The Reformed Calvinistic Church upholds the free and sovereign grace of God.

The Anglican witnesses for a scriptural creed, apostolic orders, and a settled liturgy.

The Presbyterian asserts the authority of the Presbytery, as derived immediately from the Holy Ghost.

The Congregationalist claims unlimited right of private judgment, and the independent authority of each congregation, as a perfect Church, over its own members.

The Wesleyan preaches spiritual awakening, sensible conversion, and social religious exercises.

The Baptist contends for personal religious experience previous to admission to the Church.

Every one of these principles is substantially, though not exclusively, true. When their mutual relations are forgotten, each becomes exaggerated; the beauty of proportion is lost, and a faulty extreme is made the Shibboleth of schism. Is there no analytical process possible, no law of affinity, by which the spiritual mind could precipitate the error, and leave pure and limpid the Gospel stream? or remove from the much fine gold of the Temple the dross with which it is alloyed? Would there not still remain a scriptural truth, a godly discipline, a settled order, a common altar, a united ministry, a visible union as well as fellowship in the Spirit? Might there not still be variety in unity, partial diversity of usage, and a regulated latitude of Divine worship? The Episcopalian, the Presbyterian, and the Congregationalist might consent to harmonise what they cannot exclusively enforce; they might surely " in understanding be men," and exercise the great privilege of spiritual men—that is, combine freedom with submission to law, and general order with specific distinctions.

18. But it is time to draw these general remarks to a close, and define, with somewhat more of precision, that Church of the future which is to conciliate all affections, and unite all diversities. I scarcely know which to admire most, the pleasantness of the dream, or the fond imagination of the dreamer. Still, let me speak, though it be " as a fool." My object is not to dictate proceedings, but to suggest consideration; to provoke inquiry, but not force conclusions. And since concession in matters not absolutely essential to salvation, or positively enjoined, must be the basis of the system adopted by the various Evangelical Churches, it may be fairly put to me in the language of the proverb—" Physician, heal thyself." I will begin, then, with the Church of England, and will state what it appears to me can be given up for the sake

of union.   1. A State-nominated Episcopate.   2. Compulsory uniformity of Divine worship.   Already the former has given place in Canada and New Zealand to an Episcopate freely elected by the Church itself.   The latter, it appears, even in England, is only required from the clergy in parish churches, but not when preaching in the fields, or streets and lanes of the city.   In addition, then, to the separation of Church and State in this colony, and the absence of the legal machinery connected with that union, greater freedom and diversity in the modes of worship seem attainable; and an Episcopate, moderate in its pretensions, as well as constitutional in its proceedings, associated with, and not lording it over the Presbyters; above all, chosen by the free suffrages of the united clergy and laity.

I believe the doctrinal articles of the Church of England and many others among the Thirty-Nine are allowed on all sides to be scriptural.   I conceive, then, that a settled form of sound words, a deposit of objective faith, would not be deemed a yoke of bondage, but a guide to truth.   I conceive, also, in order that all might worship with the understanding as well as the spirit, that certain liturgical offices, such for instance as the litany, might form part of the stated services, but not to the exclusion of extempore prayer in connexion with the sermon at the discretion of the preacher.   So, also, in the administration of the Sacraments and conferring Holy Orders, a portion of the office might be fixed and invariable, and a portion left to ministering pastors.

19. These points being settled, the trial, nomination, institution, or designation of pastors, the dissolution of

their connexion with their flock, or removal, their mode of payment, the internal discipline of the congregation over their members and officers, are details which may well be left for after regulation; if, indeed, there is really much or any injurious difference at present existing in these matters. A spirit of mutual forbearance and real affection must be largely shed abroad before such a system as here spoken of can possibly be inaugurated. Even if thought feasible for the future, how can it be made to take retrospective effect? How can we, who are *de facto* ministers, and think ourselves to be *de jure* so, besides being pledged to our respective systems, throw ourselves out of the one to enter upon the other?

Let us search the Scriptures for guidance. The beloved disciple was instructed to write by the Holy Spirit to the seven angels of the seven Churches of Asia, and Titus was left by St. Paul in Crete to ordain elders in every city, as he had appointed him. But besides these later exertions of apostolic authority, we find Barnabas and Saul separated by the Holy Ghost to a special mission, through the laying on of hands and prayers of the prophets and teachers of the Church at Antioch, Simeon Niger, Lucius of Cyrene, and Mánaen. Assuming the existing ministers of the several denominations to be recognized as *de jure* by their congregations, and *de facto* as such by the Anglican Church, might not the bishops of the latter, supposing the before-mentioned terms of union were agreed upon to take effect prospectively, give the right hand of fellowship to them, that they should go to their own flocks, and mission also as preachers to the Anglican congregations, when invited by the pastors of the several Churches? If the license of the Bishop can authorise even lay readers and preachers, how much more men like yourself, separated to the work of God, eloquent and mighty in the Scriptures? Indeed, I do not feel sure that I should have violated any ecclesiastical law in force in this diocese or province, by inviting you to give a word of exhortation to each of our congregations.* In this way, then, of mission without compromise, but on declared assent to certain fixed principles and truths, existing ministers might co-operate with us in the preaching of the Gospel, and under the benign influence of this brotherly love a Reformed Catholic Church might grow up, and, like the rod of Aaron, swallow up our sectarian differences.

20. I have said nothing about hypothetical ordination, which has been suggested (like conditional baptism where irregularity in the administration may be suspected), because it savours of evasion or collusion, neither of which is agreeable to Christian simplicity and due reverence for God's ordinances. Neither have I suggested the consecration as Bishops of existing Wesleyan Superintendents and Presbyterian Moderators, or those who, like yourself, seemed sealed alike by nature and the Spirit to be special

---

* Canon 54 of the Province of Canterbury, A.D. 1603–4, requires " conformity as a *sine quâ non* to preaching in the parish churches of England." I do not know that it is binding in colonial dioceses. It shows that persons were licensed to preach who were not disposed to take upon themselves all the obligations of the parish priest under the Establishment.

overseers in the Church of God. Missions, as preachers to our congregations, without imposing the obligations incident to the incumbents and curates of Churches, but not until full evidence had been given before license of soundness in the faith, would seem to meet the exigencies of the case so far as regards the present generation of ministers who have received Presbyterian orders.

Having attained to this step, perhaps God would reveal to us a yet more excellent way. Old systems have, in fact, been found wanting. Which of the Churches now existing is so perfect, so scriptural, so apostolic, as to ensure instant acquiescence from the inquirer to the exclusion and condemnation of all others? If there be none, will all the learning, and eloquence, and traditional authority devoted to the support of each, persuade the present or future generations to substitute another for that in which they have been brought up? A few may, perhaps, be convinced or converted, but the masses never. A fresh combination must therefore be sought; traditional prejudices must be set aside; cherished associations laid upon the altar of love, to rise like angel messengers, in the flame of sacrifice, to purer and loftier spirituality! Oh, for that millennial reign of peace, when a Chalmers or a Cumming, a Binney or a Watson, might serve at one altar, and plead from one pulpit with the bishops and clergy of the Church of England! It is the cause of God and Christ, of truth and holiness, of righteousness and peace, of faith and duty, of grace and salvation, of man delivered and Satan bound, of God alone exalted on that day, and reigning on Mount Zion gloriously. Then might the fulness of the Gentiles

come in, then Israel be restored, then Babylon overthrown, and that regenerated state of this fallen world
be made manifest, for which Jehovah reserved the last
great display of His providential love—the union in the
God-Man of the Manhood with Himself.

I remain, dear Sir, respectfully yours,

AUGUSTUS ADELAIDE.

Bishop's Court, September 23, 1858.

THE CHURCH OF THE FUTURE,

AS PORTRAYED IN THE PRECEDING LETTER,

EXAMINED.

AN ADDRESS,

DELIVERED TO THE

MINISTERS AND DELEGATES OF THE TASMANIAN CONGREGATIONAL UNION.

PART FIRST.

THE " IDEA " OF THE CHURCH.

TEKEL.

AN ADDRESS,

&c., &c.

Honoured and Beloved Brethren,

Although but a visitor amongst you, I have been placed, by your kindness and your suffrages, in this chair. I accept the distinction, believing it to be conferred not so much on personal grounds, as from the circumstance of my having long occupied a position of some importance in the Metropolis of our fatherland, and from my having frequently used the influence which that gave me, to excite in the Churches at home an interest in those of the colonies. You have been pleased to request me to preside over this meeting, and to inaugurate its proceedings by an address. In acceding to your request, I need hardly say that I assume and affect no powers but such as would belong to the president of any deliberative body. For the time being, the Chairman of our Assemblies is constituted by the ministers present (so far as they are concerned) a "Primus,"—but a "Primus *inter pares*,"—a brother presiding over brethren.

F

In the ministry and the Church he stands where he did before. *There* he has no faculty, function, or rights, but what belongs to every pastor. With us there is no superiority of office, no difference or distinction in that, in kind or degree. What is said, on occasions like the present, comes to us only with such force as it may possess from approving itself to our understanding and judgment, our consciences and hearts,—from what it may derive from its truth, its wisdom, or its love,—from its agreement with what we believe to be the teaching of Scripture,—and from the opinion we may entertain, in any given case, of the qualifications for his duty which the speaker brings to it. I have no very great qualifications for any thing; but you will put down something to the experience and observation of a public life of more than thirty years; and you will exercise confidence in the fraternal regard of one who esteems you as " brethren beloved," and who addresses you under the influence of feelings and recollections inspired by the thought of our common relation, as men and Englishmen, to the grand old land, and our joint participation, as Christians and ministers, in the privileges, the hopes, and the service of Christ's holy Church.

In anticipating the duty which I was aware I should this day be requested to discharge, and in thinking of what I could bring before you, it occurred to me that it would neither be unbecoming nor inappropriate if I called your attention to a subject which has recently been brought before the Christian public in these lands. I refer, as you will conjecture, to the " idea " of " A UNION of Protestant Evangelical Churches," contained in a letter addressed to myself, during my recent visit to South Australia, by the Right Rev. the Lord Bishop of Adelaide. The scheme or plan for the realisation of the proposed object, set forth in the letter in question, the Bishop submitted to my consideration, and requested my judgment upon it. He did not, I think, in doing this, regard me merely in my personal character, but as one who, for the time, and with a view to his object, might be taken to represent a particular religious body. I cannot, indeed, lay claim to any representative function, and must not. I have no authority to do so. I have no public mission in these parts, having visited Australia from personal considerations only, and simply as an individual. Besides, I should always hesitate to speak for others ; or, so to speak as, by implication, to involve others. While, throughout our Denomination there is on all great points substantial agreement, there yet may be, and there are, many shades and varieties of individual opinion. This being the case, there are occasions (and this is one of them) when we are anxious to have it understood that none but ourselves are to be held answerable for any views or statements we may put forth. Let this distinct and exclusive personal responsibility be kept in mind. I address *you*,—but I speak only for myself; I respond to the request of the Bishop of Adelaide, but I give only an individual opinion; the Denomination is not committed to my utterances, nor even this meeting. It is possible, indeed, that you may accept and adopt what you hear, and, so far, approve and endorse it as substantially expressing your own views.

Although the Bishop of Adelaide communicated with me by letter, and, up to the time of my coming to this colony, it was my intention—and my publicly declared intention—to write in the same way in reply, the circumstances in which I find myself placed will, I think, both account for and justify my change of purpose. Unexpectedly called upon to address a number of my brethren in the ministry, with the lay delegates of certain associated Churches,—an assembly representing the Congregational Body of a specified district,—it is natural that I should take the opportunity thus afforded of looking at a subject in which all of you are as much interested as myself;—one, too, on which it is expected that I should say something, sometime or other;—a subject, moreover, which, though submitted to me in the first instance, was confessedly thus submitted with an ultimate view to its presentation to the public,—to " the Protestant Evangelical Denominations" of this, and even of other lands. Unexpected circumstances, which were fully explained at the time, led to the premature publication of the Bishop's letter,— a thing to be lamented, but one that had become, on his lordship's account, necessary and unavoidable. Referring, however, to this, on the receipt of a printed copy of his letter, the Bishop says, " I was fully prepared to see it in print." And he adds, in relation to his purpose in writing, " The object of my letter has been answered. I have drawn attention to the possible future union of Evangelical Churches." " I am content to bide the time and allow the leaven to ferment." In taking up the subject, then, at this time and in this way, and in submitting my views in relation to it, not only to the primary pastor of one of the diocesan divisions of the Episcopal Church in these lands, but also to the assembled pastors of a portion of the Body with which I am personally connected, I am not only not conscious of violating any rule or principle of propriety or honour, but feel myself justified by the circumstances of the case, the nature of the subject, and the aim and object of my Right Rev. friend in submitting it to my consideration.

In entering on the matters to which I have just referred, I must remind you that *two* questions were started in what has been called " The Adelaide Corres-pondence,"—questions which ought to be carefully separated from each other, as they were different in their origin, and are distinct in themselves. The one referred to the possibility of an occasional EXCHANGE OF PULPITS between Episcopal clergymen and those of other denomi-nations, *things remaining as they are.* The other had respect to THE UNION OF ALL THE DIFFERENT PROTES-TANT EVANGELICAL BODIES IN ONE GREAT WHOLE. These two questions sprang from opposite quarters, were the suggestions of different minds, and, though brought simultaneously, or nearly so, before the public, were not exactly simultaneous in their origin. I had nothing to do with either, except as being the innocent and uncon-scious occasion of both. The last of the two questions was the first that came before me. Its origin was Episcopal. It was contained in the letter of the Bishop, addressed to myself expressly on the subject. The other question had a humbler parentage. It was started by certain lay-members of the Episcopal

Church. It first came to my knowledge through the public prints. I hardly know which surprised me most. I had no reason to expect such a communication as that with which I was honoured by the Bishop; and so little cognizant was I of the lay-movement that, on the Sunday preceding the reference to it in the papers, I had spoken from the pulpit of my intended departure in a few days, and had thus taken leave of my co-religionists in Adelaide.

The two questions, then, came before the public. They were both included in the first series of letters which appeared in print. But I wish it to be clearly understood that *they are quite distinct*, and that it is with *one* of them only that we have at present to deal. That one is the question which was first in the order of time,—which was suggested by the Bishop,—but which came to be very much lost sight of, in consequence of what was thought to be the more definite and tangible character of the other, and the supposed possibility of its admitting of more immediate action. The two questions got confounded, by the lay-originators of the second referring to it, in their memorial to the Bishop, as if it were something which was in harmony with, and might help the ripening into action of, certain thoughts and feelings which he had expressed in his letter containing the first. In this they were mistaken. The two parties, in fact, not only started from directly opposite points, but they did not contemplate, perhaps, the ultimate realisation of the same thing. That the laymen, however, should have fallen into the error they did, was, I think, not to be wondered at, from several expressions in his lordship's letter. These expressions, indeed, are modified by others, but this might not be obvious on a cursory perusal of his lordship's communication, nor deeply felt while the mind was excited by the first impression of its words.

But, however this might be, the laymen's question is not the one we have to examine. It may be dismissed altogether,—or at least it must be put aside for the present, as something with which we have no immediate concern. It may be referred to hereafter: but our first and main business is to consider that proposed to us by the Bishop.

His lordship's letter cannot be read without deep interest. It is distinguished by a felicity of diction, an earnestness and glow, which at once win the ear and warm the heart, and which awaken towards the writer sentiments of admiration, respect, and love. Its first paragraphs sparkle with sentences which are bright and luminous from the spirit of candour and liberality which pervades them. Even after certain ideas are introduced which tend to lower or modify our feelings, fervid and eloquent expressions occur, so pregnant with all that is comprehensive and catholic, that we are unable to resist their fascinating influence. The " pleasant dream," indeed, is so pleasantly told, and so beautifully depicted, that we do not, at first, very distinctly see what it really *is*,—what it includes,—or how far what at present exists would be affected or altered if " the words of the vision " should come to be fulfilled and embodied in facts. I shall first endeavour to ascertain what his lordship's *ultimate* " idea " *would seem to be;* and, having done this,

I shall offer some remarks upon it;—on the reception it will probably meet with from others, and on the likelihood, or the contrary, of its realisation.

The "Idea" Eliminated.

In proceeding to fulfil my first purpose, attempting to ascertain what the Bishop's idea really *is*,—the union proposed, and the Church which is ultimately to evolve out of it,—I must refer, with some minuteness, to his lordship's letter of September 23rd, in which his scheme is set forth.

After several introductory paragraphs, the Bishop proposes for consideration, the two following questions:—

" First, Whether an outward union, supposing no essential truth of the Gospel be compromised, is desirable amongst the Protestant Evangelical Churches?

" Secondly, What are the principles and conditions on which such union should be effected?"*

He then proceeds to take up each of these in order. I do not deem it necessary to enter into the *first*, or to examine the several reasons by which his lordship sustains an affirmative reply to it. That some more distinct and open manifestation of the essential oneness of the different Protestant bodies which alike hold the Evangelical faith, and are thus, by profession, spiritually united, however they may differ on secondary points of

* See preceding LETTER, page 8. In future references the reader will be so good as to bear in mind, that " LET." will stand for LETTER, as above; " p." for page; and " par." for paragraph. " APP." will refer to the APPENDIX at the end of the volume.

doctrine, or in relation to ceremony and order, "*is desirable*," I suppose we should all admit. Yet, it is fairly questionable how far this should be sought, or should proceed, in the way of making an approach to actual coalition or visible uniformity. There is a moral argument in support of the truths in which numbers agree, who differ among themselves in almost everything else, which has great force in it, and which it would be unwise to weaken without some very obvious corresponding advantage. An external change in the aspect of the Church, while a gain in one direction, might involve loss in another,—loss without adequate compensation. Without dwelling on this, however, at present, we will admit that it would be well if some more visible proof were given to the world that the different Protestant bodies are substantially one. Such proof might be given without having recourse to a compulsory uniformity, or to anything destructive of those different developments of thought and action which there will always be where there is *life*. My Right Rev. Correspondent alludes to this, as, in passing from the first question to the second, he glances at the *nature* of the union which he contemplates. He justly remarks that "unity is compatible with variety;" and he thus beautifully illustrates their combination and harmony as manifested in Nature—"God has created but one vertebrate type of animal organisms; but how infinitely diversified are the specific forms!" . . . "The union I contemplate," he observes, "is not a yoke of subjection—an iron rule suppressive of individual or sectional thought, aspiration, energy, and action: far otherwise." . . . "I know no reason why, in our reformed branch of the Catholic Church, there might not be particular congregations of the Wesleyan rule, or some other method of internal discipline, or usage, or form of worship, even as the Society of Ignatius Loyola, or Dominic, or Francis, exists in the bosom of the Roman obedience."* With this passing hint as to the union he contemplates, the Bishop advances to the discussion of the *second* question,—that with which we are are at present more immediately concerned,—namely, *"What are the principles and conditions on which such union should be effected?"*

The first principle specified would seem to be (for it is not distinctly numbered, but what is next introduced is called the second), the first principle would seem to be this, that, as "it must be evident, after an experience of three hundred years, that neither the Episcopalian, the Presbyterian, nor Congregationalist can reasonably hope to force on the Christian world his own peculiar system," *therefore,* "any negotiation for outward union must proceed on grounds of what is best and wisest, most likely to unite," &c. The principle is one which demands and inculcates, as an essential preliminary, the culture of charity, the oblivion of differences, the recognition of a judicious expediency as the rule of procedure. "We must lay aside hard words,—schism, Church authority, sectarianism." . . . "We must meet in the spirit of godly fear, of mutual respect, with the earnest desire by all right concession to promote God's truth, and advance Christ's kingdom."†

* LET., p. 10, par. 14.   † LET., p. 11, par. 15.

" The second principle," his lordship proceeds to say, " is, ' whereto we have attained,' or shall attain; that same rule must be publicly acknowledged; in that rule we must walk, and by it steadfastly abide."—Under this particular, the Bishop states it to be his " firm belief," that " the Church of the apostolic age embraced every principle for which in later times each section of the Christian world has felt it necessary to contend, even to separation from the main body of the brethren." These separate fragments of the truth, " obscured, distorted, or denied in the mediæval Church," but " jealously rescued from corruption or decay by sects or individuals," it may perhaps remain, " for this or the coming generation" to re-unite, and thus to restore the original fabric.

The Bishop then proceeds to state what he conceives to be " the leading idea," " the characteristic principle" of " each section of the Christian Church." In this sketch he includes the Church, of Rome, the Lutheran, the Reformed Calvinistic, the Anglican, the Presbyterian, the Congregationalist, the Wesleyan, and the Baptist. I must refer you to the letter itself for his lordship's definition of " the characteristic principle" of each of these bodies. He may be clear and correct, more or less, in relation to each; but it is not incumbent on me to go over all his propositions to ascertain this. We shall have to refer, by-and-by, to *that one* with which at present we have most to do; and, with the intimation of this, I pass on.

The statement referred to is succeeded by the following paragraph :—

" Every one of these principles is substantially, though

not exclusively, true. When their mutual relations are forgotten, each becomes exaggerated; the beauty of proportion is lost, and a faulty extreme is made the shibboleth of schism. *Is there no analytical process possible, no law of affinity, by which* THE SPIRITUAL MIND *could precipitate the error,* and leave *pure and limpid the Gospel stream?* Or remove from the much fine gold of the Temple, the dross with which it is alloyed? Would there not still remain a scriptural truth, a godly discipline, a settled order, a common altar, a united ministry, a visible union as well as fellowship in the Spirit? Might there not still be variety in unity, partial diversity of usage, and a regulated latitude of Divine worship? The *Episcopalian, the Presbyterian, and the Congregationalist might consent to harmonise what they cannot exclusively enforce;* they might surely in ' understanding be men,' and exercise the great privilege of spiritual men—that is, combine freedom with submission to law, and general order with specific distinctions."*

His lordship then proceeds :—" But it is time to draw these several remarks to a close, and *define, with somewhat more of precision,* THAT CHURCH OF THE FUTURE *which is* TO CONCILIATE ALL AFFECTIONS, AND UNITE ALL DIVERSITIES." Great and beautiful words! Descriptive of an august mission,—the work to be accomplished, the consummation achieved, by that which is now to be " defined !"

As this projected " Church of the Future," is to originate in mutual " concession," the Bishop deems it becoming to begin by stating what he himself is willing

* LET., p. 13, par. 17.

to concede. He specifies two things,—" 1. A State-nominated Episcopate. 2. Compulsory uniformity of Divine worship." These being given up, and there having come in their place " an Episcopate chosen by the free suffrages of the clergy and laity,"—and " greater freedom and diversity in the modes of worship," (based, however, upon a uniform substratum, agreed upon and accepted by all concerned,)—the next suggestion is, " a settled form of sound words," as " a deposit of objective faith." A foundation is thus laid, for the projected edifice, in these three things. They are more distinctly and definitely stated in a subsequent letter, in which they are put forth as "indispensable" " preliminary conditions" to subsequent action.

> " A. The acceptance in common by the Evangelical Churches of the orthodox creed.

> " B. The use in common of a settled Liturgy, though not to the exclusion of free prayer, as provided for in the Assembly of Divines at Westminster.

> " C. An Episcopate freely elected by the united Evangelical Churches." *

Such is the "idea," in basis and outline, of a combined Protestant Catholic Church, which the different denominations interested in the scheme are to agree to constitute, to which they are to give in their adhesion, and which, as we shall see, is to attain solidity and completeness by the toleration, for the present, of certain ecclesiastical shortcomings, with a view to their being suppressed and superseded by the more perfect order which is gradually

* Let., p. 15, par. 18; and App., p. 6.

to evolve, and which will eventually distinguish a carefully trained and moulded coming generation.

The necessity for, and the nature of, the process thus intimated, are stated and foreshadowed in the following passages :—

" A spirit of mutual forbearance and real affection must be largely shed abroad before *such a system as is here spoken of* can possibly be *inaugurated.* Even if thought feasible for the future, how can it be made to take retrospective effect? How can we who are *de facto* ministers, and think ourselves to be *de jure* so, besides being pledged to our respective systems, throw ourselves out of the one to enter into the other?" The difficulty involved in these questions, it is proposed to meet in this way :—" Assuming the existing ministers of the several denominations to be recognized as *de jure* by their congregations, and *de facto* as such by *the Anglican Church,* might not THE BISHOPS *of the latter,* supposing *the beforementioned terms of union were agreed upon to take effect prospectively,* give the right hand of fellowship to them, *that they should go to their own flocks,* and *mission also as preachers* to the Anglican congregations when invited?"

. . . " Missions, as preachers to our congregations, without imposing the obligations incident to incumbents and curates of Churches, *but not until full evidence had been given* BEFORE LICENSE *of soundness in the faith,* would seem to meet the exigencies of the case SO FAR AS REGARDS THE PRESENT GENERATION OF MINISTERS WHO HAVE ONLY RECEIVED PRESBYTERIAN ORDERS." . . . " In this way, then, of mission without compromise, but *on declared assent* to certain fixed principles and truths, existing Ministers might *co-operate with us* in the preaching of the Gospel; and, under the benign influence of this brotherly love, A REFORMED CATHOLIC CHURCH MIGHT GROW UP, and, like the rod of Aaron, swallow up our sectarian differences." *

Such are the Bishop of Adelaide's views in relation to the union of the Protestant Evangelical denominations,— the conditions on which it is to rest, and the issue in which it is to terminate,—its preliminaries, progress, and consummation. Such would seem to be his idea of the process by which the present characteristics of some of these denominations are to be absorbed and to disappear, and such his conception of the all-comprehending and overshadowing "rule," which is to give a substantial oneness to the whole, while tolerating, for a time, certain differences in some of the parts. Looking forwards,—through and beyond the preliminary arrangements described by his lordship,—we can perceive gradually coming into view, that "Church of the Future," which is *to conciliate all affections, and unite all diversities.* I now propose to state to you, and through you to its author and the public, my views and impressions of the subject thus submitted to our consideration. I have endeavoured to ascertain and to set forth what the Bishop's "idea" really is. I will now look at and endeavour to estimate it. To do this fully and successfully, we must notice, as far as necessary or practicable, whatever there may be in his lordship's original communication, or in any subsequent one, which shall seem to throw light on the ideal structure which is now standing before us.

* LET., p. 16—18, pars. 19, 20, 19.

REMARKS.

I.

DISAPPOINTMENT.

The first remark I would submit is this:—On attentively listening to his lordship's letter, there is felt, every now and then, a sort of jar. Somehow, there is a discord. Two opposing tones seem to run through the document which destroy its effect, leaving us with confused and contradictory impressions. On the first perusal, we are struck by a number of notes of most musical sweetness, which fall pleasantly on the ear, as paragraph after paragraph utters what is in it;—notes, eloquently expressive of what is considerate, candid, liberal, and just. Detain, for a moment, as they float past, and notice, a few of these.

In referring to the fact that English Christians in these colonies had the advantage of occupying "an historic stand-point, whence they can look back on their social, political, and CHURCH-LIFE in the old land," his lordship observes, among other things equally striking, "the survey would not be unprofitable if it should lead us to perceive how we had been blinded by its attractions so as to become unconscious of its faults; and so hurried away by its feelings and associations as to be insensible to the conventional bondage in which we then lived and moved." . . . He goes on to say, that "clergymen are too apt to exaggerate the importance of certain truths which they conscientiously hold, and to treat as the essential principles of the doctrine of Christ, matters of *inferential* or *traditional authority*." . . . Looking with regret at the fact that " a middle wall of partition should have separated kindred souls, pledged to the same cause, &c.; —by the very discomfort of thus ' standing apart,' being thrust rudely back upon the principles in which we have been brought up," "we are constrained," his lord-ship remarks, " to put the question to our own conscience, ' Are you as sure of your ground as true to your convictions? *Are your views so authoritatively scriptural as to put you exclusively in the right?*" . . . Then, after other wise and weighty words, he speaks, as with pain, of " the fellowship of the Reformed Evangelical Catholic Church," having been broken up " for non-essential points," and its communion narrowed " on matters of Christian expediency rather than Christian obligation." . . . Harmonising with these utterances, we find subsequent expressions of large and compre-hensive meaning, used to enforce denominational modesty in respect to exclusive ecclesiastical pretensions, and to remove sectarian obstacles to the union of the various Evangelical bodies in one great confederation:—neither " the Episcopalian, the Presbyterian, nor the Congre-gationalist " is permitted to hope that he can " force his own particular system on the Christian world;" they must " lay aside," says the Bishop, " hard words— schism, Church authority, sectarianism;" " they must meet together as brethren who have long been estranged . . . . resolve to forget the subject of their dispute, and walk together in the house of God as friends . . . . It will be unnecessary to ask ' which man did sin—this man or his parents?' or to say 'thou wast altogether born in sin, and dost thou teach us?' or 'we forbade him, because he followeth not us.'" . . . Towards the close of the letter we read, "Old systems have been found wanting. Which of the Churches now existing is so perfect, so apostolic, as to insure instant acquiescence from the inquirer to the exclusion and condemnation of all others? If there be none, will all the learning, and eloquence, and traditional authority devoted to the support of each, persuade the present or future generations to substitute another for that in which they have been brought up? A few may perhaps be convinced or converted, but the masses never. A fresh combination must therefore be sought: traditional prejudices must be set aside; cherished associations laid upon the altar of love, to rise, like angel messengers, in the flame of sacrifice to purer and loftier spirituality!"*

Such are some of the first class of notes to which we referred. In other words, such are some of the glittering wavelets of the golden thread which runs through portions of his lordship's letter;—bright jets of feeling and thought, which appear to rise out of irrepressible longings after a Protestant Catholic communion, and which, thrown out tinted and modified by the action of a candid and liberal judgment, and " a course of thought into which an Episcopate of ten years in Australia has gradually led,"† seem to shine and sparkle as in the sunlight of love! It is hardly possible not to be dazzled,— quite impossible not to be surprised,—for surprise *will* come when we recollect that this is the language, these

* LET., pars. 1, 2, 3, 15, 20.   † LET., par. 5.

the utterances, of a Churchman and a Bishop! I do not mean to insinuate, by this last remark, that, in such an one, warm and loving words, earnest sympathies, and liberal sentiments are, simply as such, things to be wondered at. Among Churchmen and Bishops there have been men of the most enlarged charity, the purest zeal, the holiest aspirations, the most Evangelical catholicism. What I mean to imply, and what *does* surprise me, is this: that one in the position of the Bishop of Adelaide,—with what must have been his educational training, with his unavoidable prepossessions and his professional antecedents,—that he should thus volunteer statements and make admissions which have no meaning if they do not involve the abandonment of those exclusive claims and pretensions on behalf of his own Church—its undoubted apostolicity, its *jure divino* constitution and form—based on antiquity and buttressed by tradition, adherence to which has always been characteristic of his class and order.

But the impression and effect of what you have just heard are greatly lessened, if not almost entirely destroyed, by a jarring note that keeps ever and anon obtruding its dissonance and marring the music. In spite of the soft and soothing intonations which affect us as we have seen, there come forth from the same instrument—or are struck off from others by the same hand—sounds like these:—" The rule of the Church of England, A TRADITION *of eighteen centuries,* declares *your orders irregular, your mission the offspring of division, and your Church system*—I will not say schism, but—

dichostasy."* "Hard words," these, after all! Something like *not* "forgetting the original subject of dispute." We were warned against treating as "principles," matters of "*inferential* or *traditional authority;*" told that "*traditional prejudices* must be laid aside;" and informed that in the colony of South Australia, men "are placed in so peculiarly favourable 'a position," that no "*ecclesiastical* distinctions interfere to distract their view, or irritate their feelings;"—and yet, *a purely ecclesiastical matter,*—and one, too, whose modern *form* is confessedly very different from the primitive arrangements out of which [or, as some would say, out of the perversion of which] it rose,—is based on "the *inspired authority* of an apostolical *tradition !*"† In spite, too, of the "who did sin" inquiry,—"this man or his parents?"—being put aside, we are reminded of it thus:—"the Congregations to which these teachers belong *have separated in time past from the Church of England.*"‡ Still further; in spite of "the experience of 300 years making it manifest that no one can hope to force on the Christian world his own particular system;" hints and suggestions are constantly occurring, which seem to indicate (as we shall see presently) that the scheme of the Bishop is to terminate in this—that *his* system, in effect, is ultimately to become universal and predominant. And finally; in opposition to all having to give up something—all having "been found wanting"—and "a fresh combination sought;" that no Church now existing can be considered "so perfect, so scriptural, so apostolic, as to insure instant acquiescence to the exclusion and

<hr>

* Let., p. 6, par. 6.   † App., p. 6.   ‡ App., p. 48.

condemnation of others;" we are told that the writer is not to be imagined to be " willing or able to compromise one single principle or time-honoured characteristic of his own Reformed Branch of the Catholic and Apostolic Church;"* and that, as to us Nonconformists especially, " the hope is cherished" that the best of us—" the wise and good" amongst us,—" may eventually find *a spiritual home* WITHIN HER PALE!"†

There seems to me, then, to be a discord, " an uncertain sound," or an opposition of sounds, in the Bishop's letter. There is one vibrating chord, distinct and telling, which at first captivates the ear, making itself heard as if it lay on the surface; but there is an undertone, harsh and rugged, which keeps constantly interposing an implied or murmured contradiction to the first. Now, I beg to say, that I don't at all find fault with my Right Reverend friend for his employment of this second note. I think it natural to the instrument over which he presides, and that it cannot but come in answer to his touch. What I venture to call in question is, the employment by the Bishop of the other note,—or, in plain words, his use of language which *must* to others seem to imply more than he means, or which means more than he can adhere to;—language, which would " deceive the unwary" if they understood it in its " plain and grammatical sense." The fact is, that his lordship sat down to write under the influence of feelings most honourable to himself. His heart uttered, when glowing and excited, what, half unconsciously, he had to modify or reduce. The impulses of the man got the better for

* APP., p. 14.   † APP., p. 52.

a time of the spirit of the ecclesiastic. But the vision which rose before him, when giving way to the luxury of sentiment, collapsed and vanished, when touched by the fettered finger of the traditionist. The candid admissions and liberal allusions of the Bishop's letter, which please so much when first heard, come at length to affect us painfully. We discover that, with him, they can never have an embodiment in corresponding action. Conscientious attachments, fixed ideas, determined adherence to the " time honoured" and the " traditional"—all perfectly consistent with his principles and position—prevent their ever being to us any thing but words. With the best intentions, on his part, he can give us little else. We feel that we have been tantalized, by having had held to our lips an elaborately moulded but empty chalice, and we can hardly help thinking that we have a right to complain,—though, if we did, it would be much more from grief than resentment.

II.

DENOMINATIONS.

The next remark I submit to you is this:—The Bishop's scheme, while apparently beginning with the recognition of the different Protestant Evangelical denominations as equal parties to the proposed union, does yet practically give authority and pre-eminence to the English Episcopate,—is to be worked through the exercise of its peculiar functions,—and to be consummated, it would seem, by the Episcopal " Rule" becoming universal and predominant. The " orders" of all Nonepiscopal Churches are assumed to be defective; they are ultimately, therefore, to be suppressed or superseded; in the meantime, those who have only received such, are to be treated with tolerance, tenderness, and condescension.

I do not myself attach much importance to "orders," as they are termed. I look more to the prophetic impulse,—to that gift and call which the Church of England recognizes in requiring every candidate for ordination to express his belief that he is "moved by the Holy Ghost," to take upon himself the ministry of the word. A solemn and wonderful declaration that! One which, when a reality, indicates something impressive and sublime. It stamps a man with the Divine seal; sets him before us as inwardly impelled by God to do a Divine thing. Office in the Church is not to him a "profession," but a *vocation;* it is not something which he chooses for himself, but for which *he* is chosen;—which he does not advance to because he will, but because he *must.* The man is not at liberty to decline the call of God! Such men, are the men to do something for the world. The words quoted from the Prayer-Book present to us, I repeat, what is grand and impressive,—that which, in the language of heaven, constitutes being "duly called" to the office and work of the ministry considered as a spiritual service; without which, however much mere ecclesiastical regularity may have been secured, a man is not "duly" or divinely "called" at all. Now, although I should shrink from personally appropriating the words in question, and think it highly inexpedient that they should be forced as a formula into the lips of numbers, I yet hold to them as exhibiting a great truth. In proportion as that truth becomes, in the spiritual guides of any Church, an embodied fact, just in that proportion, and in no other, will such Church have a really " called " and adequately qualified ministry. Attaching, then, as I do, far more importance to what God imparts than to what man can confer, I care comparatively little for " orders " of any kind, simply as such, with whatever rites, or by whatsoever hands they may be given,—although I think that admission to the ministerial office ought, in all Churches, to be jealously watched, and solemnly conducted.

But the Bishop of Adelaide's scheme for creating a " Church of the Future," which is not only to " unite all diversities," but to " conciliate all affections," (?) starts, as it seems to me, by proposing the most humiliating terms to the clergy of every community but his own. It is not merely we Independents to whom the Bishop offers a temporary tolerance—we, whose schism, or " dichostasy," we can easily understand, must, in the estimation of the Anglican clergy, deprive us of all claim to anything like legitimate or available ordination—*all* ministers, in every Church, the world over, " who have only received Presbyterian orders," are contemplated by his lordship in what he proposes. Not only is there the comprehensive phrase, just quoted, in his first letter, but, in a subsequent one, he expressly refers to and enumerates " *the Lutherans, and Reformed Churches of Europe, with the various sections of the Presbyterian communion in Scotland,*"* as included among and constituting a part of those ecclesiastical bodies to whom

* APP., p. 50.

his " Church of the Future" is presented. To " the present generation of ministers," *in all these Evangelical denominations,* who have only been ordained, according to their own customs and laws, " by the laying on of the hands of the Presbytery," his proposition is—that, with a view to a visible unity of action, THE ANGLICAN BISHOPS might *begin* by recognizing them as *de facto* ministers (waiving, so far as they are concerned, the *de jure* question); that they might give them " the right hand of fellowship," and thus countenance their going to their own flocks as ministers; and that they might also " LICENSE" them to " mission" " as preachers" to " Anglican congregations." This, however, it is carefully provided, should not be without " full evidence being given *before license* of soundness in the faith." " In this way," says the Bishop, " existing ministers might *co-operate with us* in the preaching of the Gospel;" they might thus, *as missionary preachers, be admissible to our pulpits;* PROVIDED the " *before-mentioned terms of union were agreed upon* TO TAKE EFFECT PROSPECTIVELY." These arrangements, it is concluded, " would seem to meet the exigencies of the case *as far as regards the present generation of ministers, who have received Presbyterian orders."* And as to the *future?* you ask ;—Why, as " the terms to be agreed upon to take effect prospectively," *include an Episcopate* elected by the whole of the associated bodies, then, whatever minor varieties of rule may be permitted, like those of Loyola or Dominic, all, for some general purposes, will be under that of their elected primary pastors, who, of course, will exercise *their peculiar function in respect to ordination,* so that, by hypothesis, there would, in another generation, be no ministers at all who had only received "Presbyterian orders." Just as by the gradual, and at first almost imperceptible, change of colour and object, one picture is replaced by another in a series of dissolving views, so is it to come to pass, through the working of an arranged and adapted machinery, that the present existing ministerial orders of the greater number of Protestant Evangelical denominations shall " vanish away," and one alone remain, universal and permanent.*

If I have not misinterpreted the documents before me, —if I have succeeded in discovering their real meaning, —*that* is the ultimate object of the suggestions they contain. Of the probable acceptance of the scheme, by the Non-episcopal Churches of Europe and the world, I am requested to give my opinion. In doing this, I am not called upon to defend or justify the views of any man, or of any denomination. I only give my impressions, such as they are, arising from any knowledge I may possess of the way in which ecclesiastical matters are looked at —or under certain supposed circumstances are likely to be looked at—by those who stand on different ground from that occupied by the Bishop. So far, then, as that knowledge extends, I fear I must say that my *impression* is, that little would be required beyond the bare statement or exposition of the scheme itself to insure its almost universal rejection. Different parties would take exception to different parts of it, or different aspects. What I should myself say, I will mention last; what *others* would say, I can imagine

* LET., pp. 16–18, pars. 19, 20.

might come forth in separate and successive utterances like these.

A. "Looking only at the *first* letter, I think there is a discrepancy in it something like the discord you spoke of before—perhaps a part of it. Again and again the Bishop uses language which places all the different denominations on a level:—the Episcopalian, the Presbyterian, the Congregationalist are alike to be content with harmonising what they cannot enforce; neither can hope to prevail with those brought up in a different school. Certain phrases, indeed, are employed which have no meaning, or no force, if they do not involve the admission that 'dichostasy' belongs to the Bishop and his brethren as well as others, for 'standing apart' is represented as a sin *common to all;* one Church or Denomination stands as much away from others, as others do from it;* yet, the remedy, it seems, is to consist in the Officers and the Regimen of One gradually attaining universal ascendency, all the rest becoming subject to it, or being absorbed by it! When this process is complete, outward and visible union will be perfected! Such is the inevitable *ultimatum* of your friend's scheme, though it may not seem so to himself from the concessions he thinks he has made,—or may be hidden from others on the first perusal of the letter containing it, by the glowing and beautiful words in which it is put forth. The Bishop did not know, did not suspect, while he was indulging the fond imagination, and inditing his mellifluous sentences—what is nevertheless true— that, in the document referred to, ' the voice is

* LET., p. 4, par. 3.

the voice of Jacob, but the hands are the hands of Esau.'"

B. "But there are other documents,—letters explanatory of the first, in which what ·you [A.] regard as the inevitable result, is admitted to be *designed*, and the design itself excused or justified. In allusion to one of these, *I* should say, that it may be perfectly true that 'Luther and Calvin admitted Episcopacy to be lawful; that Independents deny the Divine right of Presbyterianism; and that the Free Kirk would hardly insist upon it as a dogma of the faith ;'* nevertheless, there *are* those who actually believe that Presbyterianism or Independency is *more* scriptural than Episcopacy; and others who, though deeming all three as alike *authoritatively* indifferent, yet prefer the one or other of the former on the ground of what is wisest and best, and who would deprecate the extinction of either as a calamity to the world. Besides, the admission of the lawfulness of a thing, and that as such it may be allowed and used, is something far short of recognizing its Divine claim to exclusive rule,—or quietly acquiescing in the persuasion of those who, so regarding it, make it a 'dogma' of their system,—or being willing to accede to their request to allow it the ascendency because *they* believe it to be Divine and apostolic."

C. "It is proposed, however, let it be observed, that we should consent to this ascendency as a means to an end. It is put to us, whether, for the sake of securing a formal and visible union, which would impress the world and render access to the Church easy on all

* APP., p. 13.

sides, we might not throw all our distinctive views into the gap between us and Episcopacy, and thus make common cause with its adherents who occupy a fortress 'they cannot abandon;' and it is suggested that *we* might do this, because, while *we* do not claim exclusive apostolicity, they do.* I, however, for one, do not admit the propriety of the appeal. The gap, or sunk fence, *we* believe to have been dug by human hands. The sacrifice asked, is not therefore required by God; it is too great to be made at the suggestion of man, on any supposed calculations of expediency, or any appeal to modesty or love. It is not necessary to the end proposed; *that* might be reached better by other means, if good sense and good feeling really prevailed on all sides. However little we may boast of 'Divine right,' or 'exclusive authority,' in respect to our denominational characteristics, we think it is asking of us too much that we should consent to shoot them, as so much rubbish, into a great hole, seeing that, in doing so, *we* should feel that we were parting with much that is great and valuable, accordant with the Scriptures, conservative of the spirit of apostolic times, and which the Church, as we believe, could ill spare. I am willing to admit that 'a goodly number of the traditions and customs of past ages' might be used for the purpose of filling up the gulf referred to. But they should be contributed by both parties. The Bishop's suggestion has too much the look of 'a one-sided reciprocity.'"

D. "I should add to that a consideration which, I think, is sometimes overlooked. In adhering to what

* App., pp. 31, 30.

we ourselves regard as wisest and best, it does not follow that we require others to conform to us, or even wish them to submit to a ' fraternal curtailment.'* They are perfectly welcome to tail, mane, hoof or horn, or anything else, which they think becoming, or esteem and value as a gift of the gods, so long as they do thus regard it, and do not use it offensively against others. We accord to all the liberty we exercise ourselves,—liberty to form, to cling. to, and to carry out personal convictions. We have no quarrel with those who see in the New Testament a diocesan Episcopacy fully developed, or who prefer it as a rational and wise induction from what is there, and who conscientiously adopt and zealously adhere to it. We have no desire to interfere with them, or to ask them to do anything merely to please *us.* All we say is, that, for ourselves, as we not only do not see their system in the Record, but seriously believe that, in its modern form, it violates or ignores important rights both of presbyters and people, we could not consent to admit its pretensions or forward its ascendency."

E. "Besides, think of men being ' *licensed* ' to preach in the manner proposed! Licensed, in some instances, by those who should rather be licensed by *them;* and in others by some whom they would *not* license !"

But enough of this, and more than enough. Suffice it to say, that I can imagine individuals in the different Protestant Non-episcopal bodies expressing themselves thus, in relation to the scheme before us. These utterances of theirs may be right or wrong, wise

* APP., p. 31.

or foolish; into that question I do not enter. I content myself with saying that, for my own part, I don't think it of the slightest use to go into such questions *with a view to any united action.* They may be important and interesting, and not without results, as matters of argument and of individual research; but as to the whole Protestant world coming to an agreement to act as the Bishop proposes—in "the present generation," or any other—it is so utterly out of the question, that it is no use, as it seems to me, to canvass the scheme. It comes several generations too late. There was a time when many of the nice questions it involves influenced the world, and affected the destinies of nations; they have comparatively little interest now, except to us ministers, who, living in our own spheres of speculative thought, fall into the habit of attaching importance to matters of a theoretic or traditional character, regardless of the fact that the great machine of actual life is moving on and whirling away, not only without submitting to be controlled by them, but as to some, grinding them to powder. Schemes of "comprehension,"—plans for the coalition of different bodies,—the "reduction" of some to the bosom of another, or their subjection to its "dominion,"—these once had their day; they were talked of, suggested, proposed, and *died;* died, as it was thought, never to live again. And they never will. Any attempt to revive and resuscitate them will be vain. The divisions into sections of the Christian Church, the existence of distinct Protestant Evangelical denominations, must be accepted as a great fact. It must be dealt with as such. It is no matter who was right or who wrong, at the time of the original dispute,—unless, indeed, the subject of dispute still exists, and is on either side regarded as vital. As to sectional divisions on the ground of forms and modes of administration and discipline, these are most likely inseparable from the condition of the Church in the present world. It is by no means certain that great ceremonial differences did not exist among the first Christians in apostolic times; it *is* certain that, in proportion as the Church got consolidated into a vast association,—compact, uniform, dominant,—it became a merciless and intolerable tyranny. If it were possible for all Protestant Evangelical denominations to be fused together into one Church to-day, and as such to have a fresh start, it would be split into innumerable divisions to-morrow; or, if not, it would become a power inimical to freedom in all its forms,—and that, too, even though it commenced on the principle, and with the profession, of securing and recognizing the rights of individuals, and " the liberty of sectional aspiration and action." But, whether these views are correct or not, in relation either to the past or the future—as to primitive facts or anticipated probabilities—the one great fact stands there sternly confronting us; *divisions and subdivisions exist;* they are to be found even within communities ostensibly and formally one: the fact must be accepted and made the best of, whatever that may be;—but, as to supposing that thousands and tens of thousands of professedly free men, composing numerous and influential religious denominations, with principles, organizations, and customs established and in action,—mighty living powers,—to suppose that these could all be brought to coalesce and amalgamate, to give up, in some measure, their separate existence, and to agree and consent to some species or other of uniform rule;—still more, to suppose that the vast majority of those composing these great masses could be brought to concede, and to see the propriety of conceding, what is suggested in respect to the ministers of *one* communion,—why, even if all this were right and proper and most desirable in itself,—to suppose that *it could be*, in the present state of the world, or under any probable future condition of things, is simply to dream of an utter impossibility. Whether right or wrong, theoretically speaking, it is practically naught; for any *use*, it cannot be seriously entertained; to discuss it would be a waste of words,—you might as well discuss the restoration of the Heptarchy.

III.

DOCTRINE.

The third remark I submit is, that the sort of union proposed by the Bishop would so closely connect the different denominations with each other, that each would feel itself responsible for what was retained and professed by any. This, I apprehend, would have results in respect to his own community which his lordship has not thought of, (and could hardly be expected to have thought of,) and for which he is not prepared.

In proposing to throw into the furnace all existing Churches, and to construct a new one out of the mass,— in desiderating some "analytical process," some "law of affinity," that might aid this result—the Bishop uses language which goes far beyond matters of discipline and ceremony, and such formal and secondary things, touching, as it does, the sphere of inward and vital truth. The "analytical process" sought, is to be one "by which the *spiritual mind* may precipitate the *error*, and leave pure and limpid THE GOSPEL STREAM."* If such a process as this was to be set in action, whatever might be its effect on other bodies—which might doubtless be considerable, but which is not at present the question before us—its bearing on the Anglican section of the Church would be such as the Bishop does not conjecture. In *it*, some important changes would be required:—changes which would be called for by the deep convictions of "the spiritual mind" in other communities,—and called for in proportion as the mind of such communities *was* spiritual, and spiritually enlightened, alive, and active;—changes which would be demanded on the very ground of such a union being aimed at as the scheme proposes,—such an identity of the parts with the whole and with each other as could not but be felt to have serious results. There may be much in many Churches which the adherents of others disapprove; but friendly relations may be maintained amongst them without their becoming mutually responsible for each other's errors. The ministers of several communions, as alike holding great primary truths, though mixed up in all with something of alloy, may have kindly intercourse, exercise fraternal recognition, and even exchange pulpits, without their being involved in, or accountable for, *all* that the different Churches maintain, or with the things

* LET., p. 14, par. 17.

in each which are disallowed by the others. I hold the Bishop of Adelaide to be mistaken in stating that I " morally subscribed " to 'the whole of the Wesleyan *creed* " before I preached in their Chapel;"—a creed " tolerably long," as he says,—consisting of " what is contained in Wesley's Notes on the New Testament and his four volumes of Sermons!"* I did no such thing. I was by no means so committed to all the peculiarities of the Methodist confession by the mere act of preaching in one of their Chapels,—and that, too, to a mixed general audience gathered from the public at large, in a place eligible from its size, and selected on that account, and for a collection on behalf of the Bible Society! The Bishop would hardly apply this canon to himself for preaching in the Nonconformist Chapel at Angaston,—or, if he prefers it, accepting its use as a place appropriated for worship, and using it accordingly. If, however, the Bishop thinks that subscription to the entire creed of a denomination is involved in the mere act of preaching in one of its Chapels, *how much more must that be involved when each denomination constitutes an integral part of a great united visible body,* and all are so intimately associated that there is the recognition and display of this identity! Reponsibility for, participation in, other men's beliefs *would* follow from belonging to such a confederation as the Bishop contemplates, and would be felt by some of the constituent parts to be very serious, if what they deemed " the error" of others was *not* " precipitated" in the process of formation. I can easily understand that great changes might be effected in any

* APP., p. 35.

supposed union of Churches, so far as matters of form, or order, or governmental construction and action are concerned,—changes, which might be accepted by some without hurting the conscience, acquiesced in by others without resistance and without inconsistency. But there are other changes that may be thought of:—things might have to be touched, handled, modified, removed, which belong to a higher sphere, and connect themselves, in the " spiritual mind," with the deepest feelings and most momentous results. To enter this sphere, and " precipitate" these things, (equivocal term!) would, in the case submitted to us, if it ever came to anything, be conscientiously demanded by some of the " Evangelical Protestant denominations ;" while, by a portion, at least, of the adherents of one—the Anglican Church—that demand would be as conscientiously and resolutely resisted.

Let us take the Bishop's statement of the " ruling idea," the " characteristic principle," of the Anglican Church. She " witnesses," he says, " for a Scriptural creed, Apostolic orders, and a settled Liturgy."* We may pass over the liturgical point without remark. When we look, however, at the other two, ideas rise out of them and force themselves upon us which are not to be so easily dismissed.—" ORDERS ?" " CREED ?" What do these comprehend? What do the words imply *in the lips of an Anglican prelate?* The first, not simply admission to the ministry, but, as *we* think, ordination to the priesthood: the second, *this* profession among others, " I believe—in one baptism for the remission of sins."†

* LET., p. 13, par. 17.   † Nicene Creed.

The Bishop says to me, "before you could preach in our pulpits," "I ask of you and other Non-episcopalian ministers," "subscription" to "a creed in accordance with the Nicene Confession."* Now, whether right or wrong in their interpretation of the Prayer-Book,—the meaning of the term "orders," *as looked at in the light of the Ordination Service,*—the import of the article just quoted from the Nicene Creed, *viewed in connexion with the baptismal formularies;*—whether, I say, right or wrong in their judgment touching these matters, there are those who believe—the protestation of many of the Clergy notwithstanding—that the "creed" and "orders" of the Anglican Church include in them together a *sacramental* and *a sacerdotal* element at variance with the teaching of Scripture, and likely to be spiritually injurious just in proportion as they are believed and confided in. Spiritual regeneration "*in* and *by* baptism," the giving of the Holy Ghost in conferring "orders,"— the consequent power of priestly absolution, [" by Christ's authority committed to me *I* absolve thee from all thy sins ;"†] these and other things which come out of what we understand the Anglican Church to hold and teach, are all suggested to us by what the Bishop describes as her "testimony"—that to which she "witnesses." The rest of the Evangelical Protestant denominations, how-ever, would, more or less, protest against these things, require them not only to be "re-considered" but removed, and would refuse all such union with those who adhered to them, as would involve them in a "moral subscription" to their truth, or make them in any way

* APP., p. 35.   † " Visitation of the Sick."—*Prayer-Book.*

responsible for them. We, who here represent the English Nonconformists, have an especial right to refer to the matters in question as now set forth, because the points mentioned were among those which led to our ejection from the English Church, or prevented our adhesion to it, "in times past." Some of us had no great or insuperable objection either to Episcopacy or to Liturgies. We could have fallen in with arrangements which might have included both these; but we could not conscientiously use services and forms which, *in our view*, obviously involved the sacerdotal element, and explicitly affirmed sacramental efficacy. Many of our party, while agreeing with us in this, went much further, and could hardly have been retained by any modification of ecclesiastical arrangements; but many stood simply where I have described, and though some have since advanced, there are those who stand there still. Our objections were over-ruled, our scruples disregarded; we were obliged by the dictates of conscience and honour to submit to be cast out. The Bishop himself recognizes the propriety of our thus speaking, for he says, in words already quoted, that we "separated in times past on some not unimportant points of doctrine and discipline;" and that we "still differ in our views and teaching respecting the SACRAMENTS and MINISTRY;"—that is, as to the "*creed*" and "*orders*" on behalf of which the Anglican Church "witnesses." We do. And not only so, but we deem our differences to be so great and serious, that we could not consent to be comprehended in "the Church of the Future," over which, as we saw, the Anglican discipline is to wave, if, along with that discipline, it continued to adhere (as of course it would) to some of those things which it regards as constituting its special testimony;—things, however, which we reject; which are not, as we believe, in accordance with the Scriptures, but which, flowing from no higher source than the teaching of that Church which once enthralled and corrupted every other, we regard as errors,—errors which, in the Anglican Church, are more or less the marks and monuments of its imperfect reformation.

The priestly and sacramental elements which, in our view, pervade the " offices" of the Anglican Church, are the principal grounds of our " standing apart;"—grounds which justify such " dichostasy" to our own consciences and before God, and make it a duty and an obligation. With such convictions, we could not belong to any union, confederacy, church (present or " future"), adhesion to which would involve the sanction, recognition, and maintenance of these things. We judge no man; but we think that we should be permitted to judge ourselves. Others, to the best of their judgment, in good faith and with a good conscience, may so interpret the Anglican formularies as not to see in them what we see, and to be able to use them with inward satisfaction; while others, again, because of the very things which are obstacles to us, and which they see in the book just as we do, rejoice in it *for their sake*, and would cling to and contend for them to the death. Be it so. " Let every man be fully persuaded in his own mind." " To his own Master he standeth or falleth." So long as they are distinct in their Church organizations, the ministers of different communions, who think and feel alike,—though with their respective lights and convictions they could not conscientiously *change* places,—may yet honour and esteem each other, meet and fraternize, join in such services as are at any time possible (as they might in others if permitted), without being involved in all that the Churches may respectively hold, or be supposed to hold; but the case would be altogether altered if a number of denominations were to be consolidated into one united body, and to constitute in any sense a Church, however there might be permitted in different congregations " a diversity of rule." All would be responsible for whatever touched vital truth, and " the spiritual mind" would feel compromised by any thing that, in its estimation, did *not* leave " pure and limpid *the Gospel stream.*" Since, therefore, it appears to me that, in respect to several of the " Protestant Evangelical denominations" on the one side, and the " Anglican" on the other, there is so great a difference in their " views and teaching respecting the sacraments and ministry," that what *those* regard as impurities in the stream, *this* values as giving to it richness and flavour, and as being the source of its medicinal virtue, I do not see much likelihood of such a coalition between them as the Adelaide " idea" of the " Church of the Future" appears to involve,—certainly not, on the hypothesis of the Anglican Confession and Rule occupying so predominant and regal a position that, in the person of its bishops, it is to preside over the subscriptions to articles of faith of all other ministers, to allow and license them (" the present generation"), and to secure to their successors something more than " Presbyterian orders." The

Bishop's proposed creed " in accordance with the Nicene Confession," might consist of a few simple articles, and his service for " the conferring of orders," might omit what to other Protestants is objectionable (though, who, conscious of the power of creating a priest, would consent to that?)—but, even if such were the case, the Anglican teaching, its creed, orders, offices, ordinations, would remain for itself the same, and the point is, that " the spiritual mind," *in other communions,* would, as I think, revolt from any such identity or confederation as would make them " morally " responsible for these.

On these several grounds, then, it appears to me, that the scheme of the Bishop of Adelaide for the formal " union of all the Protestant Evangelical denominations," with a view to the formation of a " Church of the Future," can never be 'any thing but an ideal sketch. As a speculation, or theory, it is not likely to find general approval; as to its being realized in fact, that would seem to be utterly hopeless. It aims at far too much. What it seeks is not possible, if it were ex- pedient; and many will think would not be expedient, if it were possible. In liturgical and other matters, it has been thought to offer, in the name of his own communion, concessions and changes which many of its members would deprecate and resist. It asks of others what it is not to be supposed they would be willing to grant, and suggests their acceptance of, and submission to, that whose claims to pre-eminence they have learnt to deny. But worst of all, the project is impeded, as we think, by the nature of the proposed union being such, that if attempted, it would involve serious responsibility in respect to doctrine, which could not but have corresponding serious results; results on all sides,—certainly some for which his lordship is not prepared. The soundness of the conclusion at which I have arrived, and have thus stated, does not depend on the rightness and trueness of the creed and confession either of the Bishop and the Bishop's Church on the one hand, or of those of the Non-episcopal communions on the other; but simply on *the fact*, that such and such are their views respectively, and that the present condition of the Protestant world is what it is. I have gone more minutely into the matters before us, than, perhaps, was at all necessary; but the nature of the document first submitted to me, and the quarter from which it came, have very naturally led to this. In one of his latest communications, the Bishop still expresses his anxiety to know " whether *such a union as that proposed* would be deemed by Non-episcopal bodies unnecessary or inexpedient,—or whether there are any such difficulties or objections in the way, as, if not removable, would form an insuperable barrier *to a complete fellowship of the Churches.*"* I have tried to answer these inquiries; or, at least, I have tried to contribute something *towards* an answer. Having done what I could in that respect, I shall now add a few further remarks on some things which have been obtruded on our attention by the recent correspondence, or by events arising out of it.

* App., p. 50.

PART SECOND.

HINTS AND OBSERVATIONS

ON

SEVERAL SUGGESTED ECCLESIASTICAL QUESTIONS.

I.

Episcopacy.

The Bishop, throughout his communications, seems to confound Episcopacy as it at present exists, with that of the apostolic age,—to assume the identity of the two —and to claim for the one what he thinks was due to the other. This is not the time or place to argue the question; it may not, however, be improper to state that whether right or wrong in our convictions and belief, we do so apprehend things as to be obliged to disallow his lordship's assumption. The bishops of the New Testament were presbyters, and presbyters only;* and although the office of Timothy and Titus, and the direction of the pastoral epistles, would seem to countenance something like official ecclesiastical presidency in a district, there is no proof that Timothy or Titus was ever fixed as a *stationary* " overseer " in any defined sphere, extended or limited like a modern diocese. The presumption is rather on the other side;—it would seem to be, that, " *having* set in order the things that were wanting, and ordained elders in every city," the Churches were then complete (each with its presbytery, or elder-

* Acts xx. ver. 17, compared with ver. 28. The identity of the " presbyters" of the one verse, with the " bishops " of the other, is concealed by the use of the word " overseers," which is at once equivalent and equivocal. Phil. i. 1; 1 Tim. iii. 1—7; Titus i. 5—7, compared; 1 Peter v. 1, 2.

ship), and, thus constituted, were henceforth competent to govern themselves. The Christian congregations in any region, were the *Churches** of that region, not " the Church;" each was independent of the others as to rule or responsibility, though all were united by love and reciprocal recognition. Even in the second century, it is on all hands admitted, that many of those who are designated bishops in certain ecclesiastical gatherings, were simply the pastors of separate congregations, not a few of them of small country churches. This fact should not be forgotten in estimating Chillingworth's celebrated argument. But, however these things may be,—or a hundred others that might be suggested, springing out of certain expressions in the New Testament, or certain facts in Church history,—I should be quite willing to allow, for my part, that the customs and usages of the apostolic age were such, that something like an Episcopacy was a very natural result from them. Just as I have a leaning towards a liturgical service, so have I convictions and preferences which would render an Episcopal rule no objection and no burden to me. If it were possible for the different religious bodies to come to an agreement to unite and act together, something of the kind would most likely evolve, and take form and movement, by way of natural consequence,—as the result of necessity or expediency, and the action of great general laws. In this way Episcopacy arose at first,—though it was sometime before it acquired many of its modern attributes. Hence, however it may be preferred, and lawfully used, by any portion of the Church, it is not

* Gal. i. 22; Acts ix. 31; 1 Cor. xvi., verses 1st and 19th.

right for its adherents to employ in respect to it words
and terms which meant one thing in the first century and
mean another in this, as if, in each case, they weighed
exactly alike, and stood precisely for the same thing.

I do not wonder at the Bishop of Adelaide's regarding
Episcopacy, with its three orders, as a Divine institute,
as that would seem to be the "dogma" of his Church.
It believes that there have been, "in Christ's Church,
from the apostles' time, bishops, priests, and deacons."
The Bishop accepts this; and, as one "diligently reading the holy Scripture and ancient authors," is honestly
persuaded that the thing is "evident to all men" doing
the same. At any rate, for himself, he feels "bound in
conscience" to adhere to it, as of "apostolic origin and
scriptural authority." I am not surprised at this. At
the same time, it should be remembered that there are
those—men of like ecclesiastical rank, and even higher
—who think that the very statements he quotes* admit
of an interpretation which would authenticate as "duly
called" those who have "only received Presbyterian
orders;" while others, again, treat Church Government
as altogether a matter of expediency, without anything
about it to make it of permanent or universal obligation.
The present Bishop of Melbourne thus expressed himself
in his Primary Charge:—"The order of bishops, although
we believe it upon most conclusive evidence to have
been derived from the apostles, is not anywhere in
the Scriptures expressly commanded to be retained;
and therefore is not in any of our formularies, or in the
writings of any of our earliest and best divines, affirmed

* APP., p. 30.

to be essential to the constitution of a true Church." In a note to this statement of his own opinion, he refers to that of the Archbishop of Canterbury as being coincident with it; and quotes the following historical statement:—"It appears to be a well-established fact, that during a considerable period after the Reformation, many English benefices were held by divines, who had been admitted to the ministry in the Calvinistic form used on the Continent; nor was re-ordination by a bishop in such cases then thought necessary, or even lawful." Dr. Arnold says, that "Episcopacy was never commanded, the reason being that all forms of government and ritual are in the Christian Church indifferent;"—he speaks of uniformity as "that phantom which has been our curse ever since the Reformation."

While it may be admitted that *some* ecclesiastical modes and forms may approach *nearer than others* to those of the apostolic age, there is no doubt that if the apostles themselves were to rise from the dead they would rather recognize the "others" than the "some," if they found in them more of apostolic life, simplicity and power. Society understands this, in spite of all modern attempts of cloister or college to invest certain pet formulas with awful and authoritative attributes. The time is past for governing the world by *names*,—however powerful they may have been once, when they stood for that which really ruled. In these new lands especially, the days of prescription and formula are numbered. Things are real here, or tending to reality. If on the other side of the world, much more on this is he the true Bishop who actually influences thought and life, and who thus really governs and guides, by whatever title he may be distinguished, or wherever he may be found. It would be far better, if all of us who profess to be pre-eminently the "light" and "leaven" of the world, its "prophets" and "priests," were seeking to serve it by the power of truth, holiness and love, instead of spending our time in putting forth questionable claims, or in discussions about "endless" ecclesiastical "genealogies," which "minister strife rather than godly edifying." We but impose upon ourselves by trying to conjure with words, which have lost their power to divine; seeking to revive, and to give range and permanence to imbecile externalisms, which might be made to cover the whole earth without an inch of it being brought nearer to the kingdom of heaven! That kingdom "is not meat and drink; but righteousness and peace and joy in the Holy Ghost." It is not form, but substance; not order, or rule, or symbol, or ceremony, but "the life of God in the soul of man;" and, though it may be true that certain ecclesiastical customs and arrangements may, more than others, be promotive or conservative of that life, it may exist and grow, and be a reality and a power, vigorous and fruitful, under any. All may exist without sin. They might act without rivalry, dissonance, or disorder. By each, men may spiritually live;—some best by one, some by others. It is wrong to think that the adherents of this or that Ecclesiastical "Rule," must, simply as such, necessarily wish to supplant or destroy all the rest; or that attachment to their own, implies a desire to reduce others to their standard; or that an approach to friendly relations, means covert invasion and attempted conquest. The Adelaide memorialists had no intention of " blowing up the counterscarp of the ditch, and planting their banners on the breach of a ruined Episcopacy !"*   They no more thought of such a thing, or that what they asked would *be* that, than I—in stating that some of the Non-episcopalian bodies would be hard to persuade to give up their " idiosyncrasies "— meant to imply, that the " Greek, Roman, Syrian, or Russian, Churches " would, to meet their demands, have to be " reformed *down* to the platform of John Knox !" But they who confound, under one name, primitive customs and *modern,* and who think that the present age, to be in harmony with the first, should accept their traditions in respect to them, would seem to suppose (perhaps very naturally) that the members of every other communion must necessarily do the same,—have the same theory and the same thought,—must believe in the exact and the exclusive identity of their customs with what in the beginning had apostolic sanction and inspired authority, and must wish for and seek their adoption in the place of, or their ascendency over, others.

II.

The Spirit of different Church Systems.

It may be proper also to remark—or to explain—that the spirit of our Church system does not limit or narrow communion by non-essential points ; and that it does not interfere with or repress an enlarged Christian sympathy by interposing checks and hindrances to its manifestation.

* App., p. 31.

Whatever other Church systems may do, ours, we think, is free from this sin. One of the grounds of our " standing apart " from the Episcopal communion rises out of the very opposite spirit. We cannot bring ourselves to consent, by belonging to that, to be practically separated and cut off from all other Protestant Churches. Once within the sacred enclosure of the Episcopal " Rule," there is no longer intercourse or reciprocity possible between us and other ministers in any public acts of Church-life. If we believe this to be the ordination of Christ and the will of God, as the Bishop does, we should of course submit, though our feelings, like his, might " kick against our judgment." But distinguishing, as we do, between the secondary and the essential, external forms and spiritual life, we are happy in the thought that we need not, on the ground of mere outward order, decline to approach those " who have received the Holy Ghost as well as we," and, by such " standing apart," to obstruct Christian fellowship " for non-essential points," and " narrow communion through matters of Christian expediency rather than Christian obligation ?" We neither think such " dichostasy " enjoined, nor covet the isolation it leads to, however partially concealed under fine names. With our views and feelings, impassable limits, not imposed or required by loyalty to fundamental doctrinal truth, would be " bonds "—" a wall of separation " *not* of God's building,—things unlovely, however gilded and ornamented,—not to be endured, though covered over and made to look imposing by the tapestry of faded traditionary emblazonments. We not only do not wish to forbid others to cast out devils, "because they follow not us;" but we do not think it is "*following* them," if we join with them occasionally, on equal terms, in helping to deliver distracted humanity from the thraldom of the Evil One.

The Bishop is mistaken in thinking that we have only *just now* come to see *why* it is that the Episcopal clergy cannot unite with us in ministerial acts; that this proceeds not from the " mere pride of social position, or the domineering spirit of a State-favoured Church and a Baronial Episcopate," but because, "they cannot recognize our orders." * We have long been aware of that. We have long been familiar with the distinction between an Establishment and a Church, and have known how the latter might come out of the environment of the former, and be delivered from all legal disability of intercourse with others, and yet retain, in all their force—perhaps guard with greater vigilance than before, and obtrude with increased iteration and emphasis—those claims and pretensions which, far more than any thing else, separate it from the rest of the " Evangelical denominations." My Right Rev. friend cannot, of course, forego his conscientious convictions. He is bound to adhere to them, though they compel him to " stand apart " from all the Evangelical communities of Protestant Christendom, as if his Church stood alone in the midst of the earth, or was the only Divine thing on the face of it. We do not ask him to " follow us; " nor to give up, on the ground of expediency, and as a matter of compromise, the smallest atom of what he believes to be of Divine obligation; nor would we wish him, or any

* App., pp. 28, 29.

one else, to break through what he regards as a Divine barrier;—but we may be permitted to rejoice that his convictions are not ours; that "we have not so learned Christ;" that we are free, without compunction or inconsistency, and as "of faith," to hold intercourse with those who also belong to the Christian "household;"—that we can not only meet them on the common stair, and talk with them on the landing, or over the rail, but that we are able to look in, occasionally, into their apartments, in a friendly way, for a morning call or an evening visit, without feeling bound to take up our abode in them, or to adopt their peculiarities of accommodation or ornament, coming home to cut and fashion our own furniture to look like theirs. It does seem to us rather a depressing and melancholy thing, and one that argues that something is seriously wrong *somewhere*, that "kindred souls, professedly pledged to the same cause, rejoicing in the same hope, and devoted to the same duty of preaching Christ and Him crucified to a dark and fallen world," are yet forbidden, not only to exchange pulpits with each other, but even to "co-operate in the distribution of religious tracts, missions to the bush, or Sunday School Teachers' Unions." The views of one class, in respect to "orders" and "the prophetical office of the ministry," interfere. The "cause," the "hope," the "duty"—preaching "Christ and Him crucified,"—are, by hypothesis, "the same." There are those who think that a great, common object might be unitedly aided and advanced by *some* forms of co-operative action, and that it would be well if it were so; —and they further think, that it is *not* they—their principles or spirit—that prevents it.   They respect the convictions and admit the conscientiousness of those with whom the obstacle lies.   All that they ask for themselves is, that it should not be attributed to *them ;* and that they may be permitted to rejoice in " that liberty," with which, as they believe, " Christ has made them free."

III.

SYSTEMS AND MEN.

Unconscious Revelations.

The Queen, it has been said, is not a person but an Institution.   Her official acts are not to be regarded as the acts of an individual, but as the *actings* of a system. They do not indicate, therefore, personal character, but are merely illustrative of the spirit and working of the Constitution.   The same may be said of ruling ecclesiastics.   In officially carrying out their policy, and thus showing (unconsciously, it may be,) " what manner of spirit it is of," they are not to be judged as persons, but to be regarded as institutions.   Their personal-qualities, their individual dispositions and character, are separable, and should be separated, not only from their official acts, but even from many others, not strictly official, which they may either feel bound to do, or be induced to do, as entrusted with the working, or being themselves a part, of the machinery of a Church system.   This principle I hope you will keep in mind in going through the " Adelaide Correspondence."   All who were engaged in it, will be discovered to stand in need, more or less, of its charitable application, or of those charitable allowances which spring out of it. I am not myself a " ruling " ecclesiastic, (nor perhaps, in reality, or as some think, an ecclesiastic at all,) yet, as having long been accustomed to look at ecclesiastical matters from a particular point of view, and being necessarily, therefore, subject to the influence of one-sided habits of thought in respect to them,— though I have all my life struggled against that,—I frankly confess that I often found myself very quietly using expressions, which, though natural to me, and seemingly innocent, I saw, on reflection, could not but be offensive to others. Many of these merely breathed and died; but some of them, doubtless, escaped death and still live. When they cross your path, be so good as remember what I have just been saying. They will tell their tale,—betraying the secret unconsciously confided to them; but you can give me the benefit of the distinction to which I have referred. In no sphere of thought is it so necessary as in the ecclesiastical, to keep in mind the distinction between things and men,— official acts and personal character,—moral disposition and mental habitudes,—the spirit of a system, and the spirit of those who advocate or belong to it. I insist upon this, because, in connexion with the point at present before us, I deem it right to refer to some particulars which singularly illustrate *the spirit of the system in which the Bishop of Adelaide, his official colleagues, and special friends, live and move,*—THE SYSTEM as distinct from *the men;* and what I have asked for myself, I ask for them.

1. You have already seen how, when under the influence of his own genial nature, his glowing and gushing

sympathies, *Dr. Short* was pouring out his soul in his first letter, the hand of *the Bishop* kept infusing into his utterances what virtually nullified them.   In what subsequently occurred, in writing or act, little appeared *but* the Bishop.   Receiving information, when at a distance from Adelaide, of what had occurred there, he became alarmed, "doubting of himself whereunto this would grow."   He either misapprehended the movement, exaggerated minor circumstances, or saw what those on the spot did not see.   He therefore suddenly stopped at the first step, yet with the manner of one who had long been engaged in severe and somewhat disheartening labour. He finds, "when he speaks of peace, some make themselves ready to battle;" and, discovering that the " Evangelical watches *do not seem at present disposed to go together,*" retires, feeling like Charles the Fifth, who after " his life-long endeavours" to get men "to walk by the same rule," was taught, by a sort of parable, " the folly " of the attempt.* Now, I am really not aware that anything had occurred to warrant either of these statements, or at least to justify so sudden and precipitate a withdrawal from the world.   The laymen had mistaken the import of his words, and had mixed up that mistake with their own object; but a friendly and immediate explanation might have been given, and was certainly due.   But THE SYSTEM was surprised.   The *man* appeared to have raised a spirit which the *institution* did not mean to call,—was not prepared for, and could not welcome.   Its only thought, therefore, was at once to avoid or lay the apparition.

* APP., p. 7.

2. The Bishop returned to Adelaide on the 10th of November. (He wrote to me, from Bishop's Court, on the evening of that day, forwarding his note of the 5th.) The first memorial had been waiting for him *from the 18th of October* in the custody of his official friends. It seems neither to have been *asked for*, nor *presented*, up to the 15th November, as, on that day, the Bishop states that " he had been informed" of something respecting it, but had " not yet received it,"—a singular fact, considering that the Dean and the Archdeacon had recommended the publication of the Governor's letter containing a distinct reference to it. *On that same day*, however, the Bishop wrote a long reply to a second memorial, got up after, and in opposition to, the first; it was not till the 19th that the first was acknowledged, having only been received on the 17th " at 2 p.m."*—*All this is deeply significant.* But justly and candidly to estimate its import, you must distinguish between the *system* and the *men*,—and between the men in their personal and their official character. Things which, without explanation, seem to imply something like discourtesy to a number of respectable persons, of good social position, members of their own Church, are not to be regarded as the *acts* of Dr. Short, and the Rev. Messrs. Farrell and Woodcock, *in their personal character as gentlemen*, but should be reckoned as the *actings* of an impersonal polity through the almost unconscious movements of its official institutions.

3. The difference between the " note" and " letter," respectively acknowledging the two memorials, is, you

* App., pp. 8, 9.

will observe, somewhat remarkable,—the off-hand, curt brevity of the one, contrasted with the extended and minute particularity of the other. Nor are the contents of the documents without significance. In the " note," the Bishop states that " the obstacles in the way of giving effect to the principle involved in the request of the memorialists, are in his opinion little likely, under the present circumstances and views entertained *in the various sections* of the Protestant Church, to be overcome." I submit that so far as the *Non-episcopal* " sections " of the Protestant Church are concerned, *their* " circumstances and views " will hardly sustain this statement *in respect to the laymen's object in itself considered.* The " circumstances and views," however, of the Anglican " section," as felt and held by the Bishop, would not only sustain it, but, as watched over and carried out by him, do now, as we have seen, frown upon and forbid the slightest approach to ministerial co-operative recognition.*

4. I do not like referring you to a passage in the reply to the second memorial, it is of so personal a nature, yet I believe I must do so—though it will be at some cost of feeling to myself—it is so singularly demonstrative of *what it is* that " interposes a mid-wall of partition between kindred souls, pledged to the same cause, rejoicing in the same hope, and devoted to the same duty of preaching Christ and Him crucified." The emphatic words, in the extract, are the Bishop's. " For my views," he says, " I have only to *repeat* that portion of my letter to the Rev. T. Binney, in which I said, ' neither the power of your intellect, *nor* the vigour of

* Ante, p. 77 ; and App., p. 29.

your reasoning, *nor* mighty eloquence, *nor* purity of life, *nor* suavity of manners, *nor* soundness in the faith, *would justify me in departing* from the rule of the Church of England, a tradition of eighteen centuries, which declares your orders irregular, your mission the offspring of division, and your Church system, I will not say schism, but dichostasy—that is, standing apart.'"—[Hush! don't manifest any feeling. When you have lived as long in the world as I have, and have learnt to discriminate, as constantly and carefully, between *things* and *men*, you will be able to take from the One, with perfect equanimity, what you might not be willing to accept from the Other. It is the "Church," or its "Rule," that speaks; and it is with *it* only that we have to do.]—"*Neither your purity of life, nor soundness in the faith, would justify me in departing from the Rule of the Church of England, a tradition of eighteen centuries, which declares your orders irregular, your mission the offspring of division, and your Church system, I will not say schism, but dichostasy—that is, standing apart.*" Very well. Be it so, I reply. So far as I am personally concerned, I am quite content. Let rules and traditions go for what they are worth. The Bishop *repeats* his words in allusion to the laymen's request. But the laymen's request was not mine. My name appearing in their memorial, was an accident. I had nothing to do with it. But I *have* something to do with my own "mission" as a servant of Christ, and the spirit of the "Church system" within which I live; and, *in consequence of the Bishop's own voluntary act,* I have a right also to speak of *his* "Church system," especially as to its "standing apart,"—not (he himself being witness) on the ground of what is essential, in respect to "doctrinal soundness," or "Christian character," but on matters of mere "traditional authority." I have no claim to any thing like what Dr. Short, in the kindness of his heart, attributes to me in the extract just read, and would rather avoid looking at the question as a personal one. This can be easily done by transferring our friend's word-portrait from myself to Apollos. It is a very good likeness of *him*. [Acts xviii. 24—28.] Now, without going into argument or proof, (of which, however, I think there is abundance,) I will only say, that from all that appears in the apostolic history respecting Apollos, and from other scriptural facts and statements, I cannot but concur with those who believe that he was exactly in that condition in regard to "orders," that, if he were now to rise from the dead, and appear in Adelaide, the spirit and principle of the Bishop's system would oblige it to "stand apart" from him;—" neither the power of his intellect, *nor* his mighty eloquence, *nor* the vigour of his reasoning, *nor* the purity of his life, *nor* his soundness in the faith," *nor* any thing else, would be of the least avail against the authority of "a tradition ;"—or, if the system yielded, and the man who had never been ordained by a Bishop, was admitted within its sacred and guarded precincts, the agents of the irregularity would be in danger of being "contended with," as Peter was by the Jerusalem traditionists,* for consenting to eat with one uncircumcised. I hardly know of any thing more unlike the spirit

* Acts xi. 1, 2.

of the New Testament, and the customs of the apostolic age, than the Bishop's own representation of the " circumstances and views" of the Anglican section of the Protestant Church.

5. Still further; in consequence of his first letter having been misunderstood,—its glowing language and catholic yearnings leaving the impression that he was prepared for something practical,—he publishes a previous correspondence, " in self-defence, and *to re-assure* the Counter-memorialists."* I find no fault with this. I think it was quite right, seeing that he *had been* " misunderstood." But observe how it illustrates the nature of *the system.* The *Genius Loci,* the Spirit of the place in which the Bishop officially dwells, was affronted, one might say,—certainly affrighted, by the tone and tenor of his speech. In spite of himself, and of all his lowering and modifying phraseology, the flashing of the burning words which his personal feelings impelled him to utter, *was* thought to mean something. Those who were prepared to sympathize with that, welcomed the lustre, but in doing so mistook its nature and " object," and, misled by the mistake, sought at once to increase and to prolong it. This excited the alarm of others, who dwelt in the darker recesses of the temple. *They* thought the light was lightning,—and that the whole fabric was about to be dissolved! They made known their apprehensions in a manner hardly intelligible, by a sort of incoherent, confused cry,† but the more, on that account, indicative of terror;—and they could only be " re-assured" and put to rest again,

* APP., No. V.   † APP., p. 11.

by being told that they had nothing to fear,—that, so far as the *inside* light was concerned, the coruscations were as harmless as gala fireworks!—Now I do solemnly protest and avow that it is to me,—and I know that I may speak for you also, and for all our co-religionists, and say—that it is to us the source of joy and thankfulness that our "Church system" does not condemn us thus to "stand apart" from all other denominations of Christian men;—that it does not teach us to live in such jealous and sectional isolation;—and above all, that we have not learnt so to *like* to live in it, as not only to have no desire to go beyond it, but to be ready to take alarm at the slightest hint or symptom of the approach of others to us, or of us to them. We have no wish to persuade other bodies to adopt our forms, traditions, or customs,—nor should we care to achieve this by scheme or effort. It is enough that we are free both to cherish and to manifest the spirit of brotherhood; that we are able to unite in public acts of fraternal recognition, and thus to exhibit the substantial oneness in faith of those who may be distinguished by circumstantial differences. If there are those who cannot do this, or do not wish it, that is *their* concern, not ours. We have no desire to interfere with their principles or predilections. They have as much right—so far as man is concerned—to "stand apart" from all, as we have to hold intercourse with many;—the same liberty to be a "dichostasy," as others have to repress and get rid of the spirit that would make them that. Only, we think it right to say that, for ourselves, we could not consent to be one with *them* at the expense of being "divided" and cut off from all other sections of the Protestant Church. The spirit of our system forbids this, however far we may ourselves be beneath it, or however it and we may be misunderstood.

IV.

THE OFFICIAL AND THE PERSONAL
Further illustrated.

In the course of this last line of remark, I have had to make allusion to persons, and even to mention names; but I should feel it to be a great injustice (as I should certainly deem it an infelicity) if I was to be thought, on that account, to have indulged in *personalities*. Not only do I mean nothing offensive towards individuals, but the very object of my statements—or of my illustrative argument, if I may so call it—is, to bring out and make manifest the charitable distinction between things and men. You may as well confound the personal feelings of a judge with the law which he administers, as lose sight of the distinction, in the case of many other functionaries, between their personal and official character. But this is not all; the influence of any system in which men live, will be apt to show itself in acts not strictly official, and in feelings and expressions, or occasional behaviour, not natural to them as men,—things into which they will fall, or which they may give way to, with a perfect unconsciousness of what they imply. We have all need that this should be remembered and allowed for. Children of different ecclesiastical parents, we imbibe their humours as well as milk, and these will now and then break out, and be obvious to others though not perceived by ourselves.   He must know little of his own hereditary " sectional" tendencies and temperament, who is not aware that, after discussion or controversy with one of a different ecclesiastical lineage from himself, he has need, on some account or other, for the appeal—

> ———— " Bear with me,
> When that rash humour which my mother gave me,
> Makes me forgetful."

And he must be a poor specimen of Christian manhood, who not only does not instantly respond to the appeal—

> I will;—" and henceforth,
> When you are over-earnest,
> I'll think your *Mother* chides"—not *you* ;

but who has not wisdom to see the duty of such forbearance, even before it is sought,—or "love enough" to exercise it, whether it be sought or not, or not felt or admitted to be required.   The Bishop of Adelaide, in his letter of November 28th, refers to and illustrates the distinction on which I have insisted.   After mentioning the " real cause " of the " isolation " of the Episcopal clergy,—" not so much *personally* as *ministerially*,"— from Non-episcopal, (the non-recognition of the " orders" of the latter by the former,)—he says, " I was not sorry to seize the opportunity presented by your arrival in South Australia of making it *quite clear, why*, and *why only*, we hold ourselves *ministerially* aloof from Non-episcopalian ministers, though as with myself, so with my brethren, our *private* and *personal* feelings often ' kick against' our solemn convictions and pledges."*

* APP., p. 29.

Nothing could be clearer or more candid than this, or more strongly expressed. Indeed, the terms are such as I should not myself have ventured to employ. There is not a more radiant, genial soul in all Australia than the Bishop of Adelaide; and I have always felt that any thing, in word or act, in the recent proceedings, to which exception was taken by one or another, was to be attributed to the system, not the man. He has extended towards myself a like consideration. When *my* form of denominational thought has found for itself utterance in somewhat strong language, he has not only not been offended, but has accepted it for what it was, and allowed for it accordingly.

And here, in passing, I may advert to an illustration of the point before us in the case of one, whom, when in Victoria, I learnt, as I have publicly stated, very greatly to esteem and love;—I refer to Dr. Perry, the Bishop of Melbourne. I may say first, however, that I was indebted also to *him* for applying the rule, and judging according to the distinction, which I have been laying down. The " echoes of the King's Weigh-House sermon," referred to by the Bishop of Adelaide as having " not yet died away," were, after nearly a quarter of a century, still reverberating, I found, and making themselves heard even on this side of the world. The first time I called on the Bishop of Melbourne, there was a volume on the table, which he took up, and, directing my attention to a certain page, I found it to contain the offending paragraph. We had some conversation about it ; and I believe he saw that there was nothing so very terrible in it, considered as the words of one *system* about *another.* I accidentally found in the house of a friend a copy of my " Conscientious Clerical Nonconformity," which I asked his lordship to look through, as our conversation had turned on such matters. Again he did me the justice to say, that he saw nothing in it offensive, though the language was sometimes strong, as it was only the utterance of what was consistent with the ecclesiastical stand-point I occupied. I apply the same principle to him. No one, as an individual Christian, is more catholic in spirit, more " a lover of good men," delighting in intimate devotional intercourse with the members and ministers of different Churches, than the Bishop of Melbourne. He recognises and pleads for the recognition of the official standing and Church-state of the ministers and congregations of other bodies; and he is zealous and forward as a promoter of the Evangelical Alliance. Nevertheless, as identified with a certain ecclesiastical system, he feels it right to meet and mingle with other Christians exclusively as individuals, and to discountenance in his clergy every thing approaching to union, or co-operative action, with other ministers and Churches in any public way. In his Primary Charge, too, I was struck by a passage startlingly illustrative of the distinction between things and men,—the constant and thoughtful remembrance of which we all so much need. In giving directions to his clergy " in respect to their intercourse with ministers of the various Protestant denominations," he has to speak to them, as he expresses it, " with reference to those bodies which have separated themselves from the communion of the Episcopal Church." " Denying that their original secession was justifiable," which he thinks could only have been " on the ground that it had, as a Church, apostatised from the faith, and become incurably corrupt;" but, " confessing that there was much in the state of the Church, at that time, to palliate their conduct;" he is yet of opinion that " the founders of the different dissenting bodies did commit a great error in their secession."— After adding to this the statement, " we are likewise of opinion that all dissenting bodies have erred in their ecclesiastical systems, and many also in subordinate points of doctrine; and that *their ministration of the Word and Sacraments is irregular;* he then proceeds thus :— " Hence, while we may *hope* that the labours of faithful ministers among them have been, *through the* MERCY *of God*, productive of much good, we cannot but consider *dissent itself* to have been upon the whole *prejudicial to the progress of pure religion and piety.* Nevertheless, inasmuch as they are sound in all the fundamental doctrines of the Gospel, we ought to recognize individual Dissenters as Christian brethren, and to make due allowance for the circumstances in which they have been placed. It does not become us to judge them harshly. *It would be wrong for us* TO BREAK UP AGAINST THEIR WILL ANY OF THEIR ESTABLISHMENTS, (*my Lord!*) *or* TO IMPOSE SILENCE UPON THEIR MINISTERS."* (*I should think so.*) The high respect, however,—the affectionate regard, I may say—that I entertain and cherish towards the Bishop of Melbourne, prevents my making any remark on these words. They are not the words of Dr. Perry, as a

* Charge, pp. 37, 38.

loving, godlike, Christian man ; but those of *a system*,—
an unwise Impersonality, which he permitted to speak.
through him, and to speak, too, under an utter forgetfulness of the age in which it lived, and the country to
which it had come.

V.

ADMONITORY.

Throughout the whole of this address, I have kept in
view the one question which I undertook to examine—
the possible " union of all the Protestant Evangelical
denominations," as a step towards " a Church of the
Future " to spring out of it. I have not entertained, as
not being within my province, the question of the first
memorialists at Adelaide respecting the opening of
Episcopal pulpits to the ministers of other bodies. Even
my recent remarks, apparently bearing upon this, have
been intended to illustrate only what we value as our
own liberty, not in any way to persuade others to adopt
it. In the Bishop's proposition, you, and I, and all
other Non-episcopal ministers and bodies are alike
directly and deeply interested, and on the whole scheme,
in all its relations and aspects, I had a right to speak,—
not only as denominationally involved in it, but as personally solicited to " show my opinion." The laymen's
question is one which peculiarly concerns the members
of their own Church. It is a matter they must arrange
and settle for themselves. I do not know that I am
called to enter into it, beyond what I have already
incidentally done in portions of the " Adelaide Correspondence." The promoters or originators of the move-

ment are well and fully qualified to conduct their own cause. They have drawn up and exhibited their brief, in a clear, calm, and dignified manner, and have brought forth points which cannot but ultimately have results.* On the general subject something will incidentally come up before I conclude; I will only here interpose a word or two bearing upon it, that may be admonitory or suggestive to ourselves or others.

In thinking of the matter in question, and of kindred matters, we should guard against supposing that there are not large and loving souls, men of catholic spirit and expansive sympathies, within the confines of the Episcopal communion, though they seek not the liberty to manifest themselves by official, or semi-official, acts. You may think them mistaken, and they may *be* mistaken, in attaching equal sacredness, or something like it, to the external form of the Church as to fundamental and saving truth. But if they are so, it should be remembered that this is based, in the case of some, on their belief that Episcopal government is not merely an allowable mode of Church order and action, but one of positive appointment and enforced obligation, and that *within* it—as the consequence of Divine arrangement and apostolic succession—there are preserved and conveyed supernatural gifts—gifts *exclusively* so preserved and conveyed—which are essential to the validity and efficiency of ministerial acts, and to the power and

---

* *See* "THOUGHTS AND FACTS connected with a movement in 1858, to promote a closer Alliance of Evangelical Christians in South Australia." By a Lay Member of the United Church of England and Ireland.

authority of ministerial utterances. Right or wrong, that is their belief. Or, others may be thought of who take lower ground than this. Without claiming for Episcopacy so high a character, or altogether confining to it Divine gifts, this second class of persons will content themselves with saying, that it is to be regarded as necessary to the *completeness*, though not to the *being* of a Church; and that it is of such great, though not paramount, obligation, that a Church can never lose it without injury, or deliberately cast it off without sin. So long as these parties thus think and feel, it is obvious that, for themselves, they would not be at liberty to interchange ministerial services with Non-episcopal clergy-men. In the one case, the thing would not be right, but something actually and in itself sinful;—in the other case, it might be felt to be inexpedient, as not in its results likely to be harmless. You may say that conscience is to be enlightened as well as obeyed. Every one can say that in respect to his neighbour, and it is no doubt true. So long, however, as the men in question have their convictions, so long, both by us and by others, are their convictions to be respected. They are not to be urged to violate them or to allow their violation. Obliged to act according to their own views of what God has enjoined, they are no more to be regarded as *personally* chargeable with illiberality of spirit, or narrowness of heart, than those should be so regarded, who, because of *their* convictions and views in respect to Evangelical truth, can have no visible communion or interchange of services with those who deny it. True, to *us* the difference in the two things (Church Government and Evangelical truth) may be immense; so palpable, too, that submission to the supremacy of the one may seem to stand out like constructive disloyalty or treason to the other. But every man must walk by his own light. No man is entitled to demand that others shall walk by *his*. There is such a thing as the intolerance of toleration, the illiberalism of liberality. In everything we may argue, reason, controvert, persuade, endeavouring legitimately to effect a change in opinion and conviction; but in nothing is it either wise or right to urge *to action*, before the inward man, in him who has to act, himself sees the lawfulness and propriety of what is to be done, and is prepared to do it with cheerful spontaneity.

On the other hand, it should be remembered, that the men for whom we plead are not entitled to require that all should walk by *their* light, or be bound to yield submission to that which is a rule to them. Especially in a Church in which there is such diversity of interpretation with respect to almost every thing belonging to it, that there are schools and sections of every sort, *one* might surely be permitted to arise that should embody in action those principles and feelings of Evangelical catholicity, which many of its adherents profess to cherish. That the project is not without possible inconvenience, is obvious enough; and that it ought not to be adventured upon without serious consideration, is only the dictate of common sense. But that it *might* issue in blessed results—in action and re-action in many ways —to the advantage of pure and undefiled religion on all sides, " the spiritual mind," intent on general rather than sectional objects, may be disposed to hope. For the laymen's question, however, to find safe solution, or for their scheme to get practically "inaugurated," may be very difficult,—though not *so* difficult, I think, as for those to do so which it has been our duty to discuss. In England, the Church is fettered by legal disabilities; —hemmed in on all sides, by barriers and obstructions not easily to be broken. Whatever may be the theory of individual clergymen, as to the recognition of other ministers as "duly called" when orderly inducted into office according to the laws and customs of their own body; however, from the preference of substance to form, the essential to the secondary,—and from the belief that *modes* of action, traditional forms and ceremonies, are of imperfect obligation, "have at all times been divers, and may be changed according to the diversities of countries, times, and men's manners, so that nothing be ordained against God's word;"*—however, on these or kindred grounds, certain minds may speculatively recognize other ministers as Christ's servants, and other Churches as God's priesthood,—still, the law lies against and forbids any thing like a practical manifestation of the conviction. For a clergyman even to enter a conventicle, as a private worshipper, is, I believe, an offence; to cleanse and purify the minister of one, that he may be fit to enter the Anglican pulpit, requires a purgation of three years; silence is imposed for that period,—separation from all persons and places whose stain and taint are so deadly! In these colonies I am by no means sure that there is any *law* at all touching such things, except

* Thirty-fourth Article.

what the clergy make for themselves. They bring with them—and who does not? or who would not?—the associations and traditions of the old land. With a feeling with which every man who has a heart can sympathize, they and their flocks cling to the idea of being component parts of the Parent Church. The most of them have an underthought, especially the younger of them, that " this is not their rest;" they cherish the hope of one day returning and settling at " home"—the fond and favourite term, I find, universally employed in speaking of the mother-country, even by the native born who have never seen it—and they cannot be blamed for being slow to contemplate and reluctant to do *here* any thing which, if done in England, would be a bar *there* to professional service. This, from statements personally made to myself, I know to be a strong point with some. To the " tradition of eighteen centuries,"—to the felt superiority arising from the thought of their " succession" and " orders,"—there comes to be added the fear of damaging their ministerial prospects ;—the possibility—I would not say of their advancement and preferment being impeded, but—of their being cut off from ministerial duty altogether, or for some time, *hereafter*, in consequence of their doing something uncanonical now. No one can wonder at this; no one ought to blame ;—the feeling may have its roots in deep and genuine ministerial earnestness. The difficulty really is, as far as I can gather, that no one seems to know what ecclesiastical or canonical laws are in force in the colonies, or whether any of them have existence or authority beyond the limits of England. It is the opinion of some,

I know not whether it be correct, that although a clergyman, who, on his return home might have to take a
curacy, and who would be thus dependent on the mere
will of a bishop who can refuse license without assigning
a reason,—although such a one might be prejudiced by
having done something irregular here, one who received
an appointment to a living could not be legally called to
account on such a ground, or refused institution because
of it.   The ministers of a colonial Church, it is believed,
might, as such, do many things abroad which they could
not do in England, without at all ceasing to be *spiritually*
related to the Parent Church *as* a Church.*   The things
in question might be illegal in them at home as clergy of
an *Establishment*, but would not be illegal where the laws
of the Establishment do not reach, ("where there is no
law, there is no transgression") while, as ministers of *the
Church*, considered apart, they (the things supposed)
would not interfere with their position in, or their connexion with, *it.*   On this very ground, ministers of the
Established Church of Scotland, who, in their own land,
could not have gone into the pulpits of any other
denomination without committing an ecclesiastical
offence and exposing themselves to censure, have preached
in my pulpit, feeling that they could so act without
either doing wrong or incurring blame.   When the
colonial Churches are really such,—when they are composed of the native born, and their ministers belong
rather to the new, than to the old land, they may come
better to understand their position, their liberties and
their rights, and, without ceasing either to be dutiful

* APP., No. VII., p. 56.

and loving children of the Parent Church, or to be proud
of their privilege, or to be earnestly anxious to preserve
their connexion with it, dreading the severing of the
bond that binds them—without anything of all this
coming to pass, they may yet find that they can venture
on new forms of thought and action, not only without
falling into filial disobedience, or incurring personal loss,
but with the maintenance of sincere loyalty of heart to
their spiritual Mother, and with great and manifest
advantage to themselves.

PART THIRD.

PERSONAL AND OLD-WORLD MATTERS.

Before closing this already too protracted Address, and—dismissing you from attending to it and me— proceeding with you to the business of the Session and the Assembly, I think it right to advert to at least two other matters;—matters which bear, indeed, on what is personal to myself, but which cannot be referred to without glances at higher objects,—at things involving questions of principle, and the advancement of the cause of Truth and Love.

I.

Nonconformity.

Suffer me to say then, in the first place, that I greatly
regret that circumstances have obliged me to come
forward in these colonies in the way of an apologist for our
Nonconformity (as we call it in the old land), involving
as it does the exposition of the errors, *as we deem them,*
of the Anglican Church. I had no idea of such a thing
on leaving home. I came away broken in health—
incapable of contemplating public duty without dread.
I declined arrangements which friends here would have
made for me in the prospect of an expensive tour,
because I felt that I must be free from all sense of constraint—from the slightest approach to any sort of
prospective obligation to open my mouth. It was more
than within the limits of possibility—it approached the
probable—when I first contemplated my voyage and
visit, that I should go from colony to colony in
weakness and silence. As to writing any thing—
publishing letters in the newspapers even—why the
very sight of my name in the journals of the day gave
pain; every paragraph that appeared was like the inflic-
tion of a wound. And as to Church questions, or any
thing of the nature of controversy, I had long been tired
of all that. Just before I left England, I remember, I
expressed to a friend my great regret, on looking back on

thirty years of ministerial and metropolitan life, that I had so often bestowed time and thought on ecclesiastical questions and controversial pamphlets, that might have been given to higher and better themes, and been productive of something of more lasting utility. When I came to these Australian colonies, I had no idea beyond moving quietly "among mine own people," and no wish but to "live peaceably with all men." So far back as July last, when a deputation wished to wait upon me to solicit my services at the opening of a Free Episcopal Church, I declined to accede to the request, or to undertake the service, because I would not, as a visitor and a stranger, mix myself up with misunderstandings in a religious body to which I did not belong, and, by sanctioning the dissidents, seem to judge the cause, and to give a verdict against their Diocesan:— The Bishop of Melbourne,—with whom I had not then become personally acquainted. I did not know, and I did not care to inquire, who was right or who wrong. That with me was not the question. The point I felt was, that I did not come here to have any thing to do with quarrels or controversies; and that I wished to be permitted to stand clear of these, and quietly to cherish and cultivate feelings of kindness towards all good men. In Adelaide, when things took so unexpected a turn, I said and did nothing till circumstances appeared to make it imperative, and then —I can appeal to all men cognizant of the facts, or careful to understand them—the tone and tenor of my speech and writing were (I am sure they were intended to be) on the side of whatever was conciliatory and fraternal. Hard and offensive words, however, came to be used—used in communications of high pretensions, some of them of undoubted clerical origin; "Unordained minister," "Heretical," "Schism," "Schismatical lay-man," and such like; with observations and arguments akin to the phraseology. *Altogether irrespective, there-fore, of the Bishop,* and *without reference to his com-munications,* I thought it right to ask to be heard—not in the way of controversy or attack, but of explanation and defence;—to be heard in reply to the expressed or implied charges against my own and your ecclesiastical position;—to be permitted to state and set forth some of the grounds on which, *in spite of many attractions, from preference, taste, judgment, expediency,* which drew us towards the Anglican Church, we were obliged to remain without and to "stand apart." Why, many a time, in speech and writing, have I had it said to myself, "I wish you were with *us,*"—and that, too, at times, by individuals of no mean ecclesiastical rank; and it really did seem to me but fair, that when charged with high ecclesiastical crimes and misdemeanors for occupying a position actually forced upon us, we should be allowed to state how it comes to pass that we are conscientiously compelled to stand where we do, preferring to be *called* "schismatical laymen," to actually *being* dishonest eccle-siastics.* Meeting, by chance, in Melbourne, with a

* From the claims and pretensions of the Episcopal Church, combined with its position as professedly *Protestant,* it comes to pass that it employs the weapons of the Romanist against the Dissenter, and the weapons of the Dissenter against the Romanist. The words of Chillingworth, in meeting the charge of schism *which the Church of Rome brings against that of England,* might

copy of a pamphlet I published several years ago, entitled " Conscientious Clerical Nonconformity," I sent it to Adelaide, and had it published for the information of those of our Anglican friends there, who might not have looked at the subject from our point of view. I can honestly say that I would much rather have been spared the inroad on my leisure and enjoyment, and the distractions which have been occasioned by the " Adelaide Correspondence," if I could. But an unexpected call has seemed to come to me—a duty and an obligation to be laid upon me—which I could not escape; a duty to myself, to Truth (or what I deem Truth), to the ministers of my own denomination in these lands, and to those who wrote respecting us as they did—some of whom I am sure are ignorant (not, I hope, willingly ignorant) of our feelings and convictions, and did " not understand what they said, or whereof they affirmed."

That with the " views" we hold of " the Sacraments and Ministry," and the difference between these views and what we understand to be the teaching of the Anglican Church (matters, which are set forth in the tract just referred to),—that we are justified, on the ground of them, in refusing " orders" and declining " conformity," is a thing which must be obvious to every

have been used by those referred to by the Bishops of Adelaide and Melbourne as " having separated"—rather, " who *were* separated" from the Church of England. Addressing the Romanist, he makes the Protestant defendants say, " that they left not your external communion voluntarily, being not *fugitivi* but *fugati*, as being willing to join with you in any act of piety; but they were, *by you, necessitated* and *constrained to separate*, because you will not suffer them to do well with you, unless they would do ill with you."

individual possessed of common candour or common sense. Doubtless, the fault may be with us. We may mistake the "teaching" of the Church,—it may not be what we think it is. Or, the "teaching" of the Church, *being* what we think it is, may be Divine and true, and "worthy of all acceptation." Still, if, with all our endeavours, and with strong inducements from within and from without to lead to an opposite conviction, we can yet neither see that our interpretation of the Prayer-Book is erroneous, nor the teaching we attribute to it right,—as honest men, what are we to do? Our position, indeed, is not perplexing to ourselves, though it may be infelicitous. It may result from want of learning, or want of training, or "partly," as Blackstone says, "from weakness of intellect;" but our *duty* is clear enough. Our wrong views, are right to *us*. Carefully arrived at and conscientiously held, they are to our own minds a law which we dare not break. We do not break it; and hence we are exposed to bad names and hard accusations,—and we are willing to be so, rather than to incur what would be far worse. If we needed justification, however, beyond this appeal to common-sense principles, we are amply furnished with it by the Bishop of the diocese in which we are met. I will illustrate this statement.

We cannot accept and subscribe to the Prayer-Book, because we take it " to mean what it says." It teaches, as we think (taking, as an instance, one doctrine), "spiritual regeneration, in and by baptism;"—*in*, through the power of the Holy Ghost; *by*, by the rite as the instrumental cause. We think the book says this,—

plainly, uniformly, and in various ways, and that other things are harmonised with it. We disbelieve the doctrine; we refuse therefore to subscribe to the book,—not only on this broad and palpable ground, but as not being able to accept any of the theories by which, through some underlying, always unexplained, but possible-to-be-understood condition or hypothesis, the book is made to mean what it does not say, or to *us*, at least, does not seem to say,—if language is really to be used to express thought and not to conceal it.* To justify and vindicate our Nonconformity in this matter, I call before you, then, the Right Rev. the Lord Bishop of Tasmania, accompanied by a friend whom he wishes to be heard in vindication of himself. Some few of the Bishop's pieces have fallen into my hands, and in one of them ["Substance of a Reply, &c.," p. 38,] I find him refusing to admit, "that the compilers of the Liturgy were so double-minded in their dishonesty, as to *say* what they *did not intend;* to *assert* categorically, what they MEANT hypothetically." In support of this statement, he calls forward Dr. Wordsworth, whom he introduces as "one of the soundest theologians of the present day." The witness thus speaks:—"If the words of the English Church in the English Prayer-Book are not to be understood in their plain, simple, literal English sense; if, when she says, ' seeing, dearly

* An exposition of the various theories of baptismal regeneration, and the different modes in which different clergymen interpret the Prayer-Book, so far as the author could make these things out at the time, may be found in a small work with a large title, published anonymously, called "THE GREAT GORHAM CASE : *A History, in Five Books.*"

beloved, this child *is now* regenerate,' she is *not* to be understood to mean that the child *is* regenerate ;* then, doubt, suspicion, and scepticism will lurk beneath her altars, and steal into the most solemn mysteries of religion. Then, *faith in subscriptions to articles will be no more;* and all confidence in her teaching and in that of her ministers will be destroyed. And so a grievous penalty will be inflicted on her and them: a heavy injury will be sustained by her people, and *the English name and nation will sink low in the scale of honesty, sincerity, and truth.*"—So far then as *we* are concerned, we claim, on this testimony, honour and thanks for our " dichostasy," and do not deserve, we think, ridicule or abuse. *We*, at any rate, do what is in us to save the national character. We will not perpetrate, what, in *us*, according to Dr. Wordsworth, would be to lift a disloyal and parricidal hand against the reputation of our country,— against British virtue and the English name!

But this is not all. In the Bishop of Tasmania's " Charge," delivered in 1851, I find, at p. 61, the following passage:—" It is *perfectly incomprehensible* to me," he says, " how the denier of baptismal regeneration *can make up his mind to use the services, in which* THE FACT *is so positively insisted upon.* He must, as it seems to me, speak *with doubting lips and a misgiving heart.* He must surely use the Church's words, not in that literal and grammatical meaning, which she so evidently enjoins; but rather *in that non-natural sense,* through the application of which, an attempt was made, some years ago, so to explain away the articles as to render

* The italics, so far, are Dr. Wordsworth's, or the Bishop's.

it possible for a man to hold any doctrine of Rome, and yet to subscribe to them. *The principles of* Tract 90 (for it is to that which I allude), are, in my judgment, *so essentially dishonest,* that I have no mind to wink at *the adoption of their system of interpretation* in this diocese, whether they lean or lead to Rome *or to Geneva.*" These are terrible words. They involve a fearful moral charge,—a charge of adopting and acting on what is " essentially dishonest;" and that, too, against the " Ministers of the Altar," of whom it is emphatically to be required that their " yea be yea, and their nay, nay." But this charge *would lie against us* (that is our own feeling), if, with *our* views of the nature of Christianity and the meaning of the Prayer-Book, we consented to use the words of the latter. We should, by doing so, place ourselves in a position, where, to one listening to the words that came from our lips, and knowing at the same time our inward thought, the " making up of our mind" to *be* there, and to say and do what was seen and heard, would be a thing " perfectly incomprehensible." However weak, then, or erring, or ill-taught we may be, since we cannot see things in any other light all that we can do,—but are obliged to stand with the Bible under our arm, saying—' " *This* forbids, *as we read it;*—WE *dare not say* that;— God help us !"—I again claim that the Bishop of Tasmania be heard as a witness for our justification.

Still further, we believe that the Bishops who assembled in Sydney, in 1850, and put forth their views on a variety of subjects, gave, on the baptismal question, the right interpretation of the meaning of the Prayer-Book.

After describing " regeneration" to be " the work of God," by which those who are its subjects " die unto sin, and rise again unto righteousness, and are made members of Christ, children of God, and inheritors of the kingdom of heaven ;"—after thus separating from the word every thing like a mere outward or relative change, and restricting it to *an actual, subjective operation of the Holy Spirit on the soul;*—they add the following solemn declaration: " WE believe that *it is the doctrine of our Church* that *all* infants do, *by baptism*, receive *this* grace of regeneration." Among the names of the Bishops attached to this declaration, is that of AUGUSTUS ADELAIDE. I did no injustice, therefore, to my Right Rev. friend himself, in my previous remarks, nor imputed to his Church any doctrine which he would repudiate, when I interpreted the words " creed," " orders," as including a sacramental and priestly element. Of the first, there can be no doubt ; the Bishop himself asserts and maintains it. As to the second, though that is not at present immediately before us, it may be observed, in passing, that it does not depend on the mere occurrence of a word,—the word " priest," which some insist is a contraction of " presbyter ;"—it depends far more on what the man says and does, and on the way in which he is invested with a character sacred and indelible. The words of the Ordination Service, the form of absolution in the Office for the Sick, the " pronouncing" of absolution *being forbidden to the deacon* as one not yet qualified *by a Divine gift*, these things, *in our view*, decide this. We may be mistaken ; but so long as we cannot help seeing things in this light, we feel not only bound to walk accordingly, but we feel also that we are entitled to say to some who are ready to smite us on the face,—" *strike*, but—HEAR." The Bishop of Adelaide very properly makes the appeal " Could I, as an honest man, do so and so, having accepted and subscribed such and such declarations?" It is competent in us to make a like appeal, " Could we, as honest men, subscribe and accept such and such declarations, believing as we do?" But in the old country, the continued imposition of certain oaths and subscriptions, in spite of changes of time and circumstance, law and opinion, has, in many cases, reduced the standard both of professional and personal morality. Hence we have been recently taught from Oxford, that, " cases often occur in which we must do as other men do, and act upon a general understanding, even though unable to reconcile a particular practice to the letter of *truthfulness*, or even to our individual *conscience*." . . . . " Numberless questions relating to the professions of an advocate, a soldier, or *a clergyman*, have been pursued into endless consequences. In all these cases there is a point at which necessity comes in, and compels us to adopt the rule of the apostle, which may be paraphrased ' *Do as other men do* in a Christian Country.' "* We must be excused if we cannot accept this rather suspicious-looking " paraphrase," and if we decline to act in the spirit of this somewhat questionable Oxford Morality.

It would be a great injustice, however, to my own convictions, and to the character of many upright and good men, if I left you with the impression that I regard

* Professor Jowett.

the severe words of the Bishop of Tasmania as justly applicable to those of the clergy whose opinions he condemns. They would be applicable to *us*, if, with our views of the meaning of the Anglican " Offices," we subscribed to and used them; as they would to the Bishop himself, if, in connexion with *his* views of the teaching of the Church, he held a different system of doctrine, and yet consented to accept and employ language which would then express what was contrary to his convictions. But if other men say, that for themselves *they do really think* that the Book not only admits, but *was intended to receive*, a " hypothetical" interpretation, candour and justice alike require that they should have full credit for their honesty and integrity. Others may not be able to see what they see,—to concur in or to act upon their views; but that is not the question. It is enough that *they* can do so. Men are to be judged not by what others feel and think, or by what others regard as legitimate and logical inferences from their opinions, but by what they themselves understand and hold, profess or deny. But this is not all. The men in question, however once those of a different school might regard them as merely tolerated in the Church, are now fully authenticated and endorsed, and have their ecclesiastical position legally secured to them. The principles judicially laid down in the decision on Mr. Gorham's case, may be fairly supposed to sanction, not only *his* views, but forms of thought similar to, though not exactly identical with them. That decision may be denounced and rejected by individuals, as, *in their opinion*, repugnant and contradictory to the mind of the

Church; but it is an authoritative utterance, never-theless,—a judgment arrived at and given forth according to established legal arrangements, and from which there is at present no appeal. Those, therefore, who hold certain well-known theological views, have not only a claim to be believed (which they always had) when asserting that *they* think them consistent with the " for-mularies," but they are now legally entitled to hold them, and, *as* holding them, to be reputed and accepted as consistent members of the Church of England,—although, as members of the Church of the Prayer-Book, their position, words, and acts may be regarded by Dr. Nixon, as, to him, " perfectly incomprehensible." His severe and terrible language, which I quite accept and have willingly quoted in explanation and defence of *our* " standing apart," ought not to be employed, without very serious cause indeed, by Anglican clergymen against each other. It would point to and brand as acting upon principles " essentially dishonest," men like the Bishop of Melbourne and the Bishop of Sydney,—the one his brother in the Episcopate, the other his Metropolitan! Dr. Nixon denounces the idea " that the compilers of the Liturgy were so double-minded in their dishonesty as—to assert categorically, what they meant hypotheti-cally;" but both of the Right Rev. Prelates whom I have mentioned, and to whom, as public men, it is not improper to refer, interpret the language of the " Offices" on the principle of an underlying or conditional " hypo-thesis." The question is not whether Dr. Nixon could do this, or whether we could do it; *others can,* and that, too, with the mental persuasion that they are logically right, and in all good conscience before God. I really do think, therefore, that such men should have their convictions respected by their brethren, as they have a right, also, to be regarded as recognized members of the Church of England. I say this in perfect consistency with two things, which I merely name in passing:—in the first place, with the full knowledge of the fact that the advocates of an extreme section of the Low Church School have often spoken in such a manner as might have destroyed all faith in the mental and moral honesty of their clients; and in the second place, with the admission that I do not wonder at the way in which the Bishop of Tasmania regards, *theologically*, that deliverance of the Judicial Committee of the Privy Council, which he is determined to repudiate and resist " till his dying day."*

II.

Establishments.—Church.—Liturgical Reform.

I shall now take the liberty of explaining how, for many years past, the matters involved in *both* the questions started at Adelaide have shaped themselves to my mind. This is the second thing I proposed to glance at in my concluding remarks. Here, in an especial manner, I must be considered as speaking exclusively for myself: —neither for you, nor for others of our own body, either here or at home; and certainly not for the gentlemen in South Australia,—the lay-members of the Church of England, who originated the movement with respect to the " exchange of pulpits." They knew nothing, and know nothing, of the personal views or opinions

* App., No. VIII., pp. 56–60.

which I am going to express, and I should deem it an injustice, both to them and to myself, if, on account of what I may say, they should be regarded as mixed up with sentiments, aims, and anticipations of which they may have never thought, and with which they may have no sympathy.

It is pretty well known that some five-and-twenty years ago, and onwards, I occasionally took part in the public discussion of the *Establishment* question,—the Anti-*State-Aid* Controversy, as you would call it here. In consequence of doing so, or of the manner in which I was *supposed* to have done it, I have been long popularly regarded as a bitter enemy to the Episcopal Church. There never was a greater mistake. My error, perhaps, has rather been—certainly by many of my brethren it has been thought to be—that my sympathies with the Church, both as to its organic structure and mode of worship, have gone too far, been too ardent, and a little indiscriminating. I was an avowed " enemy " to *Establishments*,—national political institutions,—the " principle and operation" of which, I thought bad; and in England to *the* Establishment, or, (*as an equivalent term*, observe,) to the " *Established* Church,"—meaning, *not* the Episcopal community itself, and as such, but the *secular environment* in which it dwelt,—or it, as identified with that, as acting through it, and acted on by it. In speaking of this, I once expressed myself in language *almost* as bad as that which some Churchmen were, about the time, in the habit of using,—both High Church and Evangelical. One of the former, I remember, described the *Establishment*, in its relation to the *Church*, as a " Upas tree," which poisoned and blasted everything beneath it, withering the spiritual and Divine thing which it professed to aid and to protect, but which it only disastrously overshadowed;—while one of the latter, referring to lay patronage and to the working of this part of the Establishment, properly so called, said, that he had no doubt that it had been " *most ruinous to the souls of men.*" In times of controversy, men will fall into expressions which their after judgment will not approve. Neither in myself, nor in any one else, do I think language approaching the above in good taste. We ought to be very careful in making allusions to the dread secrets which·the coming eternity is to reveal. But a strong, religious conviction, in certain moods of mind, may find fitting utterance in nothing else. It happens, however, that so far as the particular expression is concerned which made my name so notorious, the echoes of which are reverberating here after a quarter of a century, which created a painful anticipative alarm in the minds of some good men in the prospect of my visit, and which has been again and again referred to in communications called forth by the " Adelaide Correspondence,"—it so happens that, looked at in connexion with all the surrounding explanations of the context, with the spirit of the remarks which follow, and with the previously published sentiments of its author, it may be seen not only to have no bitter or malignant feeling in it towards the Episcopal *Church*, as such, but actually to have its roots deeply fixed in the most sincere love to every member of God's holy Church throughout all the world, whether in the Episcopal " section" of it or any other, and in earnest longings for the removal and "end" of whatever interfered with the health and purity of any particular Church, or with the harmony and intercourse of all.

I have felt constrained to make this reference, from what I have heard and seen while travelling in these colonies, and in consequence of what has been done by some Churchmen, because others, without my knowledge, connected my name with a movement of their own,—which movement, however, they explained was for the sake of the *principle* involved in it, not on account of the person by accident referred to.   I do not regret, however, the necessity for the reference, as it naturally introduces the subject which I am called upon to touch,—the way in which I have been in the habit of viewing various matters involved in *both* the Adelaide questions;—*the Episcopal idea* of the fusion, union, or amalgamation of the Churches, to be *preceded* by settling terms and agreeing on arrangements; and *the Lay idea* of beginning with ministerial recognition and interchange of services between those of the Episcopal and other clergy who are one in faith, according to well-understood Evangelical verities, *without* previously entering into the formal discussion and nice adjustment of secondary matters,—depending more on the instincts and sympathies of the spiritual life than on written regulations, taking one step, only one, and leaving every thing else, if any thing else is ever to come, to time, to the action of general laws, to the controlling and developing influence of nature and grace, to experience, to circumstances, and to God.

I have had my "dream," then, as my Right Reverend

friend, the Bishop of Adelaide, has had his. Our visions came to us from opposite points; he and I looked at them, as we who are on this side of the world look at the sun and moon, and other heavenly bodies, in contrast to our friends in England. The central figures, or last phase, of both our "dreams" might have something in common, but the opening scenes, the imagined beginning and progressive development of each, were altogether different. Both may have been alike "pleasant" to the dreamer, but neither, I fear, will turn out to be prophetic. A church, and even a cathedral, may be built in the air, and " of such stuff as dreams are made of," as well as castles, and it is quite as difficult to get the one as the other embodied in solid and permanent masonry.

The Bishop of Adelaide, I expect, when a young man, began life as a high Episcopalian; I did so as a high Independent. I believed that a modern Independent Church was fashioned after the form of the Primitive Model, and was in exact adjustment, as far as circumstances would permit, with *that*. A few years served to modify these views. The same mistake seemed to be committed on both sides by extreme men,—the use of scriptural words and terms as if they stood for the same thing in relation to what existed in the apostolic age and to what exists amongst us now. True, the apostolic Churches might be independent of each other,—but that did not make each an independent Church according to the modern type. The large numbers constituting some, the plurality of presbyter-bishops presiding over all, were against that. Doubtless, there was competency and provision for self-government in each, and each used the liberty it had, (sometimes with rather a high hand,) and there could be no interference in the affairs of the Church of one city by the authoritative utterances or actions of the bishops or presbyters of that of another; but there was a supervision over many, by those who founded them, as we see in Paul;* and there was something like the temporary (at least) delegation of his powers to others;—and it is a singular circumstance that we have three *inspired* epistles addressed to individuals, which, on some theories, were never to find a *person,* after the first age, to whom they could directly and specially speak! I did not on these grounds feel obliged to accept *modern* Episcopacy as if that was exactly the Divine thing, and all New Testament terms found their ideas in it. I saw they did no such thing. But I also saw, that there was more of every great system of Church Government in the apostolic records and customs than the thorough-going advocate of any would confess; that the New Testament was not the exclusive property of any; that each had some portion of truth in it, which the others had not; that all had something both to learn and unlearn; that " Gospel" was far more important than " Church;" that the substance of the one was Divine and imperative, any particular form of the other not so; that different communions might exist without the Church universal being really divided; that Union in the Head, spiritual sym-

---

* But even the apostle's superintendence of the Churches was hardly a part of their constitution. Each had to act for itself. He did not visit some of them for years together; and we have not a letter to any that can be referred to the *two years* which he spent, in not very severe imprisonment, at Cæsarea. Did he write none? Or were they not inspired? At any rate, none are preserved.

pathy and fraternal affection between the parts, were the great things to be sought, *not* Uniformity; that the getting rid of hindrances and obstructions to the union of Christians, whether arising from without or within,—from the World encumbering some " sections " of the Church with help, and hedging them round by law, or from the high thoughts which others or the same had of themselves,—and the encouragement and promotion of co-operative action, in public services, on broad principles, without regard to much beyond Truth and Life,—that *this* should be the *beginning* of things, and that *out of this* might ultimately come reform and improvement on all sides, every Church both doing good and getting it,—and that in the end, perhaps, there might further arise "a new thing in the earth " altogether,—the springing up (" men not knowing how ")— the quiet growth and gradual development—of " a Church of the Future,"—a Church which " should conciliate all affections, and harmonise all diversities."

Such are the outlines of the " dream," under the influence of which it was that I and others engaged in the Anti-State-aid controversy. Despairing of anything like a visible uniformity, to be arrived at by the " reduction into the bosom of one communion " (whatever that may mean) of " all the different professions of Christianity,"* or by diplomatic conference and arrangement between them, on equal terms; yet, longing for the manifestation of visible oneness in faith and affection, if that were possible, *we really aimed, in our simplicity, only at that.* This was the religious side of the question,

* App., p. 11.

M

as distinct from its relation to social rights and political justice.   Among the unendowed Evangelical denominations, there was, on the whole, harmony and intercourse, mutual recognition, sympathy and help ; there were defects in all, " things that were wanting " both in truth and love ; but with respect to the Episcopal Church — what ought to be and might be the great central power in the land—*its* distance and " isolation " from all others were imperatively enforced by the legal net-work in which it was bound by the secular power,—*that which constituted the " Establishment,"* and which covered and clung to it like a poisoned robe.   Knowing this,—and knowing besides, that while, in its articles, it had, on the whole, a pure creed, and in its Liturgy **a** beautiful and affecting service, it yet retained in its " Offices " serious errors, and put forth in its claims as to " succession " and " orders," what, under any circumstances, would separate it (among Protestants) from the rest of the faithful ;—but, *also* knowing that there was within itself, in the throbbing hearts of many of its members, a deep, strong, inward protest against these things, a wish and longing for their modification or removal,—we thought that, if the *secular* part of the mixed institution was separated from the *ecclesiastical*,—if that which by the force of law gave. permanence to error and imposed restrictions on action, was to come to an "end," that then spiritual life would both be emancipated and manifested,—that contact and intercourse with other bodies becoming possible would be desired,—that the Church, free to take independent action, would ultimately reform itself,—that what, according to some Church writers,

" had been retained by her to meet the tastes and sentiments of a half-Protestantized people," would be made to slough off,—that other Churches, which had much in them also to alter or reform, being brought into friendly and sympathetic relations with the greatest of all, would be influenced for the better, and improve both in spirit and power, while *their* influence, too, would be felt by it,—and that thus results might be anticipated which might lead to, or be, the fulfilment of the prayer of our adorable and loving Lord,—" *that they all may be one; as thou, Father, art in me, and I in thee, that they also may be one in us; that the world may believe that thou hast sent me.*"

Such were my views, formed, advanced, and advocated nearly a generation ago.   They are, perhaps, as visionary as those of the Bishop of Adelaide, who looks through the opposite end of the instrument by which we alike attempt to discern the future.   I do not advert to them for the purpose of discussing their practicability; I can myself see many things, which, on both sides, might be urged as obstacles to *action*.   I only wish, like my Right Rev. correspondent, so to explain matters, that the " object " of myself and others, our spirit and opinions, may not be " misunderstood," nor continue to be " misrepresented."   Personally, I should deem this a very small matter, as I cannot say that I now care much for mistakes or attacks of any kind, especially such as probably proceed from unavoidable ignorance,—in young men, it is likely, who could know nothing experimentally of times which passed when they were in the cradle or at school, and who have not the means of fully understanding the character of the persons or the real nature of the controversies to which they sometimes rather flippantly refer. But, there are reasons, in the ecclesiastical condition and circumstances of these colonies, and in certain public questions which are in the course of discussion and settlement in some of them, which may excuse or justify my entering into statements with respect to these old-world matters, especially as such statements are only explanatory, not controversial.

The "dream," then, of which I have given the outlines, was what influenced myself and others in our contests with the *State-aid principle*,—as it is acted upon and carried out in England. This was our "idea" of what was necessary to bring about "a Union of the Protestant Evangelical Denominations," if such a thing was ever to be realized;—and of making "a Protestant Evangelical Catholic Church" *possible*. Rightly understood, it demonstrates that our opposition to *Establishments* was based on *religious* grounds far more than on political; and that such opposition not only may exist in the minds of devout men, (however, as such, they may be deemed ignorant, pharisaic, or Evangelically fanatical,) but that it *must* exist in them, under certain ecclesiastical circumstances, in proportion as they *are* devout, and are anxious for every Christian community to be at once free, pure, and *practically* catholic. In England, many of the men who are most decided in their opposition to the "Establishment," properly so called, are at the same time admirers of much in "the Church" as a Church, and have no wish but to see her what, with her age, prestige, learning, prescriptive position, and varied and vast resources, she is capable of being in the high service of God and man. The Leader of the Anti-State-aid agitation in England, a man whose personal character has been much misapprehended, and often, in ignorance, denounced, has recently said of himself what is equally true of many others. In the last of a series of letters recently addressed to the Earl of Shaftesbury, Mr. Miall thus speaks:—"I am reputed, as your lordship probably knows, by men whom prejudice or passion hinders from ascertaining my real sentiments, to be a bitter and even a malignant enemy of that Church of which you are one of the brightest living ornaments. *I am, in truth, no such thing.* I am, it is true, with the whole force of conscientious conviction, opposed to that worldly basis upon which, as an *endowed* Church, and as a *national Establishment*, that institution has been made to rest, and for that opposition I have assigned to your lordship certain reasons growing out of my understanding of Christ's Gospel. But, my lord, I believe that my desire to see your Church fulfil her mission with increased and ever-increasing success is quite as deep and as ardent as can be that of any of those who denounce me as her foe. I could wish to see the Christianity that is in her liberated from the shackles of a worldly policy. I could rejoice to give full scope to the faith, the liberality, the zeal, the love, the self-sacrificing energy of her children. I believe that if her faith were in due exercise she would remove mountains,—I am sure she could open up to herself resources richer and more permanent than she has yet dreamt of. I am persuaded she could win back the sympathies of the greater part of our population. Within her reach, as it seems to me, lies a truly glorious destiny."* Men who, when maligned, can face the world and so speak,—who, calm and undisturbed, can listen to the sound of their solemn asseverations as they echo through the conscience, and ascend up to heaven to be recorded there,—are not men whose character or spirit is to be lightly impugned, or whose opposition is to be little accounted of. They have something on their side far more powerful than their own arguments. Mistaken as they may be in their visions of the future, yet seeking, as they do, not the dominancy of a sect, or the triumph of a party,—not " thinking that they do God service," by " haling to prison," or " casting out of the synagogue," but praying and pleading for the freedom, purification, and spiritual advancement of all the " sections " of God's true Church,—their union in spirit, unfeigned love to and brotherly bearing towards each other,—such men are seeking that which cannot but be acceptable to " HIM," " *of whom the whole family in heaven and earth is named.*" " I speak as a fool;" but conscious as I am, of the deep religious earnestness, the unsectarian and unselfish aims, which actuated many who took part in the argumentative agitation against State-aid in England, I am not ashamed of " this confidence of boasting."

With our knowledge, indeed, of the exclusive spirit which lurks in the pretensions of the Episcopal Church, and of the zeal with which many of her sons contend for her errors as catholic truth, some of us perhaps went too far in our expectations, both as to the Church drawing

* " The Fixed and Voluntary Principles : Eight Letters to the Right Hon. the Earl of Shaftesbury." By Edward Miall. P. 41.

towards other bodies, and of its readiness to reform itself, supposing it was separated from the thraldom of the State. But these things must come. "We bate not a jot of heart or hope" in relation to that result. The different schools and parties in the Church—some of them the very antipodes of each other—are One only legally and by force, not in spirit, or by spiritual sympathy. If they were competent freely to discuss and *act*, movements would commence which, though disturbing at first, would ultimately advance both truth and love; while, if the body of the people (who are the Church),—the pious, the intelligent, the wise and good—if *they* had power, and could make it felt, there is no question as to what would be the issue. There are those among the clergy, and even in the episcopate (and that not only in the old land), who, by their high doctrinal and ecclesiastical tendencies, combined with their contempt for constituted authorities and their resistance to legal decisions, seem to many to place themselves in this position,—that, while sound members, it may be, of the Church *of the Prayer-Book*, they are virtually DISSENTERS from the Church *of England*. The great majority, however, of the lay attendants at Episcopal places of worship are *just the contrary*. For many reasons,—easy to understand, and with which it is impossible not to have sympathy,—reasons from association, preference, taste, habit, they remain members of the Church of England, though they do not hesitate, on many occasions and in many ways, to avow that they differ from the Church of the Prayer-Book;—*not* observe, in respect to its Liturgy, or its ordinary form of worship, but in respect to the apparent meaning of its "Offices." The more decidedly evangelical portions of its people reject that meaning, on what they deem scriptural ground, and sometimes with Episcopal sanction. The educated and accomplished of general society, men of sound sense and virtuous lives, but making no pretensions to spiritual religion, will mostly be found, in conversation on such matters, not only to dissent from the apparent doctrine of the Church "Offices," but unhesitatingly to admit that they could not themselves "enter the Church" on the condition of using them. Men with much of devout and good feeliug in them, but having no sympathy with Evangelical sentiment, have occupied the position to which I am referring,—*inside* the Church of England, *outside* the Church of the Prayer-Book. Southey himself, the author of "The Book of the Church," one who wrote in defence and deprecated the fall of the *National Institution* as such, was not a believer in or a religious conformist to that spiritual entity or doctrinal system which it enclosed,—or not entirely. We have the proof of this under his own hand. In the "Life" of my late esteemed friend, Josiah Conder, Esq., whose poetical genius Southey was one of the first to recognize, and who, for some years, occasionally corresponded with him, there are included, among letters from several distinguished persons, some of the poet laureat's, in which statements occur to the effect named. In one he says: —"I do not subscribe to the Church; if I could do it, I should be in orders—an office to which my inclination would always strongly have led me. My mind has undergone many changes, and is in many points nearer to the Church, than when I forbore to enter it as a minister. Still, I am far from being in communion with it, or from ever expecting to be so." Again, " Our Church Establishment has its evils; you and I would not agree as to what those evils are; my conception of them is such as to exclude me from the clerical profession. But I am fully convinced of the utility of an Establishment; though, if I were to form one for a colony, it would differ materially from our own." " My attachment to the Established Church, in preference to any other existing form of Christianity, is not founded in bigotry or in prejudice; for, though I conform to it, I do not subscribe to its articles, and am thereby precluded from being (what otherwise I should most desire to be) one of its ministers." In connexion with the second of these passages, the writer, in spite of his dissent, and of the changes he would introduce in a Church " for a colony," yet shrinks from even " wishing" to touch, or to obtain " alterations" in, the Establishment at home, dreading that the attempt might " bring upon us ages of religious anarchy, and perhaps of civil war." Perhaps. But that does not in the slightest degree alter *the fact* that Southey belonged to the Church " *of England*," but *not* to the Church " *of the Prayer-Book*."*

* " Life of Josiah Conder, Esq." By his Son, the Rev. Eustace Conder, B.A. Pp. 163, 177, 173.

This reference to the opinions of Southey, and to his idea of " a Church for a colony" as being that of one materially differing from the English system, reminds me that a friend mentioned to me lately the following words of Dr. Arnold :—" I am disposed to cling, not from choice but necessity, to the Protestant tendency of laying the whole stress on Christian Religion, and adjourning the notion of Church *sine die*. Thus I can take no part in aiding ᴵ So far as my acquaintance extends among Episcopalians, I know this state of things to be quite common. No Church can be in a healthy or enviable state, whose clergy occupy a position which many of the most thoughtful and intelligent of their hearers feel that *they* could not conscientiously occupy. A standing like that may be regarded with something like wonder or dread, but it cannot be looked up to with intelligent veneration. The laity may be mistaken—from their unacquaintedness with the subject, their ignorance of the niceties of theology, and of the light in which things can be viewed by " the clerical mind ;" but the condition of things neither here nor at home is at all calculated to correct their mistake. The four colonies in which I have principally been, do not seem to be doctrinally at one. I have already adverted to Episcopal language, the implications of which I think very serious. In one diocese, views are in the ascendant with which numbers have no sympathy ;—which, indeed, wherever they prevail in the old land, and in proportion to the distinctness and frequency of their inculcation, are productive of much which men of earnest Evangelical religion deeply lament. In another, congregations are increased in proportion as the peculiarities of the Anglican system are virtually ignored, and the broad principles of the Gospel preached as held in common by the Evangelical denominations,— but then I have known its Bishop described, by some who are under him, " as no better than a Dissenter." In one, from some cause or other, the Church is gradually

the new Colonial Bishoprics, because they seem to me to be likely
to propagate to the end of the earth the Popery of Canterbury."

decreasing in numbers, in spite of the fact that the majority of immigrants are officially described as belonging to its communion; and in all I find uneasiness, indicated by speech, writing, or act, under some exercise, some misconception of, or some insubordination to "the Episcopal rule."

I am well aware of the many unseemly and disorderly things to be found in other bodies, our own not excepted. But I am justified, I think, in speaking as I do, because of the peculiar position I have personally occupied, and the remarks with which in some quarters I have been met. In spite of the difference in doctrine and ritual between us and the Presbyterians, Methodists, Baptists, and other bodies, I have had ministerial intercourse with all,—have had access to their pulpits, and felt at one with them, in respect to the great fundamentals of the faith, and the preaching of "the common salvation." With the vast majority of the Evangelical members of God's Church throughout these lands I have thus had visible communion. I hold it to be the same in the old country; as it would be in America with the large and influential Non-episcopal bodies there, together with that of the wonderfully advanced and advancing Methodist Episcopal Church. And yet, with the strange antagonism of things within, and the co-operative union (in spite of diversity) of things without, my friend, the Bishop of Adelaide, dwells on the idea of being "associated with multitudes of fellow Churchmen" "*through the same rule and order of worship*," and wishes that "the wise and good and able of all Evangelical denominations may find it possible, by the adoption of common

principles, to join *the* great confederacy of the Gospel."*
We think that there may be, in spirit and design, such a
" confederacy," without a formal union in " the same
rule and order of worship;"—as we have reason to fear
that there may be a visible union in " the same rule and
order of worship," without a " confederacy" either " of"
or *in* " the Gospel."

Returning to the subject from which we have in
appearance, though only in appearance, a little diverged,
and referring again to that state of things of which
Southey's position gives us the type, it seems pertinent
to remark, that some changes and alterations, of one sort
or another, must surely come, and should certainly be
sought, by which such an anomaly might at length be
removed.　We, of course, think, in consistency with our
own theological views, that the changes ought to be in a
certain direction ;—but not only so, we also think, in
consistency with our belief of what is the feeling in the
devout and intelligent *lay* mind of the Church, that if *it*
had the power to make the changes, they *would* be in the
direction indicated.　Let the piety and intelligence of
the Church *as a whole* be free to influence it, and such
alterations would most assuredly be effected, as—while
some might regard them as awful departures from
catholic truth—would in fact be an approach to what is
Scriptural and Apostolic.　Such alterations would give
new life and power to the Church ;—making her strong
" to do exploits," bringing her also nearer in feeling and
action to other bodies, and conciliating the affection of
others to *her*.　But these things, though certain and

* APP., p. 14.

inevitable, will be of slow growth and tardy accomplish-
ment. In England, if the Church were to become perfectly free, and as such to discuss and act, it would
divide at once into separate " sections," as certainly as it
is a forced combination of positively antagonist elements
now, not at all a unity in itself. In the colonies, from
the feebleness of the Church in some,—the want in
others, of hearty interest in it, from various causes, of
the more vigorous and influential of the laity,—from the
fear in all of diverging in any thing from the Parent
type,—and from the principle on which the different
synods are carefully constituted, being bound not to
touch ceremony or doctrine, " to alter the Liturgy or
tamper with the Prayer-Book,"—any great change is
perhaps only to be looked for from political separation,—
a thing which we, at least, would devoutly deprecate,
but which would seem to be necessary to give to our
friends ecclesiastical independence.

In New Zealand, this is provided for. The Conference
that was called together to form a " General Synod,"
resolved, that, although " unwilling to take any step
that might appear to interfere with the supremacy of the
Crown, or to weaken the union with the Mother Church,
yet, as the property of the Church in New Zealand might
be placed in jeopardy, unless provision were made for
the contingency of the separation of the colony from
the Mother Country, and for that of an alteration in the
existing relations between the Church and the State, *it is
declared* that the Synod *may*, in the event of such contingency, *make such alterations in the* ARTICLES, SERVICES,
AND CEREMONIES *of the Church in New Zealand, as the*

altered circumstances may then require."* By this proviso being connected with securing the " property " of the Church, there seems to be indicated a sort of consciousness, or unacknowledged apprehension, that emancipated men, having got their liberty would use it, demanding certain alterations and changes, and therefore, prospec-

* " New Zealand and its Colonization," by William Swainson, pp. 410, 411. In immediate connexion with what is quoted in the text, the reader is requested to look at the following statement, which is that of one of the Church-writers whom the " Adelaide Correspondence" called forth. Speaking of the Church of England, he said :—

" The whole machinery of effective government must be employed before the most trifling change can take place in her external existence. Her doctrine is above her discipline ; it is in appearance infallible, and from experience unchangeable : *it has once been determined, right or wrong, and it can never expect to be altered, however desirable, however convenient.*"

Without testing the accuracy of this by the *past*, as to whether " experience" testifies to the " unchangeableness" of the doctrine of the Church of England,—or questioning the statement that it is " in *appearance* infallible,"—it is obvious to remark that, in respect to *the future*, the writer is evidently ignorant of the real state of the case. The Church may not have the liberty, or may not be disposed, to alter any thing on the mere ground of an inquiry as to its being "right or wrong," or because of its " desirableness ;"—its desirableness, for instance, to heal divisions and effect some loving and catholic object, consistent with the retention of Evangelical and Protestant truth. But it *has* the liberty, and is disposed to exercise it,—to anticipate, and to prepare and provide for its exercise,—if it should be " desirable " and " convenient " *for the sake of preserving its* " *property.*" *Then* not only may the " *Services and Ceremonies*" be " tampered with," but even THE " ARTICLES ;"—these, by emphasis the strong hold of the " infallible " and " unchangeable " doctrine, may be made to undergo " such alterations as altered circumstances may require," —require, that is to say, *for the securing of the object specified.* I can attach no meaning but this to the New Zealand declaration.

tively to meet what it is felt would be inevitable, the concession is granted for the sake of securing what might otherwise be lost. So the thing shapes itself to me. But whether that be the true explanation or not, the fact is the same:—On a certain "contingency," power is conferred "*to make alterations in the Articles, Services, and Ceremonies of the Church*," and, in the exercise of that power, we may be quite certain that not only would the "Offices" not escape, but that they would be the first, if not indeed the principal or only things, that would be materially modified. There is no fear of the beautiful Liturgy of the Church of England being "tampered with" by her true and loving children,—a service which, for myself, I have once and again acknowledged, that I seldom hear devoutly and appropriately conducted without tears. But that the "Offices" should be reformed, and thus brought into harmony with the mind of the living and personal Church,—the men and women who really constitute the congregation of the faithful, who have scriptural light in their purified reason, and the life of God in their holy souls,—that this should be done, is only what is panted and prayed for now, by a majority of the members of the Episcopal communion, who are alive to its interests, distinguished by intelligence, or piety, or both.

Movements are on foot in England, which are intended to accomplish this very thing. Societies are organizing to seek and agitate for "liturgical reform." The laity are foremost in these advances. But others are writing on the same side,—a series of letters having recently appeared, from the pen of a clergyman,

" advocating the revision of the Liturgy." "At present," he says, "he confines himself to five points:—the doing away with the Apocryphal lessons, the damnatory clauses of the Athanasian creed, *the* REGENERATION *statements in the Baptismal Service, the* ABSOLUTION *clauses,* and portions of the Burial Service." Such is the account as it has been brought to us. The omen is auspicious. I don't believe that much will ever be done, in the way of liturgical reform in the Church, by the fault-finding of those that are without; that only provokes resistance to aggression, the clinging to and retention of felt defects. The ground of hope is in the spontaneous action of the attached members of the Church itself. In the same way, I expect nothing effective towards "Church Union" from attempts at negotiation,—preparatory proceedings to lay down certain principles, or to fix and agree upon common forms,—each party giving up, or insisting upon, something. But, if without any such questionable attempts at arrangement, the good and wise, the energetic and earnest on all sides, could be brought into frequent or occasional contact, by loving intercourse in some mode or other of Church-life, I cannot but hope that by mutual action and re-action, improvements and reforms would gradually grow out of this, by way of natural consequence,—not, in any case, by the force of argument or appeal from without, but, in all cases, by the growth and the development of life from within.

This, at any rate, has been the way in which things have shaped themselves to my mind for many years past. If some few men were bold enough, there is scope and

opportunity (the representatives of the law so judging)*
for what is *tentative*, at least, in these colonies. It is
certainly worthy of notice, that in that colony where
State-aid is entirely done away with, and all the
Churches are on a perfect level, the first step has been
practically attempted of a movement that might be the
beginning of good to the Protestant denominations, and
to the general interests of Protestant truth. In all the
Australian colonies the days of State-aid are numbered.
The majority of the candidates for senatorial honours in
New South Wales take the negative side,—the present
premier heading the advance. The advocates of the
system are everywhere folding its mantle about it, that
it may decently die—without open struggle or convulsion—for die it must. The Wesleyans, though yet
recipients of the bounty, are beginning to speak with un-
faltering tongue. Bishops themselves are pronouncing
against it. The masses of the people have long done so:
—Some on the principle of political justice; some on
purely religious grounds, protesting against the support
and sanction of error; and some, where extreme ecclesiastical influences are injuriously affecting Evangelical
truth, earnestness, and power, on the principle of simple
common sense and ordinary pecuniary calculation.
Their thought is, "What is it we actually receive
for our money? When we get what is paid for,
what is its value? Is the thing tendered worth
the picking up?" With such cogitations stirring
within them, it cannot but be, that, one day, intelligent, good, and free men will determine to ascertain—

* APP., p. 56.

Whether what they disapprove must be suffered to be eternal.

Every denomination, in a new country, may come to discover that it has something to learn and to *unlearn*. All might feel that their circumstances call them to draw fraternally towards each other. For myself, I am ready to justify Independency as an exceptional system, —as a becoming assertion in favour of the individual,—a protest for personal conviction and action, against the error of an Age or the tyranny of a " Rule." The Ancients used to say, "where there are *three* there is a Church;" but *one* may be a Church as well as three,—as " one, *with God*, is a majority." ATHANASIUS *contra mundum :* The Church, so to speak, was once reduced to, or embodied in, *him*. But, only to recognize the principle of individualism, is not to lay the basis of a Church *fitted to achieve the conversion of the world.* Episcopacy, on the other hand, (and not only *it*,) makes the " Rule" every thing, and the individual nothing. But on both sides, there is within the different systems, a sort of practical protest against them. Independent Churches combine and act, especially in the way of missionary effort, *beyond* what is strictly provided for by the theory; many within them have views and wishes unfavourable to the idea of every congregation constituting a little ecclesiastical republic; while not only is it understood that something of personal liberty must be given up, for union in a Society to be possible, but, as the abuse of this, there may be seen at times the tyranny of opinion, restraints upon and suspicion of individual thought. Episcopalians, again, exercise individual independence in the most extraordinary variety of forms, while they ostensibly unite as if essentially one ! Interchange of services and co-operative action might possibly bring benefit to *both*. A new country needs ecclesiastical arrangements which might put to flight some of our own hereditary traditions. The adoption of these might become more easy, if we mingled more, and more heartily and earnestly, with others. They, again, might receive advantage from our distinguishing peculiarity of attaching more importance to the preaching of the Truth than to any thing else ;—our boast being—and we have a right to make it—that we think far more of "the common salvation," than we do of our own distinctive polity,—and are more anxious to make sinners into saints, than saints into sectarians. All Churches, if more broad and cordial in their intercourse, might be spontaneously impelled to seek advancement and growth, without any one urging reforms on the rest. The highest and most blessed results might then evolve out of the mere fact that there was an open field—cleared from all secular and ecclesiastical impediments—for the exercise, by the Churches, of the independent action of each on itself, and the mutual influence of all upon each other.

III.

Last Words.

It may not be amiss, perhaps, to state, that I am no advocate for rigidly insisting on an exact identity of sentiment and feeling, or in modes of thought and forms of expression, in the ministers of a religious body. I have great sympathy with the freedom which is enjoyed and exercised by the clergy of the Church of England. By many of them, "the liberty of private judgment" is far more used than by some in denominations professedly based on that very principle. In itself considered, the sight of this freedom is somewhat refreshing. It is pleasant to notice how much men in the same Church may differ from one another, and speak out their differences, without forfeiting their position, injuring their influence, or damaging their character. The difficulty is, that the privilege seems to be bought too dear. There are those who cannot consent to give the price, and to whom, in spite of every effort to the contrary, it is "perfectly incomprehensible" how some bring themselves to consent to give it, or, having given it, how they can comfortably enjoy and use the purchase. The anomaly no doubt arises from the extent and stringency of the exacted subscription. It is felt that it *must* be understood in some conditional sense; that it cannot be supposed to be taken in the strict way in which men of the world have to transact matters of business; or that a literal mental conformity is either intended or likely to be enforced.

This necessity, from the nature of the case, of assuming an allowed latitude of interpretation, has led to so much laxity (or indulgence) that with many the transaction would seem as if it had never been taken to mean anything. Hence, that *extreme sort* of "diversity in unity," (contrarieties in union,) which is seen to exist in the English Church. Within certain limits—for there *are* limits, which, under an authoritative and dogmatic revelation of truth, cannot be passed by the individual without insubordination to *God*, or allowed *in a Church* without its forgetting one, at least, of the ends for which it exists,—within certain limits, I repeat, one likes to see the practical liberty, the assertion and use of it, to which I have referred. I think it suspicious, when all the members of a particular body are so perfectly and in everything one, that they seem but the copies or echoes of each other. To a certain extent, differences of view, in opinion and modes of thought, are the signs of health; of mental activity; of vigour and maturity in the inward spiritual life of a denomination. I have sympathy with and complacency in such phenomena, looked upon simply as facts. The difficulty, as I have said, is to understand, in some cases, how men manage to get, or how they can comfortably take possession of that liberty, which they so largely and habitually exercise. It would be surely better, if it could be openly declared to be theirs *at the beginning.* But one hardly knows which is the most confounding or most humiliating mystery—the fact of men appearing to abjure, what they afterwards claim and use (and sometimes with a vengeance); or that of others, first claiming the thing and boasting that they have it, and then hardly afterwards ever using it at all.

Throughout this Address, in referring to our ecclesiastical position and to the Protestant Episcopal denomination in these lands, I have used, for the most part, apologetical forms of speech, language somewhat deprecatory, certainly defensive. I have done this, because, in my position, it is the most appropriate. It would have been quite out of keeping, both with my circumstances and

feelings, for me to have obtruded myself on public attention by voluntarily coming forward to canvass contested
ecclesiastical matters; directly to impugn the constitution
or forms of any " Church system;" to speak disparag-
ingly of its " mission" or its " orders;" or to object to
its teaching respecting the " ministry and sacraments."
I have only spoken, as to one matter, because I was
asked to do so; and on others, because things were said,
feelings indulged in and sentiments expressed respecting
them, which seemed to justify an appeal to men's candour
and common sense. Statements respecting our standing as
ministers, and our relations to the Episcopal communion,
—partly on the ground of what that communion assumes
to be, partly on that of the separation of our ancestors
from it,—statements, made generally and comprehen-
sively in relation to you all, or specially in respect to
myself, appeared to call upon some one to breathe into
the ear of impartial and conscientious REASON as it exists
in the English mind, such an appeal as I have made:—
" apprehending things, as, unfortunately for ourselves,
we do, *judge* whether, even if altogether wrong in our
Nonconformity, that Nonconformity itself may not, in
our circumstances, and with our convictions, be honourable, praiseworthy, virtuous?"

I beg now to say, however, that, in one aspect of the
matter, I think the Episcopal Church, in these colonies,
should no more refer to our ancestors' separation from it,
or raise the question as to who was right or who wrong
then, than that the Englishman and American of to-day
should refer to the disputes of a former age, before they
would have friendly relations or dealings with each

other. Even in England, the things which issued in ejectment and secession from the Church, may be argued now, not as between the Episcopal body and Dissenters from *it*, but on the broad ground whether the parties, respectively, as they exist in fact, and without regard to past relationships, are right or wrong,—their creed or customs scriptural or the contrary. In a colony, where all denominations are professedly on a level, whither many laws of the parent land, creating or perpetuating class distinctions,.do not reach, much might be lost sight of which impedes action or prolongs strife. Unless a particular denomination regards itself as exclusively the Church,—*the* Church—with claims on the obedience of universal humanity equal to those of the Gospel message, (which, whosoever believeth not, shall be damned,) it seems to me absurdly arrogant for it to set up the claim, embodied in the title of a book I met with in New South Wales,—" *Separation from the Church of England in this Colony, a Duty* or **a** Sin."* If it be the only Church, the Church of Christ,—be it so. If the question be

---

* The analogy here suggested may be thought inaccurate, since disobedience to the Gospel message can in no case be anything *but* sin; and it may be further objected, that Nonconformists themselves say that separation is with them *a duty*. In reply, I may observe, that the remarks in the text took their form from the impression the book alluded to left on the mind, namely, that the author of it looked upon separation as sin only, and could not conceive it to be duty; and that, in his hands, the *word* referred not merely to the *act* of separation under particular circumstances, but to the fact, under all circumstances, of *being* separate, or " standing apart." Lest my recollection, however, of the views of the writer alluded to should be imperfect, let my remarks be taken as bearing only on those who look at the subject in the way explained—for there are many such.

restricted to the conduct of the original Nonconformists; again, be it so :—That can be met and argued by their successors. But, to put forth such a thesis as of general application, as including all in these lands who do not belong to the Church of England, as if, by the mere circumstance of standing separate from it, they were necessarily in a state of schism, is as ridiculous as it is assuming. Even with respect to the present position of the descendants of those who, in *their* act of separation, might have committed sin, the proposition may be met by a negative; while, as between PROTESTANTS,—who have all alike access to the Book, and, individually or collectively, as persons or as communities, must recognise the law *of standing or falling* TO THE MASTER ALONE, the claim or pretension is most inconsistent. " Separation from the Church of England, in these colonies," simply in itself, is neither duty nor sin; what it is, in any particular case, must depend on previous circumstances, or on individual, personal convictions. In some, it can have no moral character at all; the men have their own national or ecclesiastical standing, and bear no relation to the Church of England that can affect them for better or worse. In others, it may be either duty or sin, as the case may be; *that* will depend on *their views* of its character and claims, and whether *their position is in harmony with their views ;*—just as, according to the personal convictions of some within the Episcopal Church, it may happen that their conformity to *it,* and their separation from some other Church, are *neither* of them duties, but *both* sins.

These things cannot be said with respect to the Gospel

itself,—the acceptance or rejection of the Evangelical message, which comes with a distinct demand on the conscience and obliges to "the obedience of faith;" but they *may* be said with respect to any system or all systems of Church Government. These are of the nature of "the meat and the drink," which are not "the kingdom of God," and respecting which it is enough, in one case or another, for men "to be fully persuaded in their own minds." True, they should be "fully persuaded;" the grounds on which they accept one system, and stand apart from others, are to be examined and understood. The claims of the Church of England have in this way a right to demand a hearing; but they have that right, just as those of other Churches have it, and no more. On the principle of Protestantism, and, *constitutionally, in these colonies,* Presbyterians, Congregationalists, Wesleyans, have as much ground for calling on the Episcopalian to account for and justify his "separation" from *them,* as he has to require that they should examine whether theirs from him is " a duty or a sin."

Unless, then, the Episcopal community claims to be exclusively the true and only Church, other Protestant bodies may be Churches as well as it; hold their position and take action with equal propriety;—as they, too, might put forth books with similar titles to the one I have referred to, if it can do so. It would have been most unbecoming in me, however, to have voluntarily originated a controversial discussion with *any* Church or denomination whatever. But events and circumstances, over which I had no control, seemed to render unavoidable an *exposition* of, or apology for, our views and standing. As resident colonial ministers, and as ministers of a known Christian community, *your* action might be different,—more spontaneous, less apologetic. If there is anything around you in any community, operating injuriously on the interests of religion, by the tacit sanction or the positive inculcation of error, you are free to utter your protest against it, and to confront it with your testimony. It may happen that the error or errors may be such as your fathers had to face, and for resisting which they forfeited position and income, accepted imprisonment, and took the spoiling of their goods. That is an accident; you are not bound, either to begin by defending *them*, or to speak as if pleading for a tolerated existence; or to argue any point on the ground of its being the matter of an old feud. You have your own independent position, authorized by the maxim of " the Bible, and the Bible only, being the religion of Protestants," and you can stand upon that and act. In the same way, as the representatives of a Christian body professedly on a level with every other, you have a right to resist the efforts of any to obtain Establishment, authority, rights, preference, or privileges, in such a way, and in such a sense, as would destroy the equality that ought to be maintained here, and to introduce into colonial life that which has been the source of so many evils, and the cause of such social separation, and of so much bitterness and estrangement in the old land.

The tendency of the colonial mind is manifestly democratic. It is supposed by some that our Church system is in harmony with that, and adapted to attract it. There are those, again, who doubt this. In new colonies,

if a denomination is to take an effective *missionary* character, it would seem to be necessary for it to act on
some form of the connexional principle. It is thought
that congregations might yield a portion of their liberty,
for the sake of effective combination, in the same way as
individuals yield a portion of theirs in uniting with
them. Some bodies have the central power exclusively
in their ministers. Others have the laity associated with
them, but so fettered, it is thought, by pre-arranged
limitations, or by prerogative or authority, that many
things can neither be discussed nor decreed. For ourselves, though we meet for united conference, we are
almost confined to the passing of resolutions which have
no binding force, which can go forth only as the expression of opinion, or as so much advice, and which some
who pass them forget and disregard. Power, placed in
and exerted by freely elected deliberative assemblies,
might actually, it is supposed, be more in accordance
with democratic tendencies, and more acceptable to a
democratic people, than the existence and action of a
number of distinct independent republics ;—while, on the
other hand, it might really be more conservative ; pro-
tective of rights and liberties sometimes endangered ;
more efficient in the just settlement of disputes and misunderstandings, and more adapted than anything else to
direct and sustain vigorous and aggressive missionary
action, especially if that was understood and declared to
be its principal business. It would seem, too, in the
condition and circumstances of colonial life, that laymen
of piety, education, and influence, should be recommended to undertake many services from which they

might be excused, or may excusably shrink, in the old land. In certain localities into which ministers seldom penetrate, where they cannot be sustained, or anything like a competent congregation formed, persons might be found who could gather together the scattered inhabitants, and encourage them to keep up the forms and habits of Church-life. In this way, many might not only be preserved from sinking down into practical heathenism, but the way would be prepared for the settled pastor, and for the customary administration of Church ordinances. Some of the things just adverted to, may be of questionable utility, some of difficult attainment; but I have given to them these passing words, as I have heard them stated, more than once, by thoughtful men in these lands.

Finally, to you, my ministerial brethren, I would especially and earnestly say:—As scripturally authorized messengers of Truth and Peace, "Preach the Word; be instant in season, out of season; do the work of Evangelists; make full proof of your ministry; take heed unto *yourselves* as well as to your doctrine; for by doing so, you will save yourselves and them that hear you." Combine and work, seeking to do your part in diffusing the light and spreading the leaven of Divine Truth throughout this great Southern world. Sustain the character of the body to which you belong for all that is earnest and evangelical—as more intent on winning souls and preaching the Gospel, than on parading and magnifying its own peculiarities. Regard all good and true men as fellow-labourers,—"co-workers of God," to whom you sustain, "in the Gospel of His Son," a fraternal relationship. Rejoice to recognize them as brethren ; to hold ministerial intercourse with them ; to advance your common object by occasionally aiding theirs ; to pray for their enlargement, and to rejoice in their success. Adopt anything new, in Church arrangements or modes of action, which approves itself to your judgment, and is not inconsistent with the general principles embodied in or suggested by the customs and procedure of apostolic times ;—arrangements or procedure by which you may more effectually fulfil your mission and your ministry, and adapt your efforts to the circumstances of new communities in which everything in some sort starts afresh, —where the future can receive benefit, not only from the teaching of the wisdom of the past, but from the admonitions furnished by its folly or its failures.

There is a grand future before Australia ; and it cannot but be the desire of every denomination to exert the greatest possible amount of power to give to that future, in the character of its people, what will ever be the fruit of an earnest and active religious faith. It is a greater thing to be a maker of men, than to be a man ;—to be the ancestors and moulders of an illustrious progeny, than to be the offspring of illustrious ancestors. It is as inspiriting to be at the beginning of things, as to be related to a splendid past ;—to make history, as to read it ;—to sow that others may reap, as to enter into the labours of those who have sown. " Righteousness exalteth a nation." Pure religion is the parent of righteousness. The reflex or secondary influence of the Church, on laws and institutions, on the habits, the tone, the morals of society, is far greater than society itself may be willing to acknowledge. Where directly spiritual and Divine results are not attained, religious influence may be sensibly felt in a lower sphere, and be at once counteractive of much evil, conservative and promotive of much good. May it be yours—and that, too, of the ministers of all other Churches—to be a perpetually operating and pregnant power in the midst of the land! May your influence be as the light and the dew—felt everywhere, touching everything,—beneficent, genial, gentle, mighty,—yet flowing only from what is moral and legitimate,—the torch of Truth in the hand of Love! May all Christian churches, as well as Christian men, " look not every one on its own things, but every one also on the things of others." " Doing all things without murmurings and disputings, may they be blameless and harmless, the sons of God without rebuke; shining as lights in the world, and holding forth the word of life." Ceremonies and forms that may separate in appearance, are of no account in comparison with the truths of " the common salvation." "*In Christ Jesus neither circumcision availeth anything, nor uncircumcision, but a new creature.* AND AS MANY AS WALK ACCORDING TO THIS RULE, PEACE BE ON THEM, AND MERCY, AND ON THE ISRAEL OF GOD."

⁎ As this volume owes its existence to external circumstances, it is of course confined to those topics, and those aspects of them, which drew it forth, and to such matters as they suggested. Had I spontaneously entertained the project and formed the purpose of writing a book on Australia,—on *all* the lights and shadows of Church-life there,—it would have been incumbent upon me to

enter into numerous subjects which I do not touch, but which it must not therefore be supposed I did not in some degree notice. The position of *Romanism* in the colonies; its relations to the State; its political influence; the feelings, so to speak, consciously indulged between it and the English Church, sometimes openly manifested, with other kindred matters, constitute subjects of deep interest and of vast importance too. *Universities, Colleges, Cathedrals, Church and Chapel architecture, generally, Presbyterian Church-Union, Bush missions, missions to the Chinese, Educational systems, the Colonial Press in its relations to religion*, with various other things, might all be looked at as, in one way or another, illustrative of Church-life. Then, there is the *adaptation* of Church-systems to the circumstances of a people, some of whom are in small skeleton settlements, or on solitary stations, all more or less widely apart, and spreading over an immense space; others of whom are in towns and cities which have sprung up with different degrees of suddenness, and into which a mixed multitude from all quarters, of all religions and no religion, has suddenly flowed. Though I don't mean to be tempted into what I never purposed,—writing a book about these or any other Australian questions, I may yet, perhaps, occasionally furnish a short paper on one or other of them to some periodical.

In the concluding pages of the preceding Address, I have thrown out a hint or two as to some things which might be looked at by Congregationalists in relation to their own polity. As to Colonial Missionary action, the Episcopal and Presbyterian bodies might, I think, *as Churches*, adapt themselves to it more efficiently than they do. They are each a unity, a whole, a body—properly so called; but they are this for government, discussion, discipline, and so on, rather than for diffusive effort. The clergyman in both systems becomes, in fact, very much an isolated minister, fixed to a particular spot, to be supported by his own parish, or congregation, permanently stationed there, unless circumstances,—*not* Church-arrangements,—prevent. This is practical Independency;—Independency in its worst aspect as a system of *isolation*, with its evils but without its compensations. In spite of Episcopacy and Presbyterianism being each professedly a great whole, the particular parts become so separated and distinct, that many questions as to ministerial adaptation, missionary agency, and pecuniary support, get entangled in such a way as to become delicate, perplexed, and difficult of solution. As a practical Independent and theoretic or doctrinal Voluntary, I do not hesitate to acknowledge that I think " the work of the Evangelist " cannot be fully carried out, nor " the voluntary principle " evince its power, on a system of ministerial and congregational isolation.

I am well aware how the one half of the thing is attempted to be met by Church Societies which provide Bishops with supplementary funds; Presbyterian sustentation funds; Congregational Colonial Mission Committees, with their grants-in-aid ; all good and right as far as they go, but they are not everything. As to the other half of the thing—missionary action—each Church, or denomination, being, as such, an advancing and aggressive institution, and for this purpose furnished with power to use its agents as necessity might require, wisdom suggest, or fields open, there is nothing like what there might be in some quarters, where the whole *is* a body, and not merely so many separate legs and arms. The Wesleyan system has great adaptations for a Missionary Church, and is free also from some of the hindrances to success arising from every distinct ecclesiastical " rood of earth" having to " maintain its man," its own individual man, and that, by hypothesis, permanently. There are many things about Wesleyanism which we that are without wonder at. Its government is so exclusively clerical, the laity having neither liberty nor opportunity, independently or by representation, of free speech and firm action. But I must say this, that the different varieties of the Wesleyan type in Australia, appeared to me to be all successful and prosperous. They are very numerous, and, in many places, the largest and most commodious places of worship are theirs.

All the different denominations,—Episcopacy, Presbyterianism, Wesleyanism, Independency,—have their mission, their sphere, their work. They have all their excellences as well as their defects. Each has some prominent, better point, where it touches some phase or some portion of society more efficiently than the others. All have principles to testify to, or to maintain, the repression or extinction of which would be a loss to the world, though each might be improved by condescending to borrow something from the rest.

LIGHTS AND SHADOWS.

APPENDIX.

Illustrative Memoranda, Letters, Notes,

ETC., ETC.

o

APPENDIX.

In the Australian edition of this book, there were added, in this place, in full, a number of the letters and papers which had appeared on both the questions started at Adelaide. It is not thought necessary to encumber the present publication with the whole of these documents. Instead of troubling the reader to wade through them, to gather facts and dates, or to detect and put aside certain colonial misapprehensions, I propose to condense into a brief statement what may enable him to understand the allusions of the preceding Address ; and merely to give such letters, or extracts of letters, as may be necessary to his seeing the bearing of the argument.

The letter of the Bishop of Adelaide on " The Union of Protestant Evangelical Churches," was received by me on the 4th of October [1858], on the eve of his lordship's starting "on a five weeks' tour." I was staying at the time at Government House. The fact of my having received such a communication was, therefore, naturally mentioned to our common friend, Sir R. G. MacDonnell, who expressed a wish to be permitted to see it. I felt that there could be no impropriety in acceding to this request, and, in doing so, coupled compliance with a wish, on my part, that he would give me his thoughts on the subject started, as I felt curious to know how the matter would shape itself to an intelligent layman. Just at that time, certain members of the Episcopal Church, on their own impulse, originated a memorial to the Bishop, soliciting the opening of the pulpits of the body to which they belonged (in my person) to the ministers of other " Evangelical denominations." To this memorial, the Governor and other influential gentle-men affixed their signatures.* They did so, simply as members of the Episcopal communion, *not* in their official capacity ; but in sending the memorial to the papers for publication, their official designation was added by the gentleman who forwarded it, and hence a very natural mistake.

The memorial was forwarded, in the absence of the Bishop, to the Dean and Chapter, who, of course, felt them-selves incompetent to act; but they took charge of the document, for presentation to his lordship on his return. So early as October 7th, the Archdeacon made an allusion in a public meeting, (in general terms, but which I per-fectly understood,) to the letter which had been sent to me by the Bishop. More distinct allusions were made to it, on a subsequent occasion, by the Governor and others. The Governor had written to me a letter commenting on the Bishop's, which, before I received it, he submitted to the Dean and the Archdeacon. These gentlemen recom-mended the publication of both. I began to feel, too, that it had become " due to the Bishop" that " what he had really written should be seen, as it might be supposed that he had gone further than he had, or meant to do, or than his words implied." Circumstances, which it was impossible to control, thus led to the publication of the letters of the Bishop and His Excellency (in the absence of the former)

* The Governor stated, in one of his published communications, that when he was applied to for his signature, he declined to give it until he could peruse the letter of the Bishop, which was then in his hands, but had not been read; and that he was so impressed with the spirit and tenor of the letter when he had gone through it, that he said he felt free to sign the memorial, but yet only on the condition that it should contain a clause stating that those - signing it " believed his lordship was most desirous of adopting all measures calculated to extend and establish the common catholic principles of faith held by the Protestant Church of Christ, into whatever sections that Church might be divided, and earnestly desired to assist his lordship's efforts in that behalf."

in the Adelaide newspapers. I sent them to the press, accompanied by a full explanatory statement, and I forwarded a copy to his lordship's residence, with a private note, to be despatched to him if there was any likelihood of its reaching him in the course of his Episcopal migrations.

On the 10th of November the Bishop returned from his visitation, and sent to me, the same evening, just in time, happily, for me to receive it, as I was to sail the next day, the following letter, which had been written a few days before.

No. I.

The Right Reverend the Bishop of Adelaide to the Rev. T. Binney.

Anama, November 5th, 1858.

DEAR AND REVEREND SIR,—On my arrival yesterday at this place, I received your note, accompanied by a printed copy of our correspondence. I was fully prepared to see it in print; but I forbore to suggest that course, being satisfied that you would choose the proper time and place for so doing. It was, however, rendered necessary by public allusion having been made to my letter, and a correspondent, on no better grounds than his own surmise, having thought fit falsely to disparage an eminent lady, with whom I was not personally acquainted until after I had been consecrated Bishop of Adelaide. I should have preferred to have received from you at your leisure the matured conclusions of your judgment on the interesting topic to which I have drawn attention. The discussion, however, has been precipitated, I would fain hope, without prejudice to the cause.

I must now beg to say a few words explanatory of my impressions on the proceedings which have taken place during my absence.

1. I think it "untoward" that His Excellency the Governor should have been mixed up with the correspon-

dence between you and myself. Church and State have been separated in this colony, and I know not why an official character should have been given to a memorial concerning the administration of this diocese, by the signature of the Governor-in-Chief and Ministers of State.

2. If I have doubts how far the letter of this ecclesiastical statute law of the Established Church of England is applicable to this or other colonial dioceses, I have none as respects its spirit, nor of the inspired authority of the apostolic "tradition of eighteen centuries" on which that law is founded. The evidence even of Jerome, and the argument of Chillingworth, are to my mind conclusive on that head. I could not, therefore, nor can I feel justified in departing from that traditionary rule, even in your case. Had I felt sure that no statute law would have been violated, I should not have transgressed the "custom" of our Church without first consulting the Metropolitan and other Bishops of the province of Australasia, as well as the Archbishop of Canterbury. Consequently, I think that I ought not to have been invited by those high in authority in this colony to take a step on my own responsibility, which though possibly not an actual, would have been at least a virtual transgression of the law of our Church. You, Sir, well enforced the duty of obedience to existing laws in your farewell speech.

3. Having stated why I was unable to invite you to preach to our congregations, I took occasion from thence to urge a consideration of the terms on which at some future time possibly that inability might be removed. The indispensable conditions appeared to me to be three.

A. The acceptance in common by the Evangelical Churches of the orthodox creed.

B. The use in common of a settled Liturgy, though not to the exclusion of free prayer, as provided for in the Directory of the Assembly of Divines at Westminster.

C. An Episcopate freely elected by the United Evan-

gelical Churches, not (as I have been misapprehended)
exclusively by our own.

No notice, however, of these preliminary conditions was
taken in the memorial addressed to me. Without them
there would be no security against the intrusion even of
heretical preachers into our pulpits.

I have now done. The object of my letter to you has
been answered. I have drawn attention to the possible
future union of Evangelical Churches ; but I have found,
like another before me, that there are those who " when I
speak unto them of peace, make themselves ready to battle."

Charles V., after his abdication, amused himself with
trying to make some watches keep time together. Finding
his hopes disappointed, he wondered at the folly of his
own life-long endeavours to make men " to be of the same
judgment and walk by the same rule."

My letter certainly has not bridged the ecclesiastical gap
which separates us. On the other hand, I do not think it
has widened the breach. I am content to bide the time,
and allow the leaven to ferment. If the counsel be of God
it cannot be overthrown. Meanwhile, as the Evangelical
watches, though all professing to be set by the sun, do not
seem at present inclined professedly to go together, I must
continue to set mine by the " old church clock," which,
after all, is probably the surest going time-piece in the
world, and as near, perhaps, as any other, to the true time
of the Sun of Righteousness.

I remain, &c.,

AUGUSTUS ADELAIDE.

STATEMENT CONTINUED.

This letter the Bishop forwarded to the papers. It
appeared the next morning, November 11th. Its allusion
to " the official character given to the memorial, by the signature of the Governor-in-Chief and Ministers of State,"
occasioned a rather unpleasant correspondence, as the
original was only signed by these gentlemen in their private

capacity. The Bishop was misled by the newspaper statement already mentioned. A reference to the memorial itself, would have at once removed the mistake. Ultimately, it *was* removed. The memorial had been waiting his lordship's return; but a second or counter-memorial had been prepared; so that there were now *two* to be acknowledged and replied to. The following papers are connected with these statements.

No. II.
THE TWO MEMORIALS.

PRELIMINARY NOTE.

The Right Rev. the Bishop of Adelaide to Sir Richard Graves MacDonnell, C.B.

Bishop's Court, November 15th, 1858.

MY DEAR SIR,—I beg to acknowledge the receipt of your letter on the subject of my reply to Mr. Binney, containing a paragraph arguing on the supposition that you had signed a memorial to me in your official character. I think it due to your Excellency at once to state that I was misled by the signatures as printed in the *Register*.

I have been informed (for I have not received the memorial), that the signatures in the original were without any official designation. When or how, or by whose instrumentality this untoward addition was made, I cannot say, nor is it my business to inquire. I can only say I regret that it compelled me to write the paragraph in question.

I remain, yours very faithfully,

AUGUSTUS ADELAIDE.

THE FIRST MEMORIAL.

To the Lord Bishop of Adelaide.

We, the undersigned members of the United Church of England and Ireland, attached to her ritual and Church Government, yet desiring to promote union and Christian fellowship between the Churches agreeing in our common

Protestant faith; believing also that your lordship is most desirous of adopting all measures calculated to extend and establish the common catholic principles of faith held by the Protestant Church of Christ, into whatever sections that Church may be divided, and earnestly desiring to assist your lordship's efforts in that behalf, seize the opportunity now afforded by the presence in Adelaide of a distinguished member and minister of the Church of Christ, to offer a sign of good-will towards our brethren of the Evangelical Churches, by requesting your lordship to invite the Rev. Thomas Binney, previous to his departure from Adelaide, to fill one of our pulpits in this city: in the belief that Christian union and Christian love will be thereby promoted and diffused in the hearts of those who, holding like faith in the great saving doctrines of our common religion, have been hitherto kept asunder by differences in matters of form and discipline.

Adelaide, October 16th, 1858.

The Right Rev. the Bishop of Adelaide to Sir R. G. MacDonnell, C.B.

Bishop's Court, November 19, 1858.

MY DEAR SIR,—To you, in your private capacity as a member of the united Church of England and Ireland, whose name stands at the head of a memorial (forwarded to and received by me soon after 2 p.m., on Wednesday, November 17), requesting me " to take steps to invite the Rev. T. Binney to occupy one of our pulpits in this city," I beg to transmit the enclosed reply, and remain,

Yours very faithfully,

AUGUSTUS ADELAIDE.

To His Excellency Sir R. G. MacDonnell.

THE BISHOP'S REPLY.

May it please your Excellency and Gentlemen,

The immediate object of your memorial, requesting me

" to take steps to invite the Rev. T. Binney, previous to his departure from Adelaide, to fill one of the pulpits of this city," being impracticable, permit me to remark that the spirit out of which that request proceeded, appears to me worthy of all respect; but the obstacles in the way of giving effect to the principle involved in such an invitation are, in my opinion, little likely, under the present circumstances and views entertained "in the various sections of the Protestant Church," to be overcome.

I have the honour to remain,
Your faithful Servant,
Augustus Adelaide.

To Sir Richard Graves MacDonnell, and the Gentlemen
who signed the Memorial.
Bishop's Court, November 19, 1858.

THE SECOND MEMORIAL.

To the Right Reverend the Lord Bishop of Adelaide.

My Lord,—We, the undersigned members of the United Church of England and Ireland, feel that we should be wanting in respect to your lordship's high office, and in faithfulness to the Church of which it is our privilege to be members, were we to withhold the expression of our deep regret, that a memorial, urging the invitation of an unordained minister, and of a denomination in separation from our Church, to teach from her pulpits, should have been addressed to your lordship by certain of her members, professing, at the same time, attachment to her ritual and government, and to be animated with a desire to promote Christian union on catholic grounds, and of aiding your lordship's personal exertions in that great object.

Relying on the forecast and wisdom of your lordship to maintain our Church in its integrity in this our adopted land, and to preserve her alike from all unauthorised measures within, as well as every intrusion from without, which may tend to obliterate even the least of her time-honoured and distinctive characteristics, we await with every confidence your lordship's determination.

Well aware that the fallacies of the positions assumed in the introduction of that memorial will not escape your lordship's notice, it would be out of place were we longer to dwell upon them to add, that while we earnestly desire and await the reduction of every profession of Christianity into the bosom of one communion, we are not at liberty, as reasoning and reflecting men, to forget that the name of Christianity affords no security whatever for substantial unity; and that Christianity in any form, without the proof of its being a revelation, is but a human opinion—reasons which lead to the inevitable conclusion that any such anticipated union as that which the memorialists so indefinitely and vaguely describe, must be considered as purely ideal.

We are prepared with abundant reason why it is not possible for us to consent, on the present, or any occasion, that our Church should unite or ally herself, or make any conditions of mutual assistance with any man, or body of men, involving the slightest compromise of principle, but aware that your lordship will anticipate us in all these respects, it seems only to remain for us to express the unfeigned satisfaction with which we have received the decision of the Dean and Chapter in your lordship's absence.

We remain, your lordship's faithful Servants.

THE BISHOP'S REPLY.

Bishop's Court, November 15th, 1858.

DEAR BRETHREN,—I should be "presumptuous and self-willed" if I did not give due weight to a memorial signed by no less than 164 members of our Church, who address me on a subject of grave importance, from the conviction that not to do so would "show a want of respect to the high office" which I hold, and unfaithfulness to that Church of which they feel it a privilege to be members, as well as in "confident reliance upon my forecast to maintain the Church in its integrity," to preserve it from unauthorised innovations from within, and "intrusion from without, which might obliterate even the least of her time-honoured and distinctive characteristics."

The memorial refers specifically to the admission of persons to the office of preaching in our pulpits, who have not been ordained by the laying on of hands of the Bishop with the Presbytery.

For my views on this subject, I have only to *repeat* that portion of my letter to the Rev. T. Binney, in which I said, "Neither the power of your intellect, *nor* vigour of your reasoning, *nor* mighty eloquence, *nor* purity of life, *nor* suavity of manners, *nor* soundness in the faith, *would justify me in departing* from the rule of the Church of England, a tradition of eighteen centuries, which declares your orders irregular, your mission the offspring of division, and your Church system, I will not say schism, but ' dichostasy'— that is, standing apart."

It is true I added " that my feelings kicked against my judgment," but not I trust to its overthrow.

It is true that "*I did not feel sure* how far" I was restrained by force of law from breaking through that tradition, but I never supposed it would be imagined that I *could, on my own authority*, settle that intricate and extensive question.

Grieving, however, at what I cannot but believe to be unscriptural "divisions" of the Orthodox Protestant Denominations and Churches, I cast about to see in what way union might be restored, and the work of God carried on in common, by the co-operation of all Evangelical ministers and people "who love the Lord Jesus Christ out of a pure heart fervently." I did not, however, flatter myself with the delusive expectation that my suggestions would be adopted. It was enough if they should be *considered;* and I was not unwilling to show that the intolerant spirit which once silenced Baxter, and failed to employ Wesley, no longer animated our Church.

By recurring to the scriptural principles and usages of primitive Christianity, the mid-wall of partition which now separates men of God in preaching the Gospel, I thought might be removed.

I, for example, have ever understood that the Orthodox Dissenters of England did not object to what are called the doctrinal articles of our Church.

I knew that a "stated form of prayer" (to say nothing of the hymnology of Watts or Wesley) was used by many Wesleyan and by some Independent congregations. I remembered that Richard Baxter had composed a Liturgy for our Church.

I had read that both Luther and Calvin esteemed Episcopacy lawful, and would have retained it, had circumstances permitted, in their respective Churches.

I knew that the old Independents, while they denied "the divine right" of Presbyterianism, did not claim it for their own system.

I imagined that the founders of the Free Kirk would hardly insist upon it as a dogma of the faith.

It seemed therefore to me *possible*, that with the growth of brotherly love among the various portions of the reformed Orthodox Church, a longing for closer union on the basis of the Primitive Church might arise, to which, in the language of Bishop Jewel, the Church of England had acceded when she seceded from Rome. If this is a dream, it is at least as harmless as it is pleasant; but if it be the counsel of God, it will yet be accomplished. Be that as it may, it cannot be brought about by rudely breaking in upon cherished associations, deep-rooted convictions, or even reverend prejudices.

From the relations of colonial dioceses to each other and the Mother Church, it is plainly the duty as it is the wisdom of each Bishop, after he has ascertained the general feeling on any given question of the clergy and laity of his own diocese, to communicate their views to their brother Churchmen in the metropolitan province, through the Metropolitan and their respective Bishops, so that in all matters affecting discipline and worship we may act in common, neither disregarding the supremacy of the Crown, nor the legitimate authority of the Mother Church at home.

It is a pleasing thought that the same rule and order of worship which link us with the earliest ages of the Gospel—those generations of martyrs and confessors which by patient suffering overcame the rulers 'of the darkness of this world—also associate us with multitudes of fellow Churchmen in more than thirty colonial dioceses, as well as in the vast territories of the United States.

I heartily wish that the wise and good, and able, of all Evangelical denominations, may find it possible hereafter, by the adoption of common principles, to join the great confederacy in the Gospel. I desire no prominence for myself; I claim no dominion for my Church; but if by the manifestation of kindly feelings, and a just estimate of a really great man, I can in the slightest degree further that object, I do not think I shall have done amiss in writing to Mr. Binney, nor yet have given just ground for imagining that I am willing or able to compromise one single principle or time-honoured characteristic of our reformed branch of the Catholic and Apostolic Church.

I remain, dear brethren,

Your faithful servant in the Lord,

AUGUSTUS ADELAIDE.

To the Hon. J. H. Fisher, President of the Legislative Council, and the other Memorialists.

STATEMENT CONTINUED.

After leaving South Australia, I was so much occupied in travelling and preaching in Victoria, that it was impossible for me to enter upon such a full consideration of the Bishop of Adelaide's first letter, as it appeared to me to demand. While moving about, however, among the diggings, I availed myself of an occasional spare hour to submit to his lordship some thoughts suggested by his second communication. These extended much beyond the limits to which I had meant to confine them, and drew from my respected correspondent a similarly extended reply. That reply cannot well be omitted here, as it is more than once referred to in the "Address," and its insertion would seem to require that the greater part of my letter should be also given. I omit, however, some introductory paragraphs referring to my satisfaction in finding that the publication of his lordship's letter was admitted to have become "necessary;"—to the non-official character of the signatures to the memorial;—and to the fact that that document had an *origin* altogether independent of his lordship's having written to me. The letter then proceeded as follows:—

No. III.

The Rev. T. Binney to the Right Rev. the Bishop of Adelaide, in reply to his Lordship's Letter of November 5.

Sandhurst, Bendigo, November 29th, 1858.

*   *   *   *   *   *

Dismissing, however, these preliminary topics, I will now beg permission to submit to your lordship some thoughts which your last letter has suggested. I look at it, of course, in connexion with your previous communication; but I begin with it for a reason which will afterwards be explained. I think it not unlikely that some of my observations may surprise you; none, I hope, will offend. It is impossible, I should suppose, that your lordship can be so acquainted with the modes of thought and feeling prevalent in the Non-episcopal denominations, or with the way in which they look at certain ecclesiastical subjects, as those are who belong to them. However, therefore, you may be surprised by some of our idiosyncrasies, or may lament them, it may yet be interesting to you if I explain to your lordship—which I shall do in the most friendly spirit—how some of the statements and expressions of your letter would, as I think, appear or shape themselves to the minds of ministers of other Churches.

Beginning with the section marked 3, I beg respectfully to submit to your lordship whether there may not appear to some to be more implied or assumed, in the first paragraph, than perhaps your words were meant to convey. *"Having stated that I was unable to invite you to preach to our congregations, I took occasion from thence to urge a consideration of the terms on which at some future time possibly that inability might be removed. The indispensuble conditions appeared to me to be three."* Such are your lordship's words. At present you are "unable" to do a certain thing; but you suggest certain "terms," "indispensable conditions," on which "possibly" "at some future time" that "inability" of yours "might be removed." Now, my lord, although *I* understand you to mean that your own Church would have to be one of the parties to these terms, in common with all the rest, I greatly fear that to others the language will seem to be pervaded by assumptions, which they not only cannot admit, but which, according to the temperaments of individuals, would be smiled at as harmless or resented as offensive. It looks like one party to a friendly arrangement beginning the conference, I will not say by *dictating* but by *offering* terms to all the rest,—terms on which alone *it* can be brought to consent to anything. Of these terms some would regard the first as unnecessary, seeing that "Evangelical Churches" must, as such, have already accepted, and be known to hold, the orthodox creed; others would think the second inexpedient to be insisted upon as a first step, and without preparation, with the present fixed habits of different parties; while the third (to say nothing of its requiring in some the abandonment of what they hold *as principles*) would appear to many to demand what it would require the interposition of a miracle to secure. But the point that would be most felt, I think, would be this :—that all is asked for, apparently, on the ground that it is required in order to relieve one party only from a certain " inability,"—an inability, the removal of which might be something to *it*, but which would be nothing to the rest worth the price they would have to pay for it,—for there are those who think, that what your lordship could grant if you had the ability to do so, is not a favour to be received, much less bought, but a fraternal courtesy which they have it already in their power to exercise if others were only able to accept it. How the matter thus put will appear to your lordship, I feel quite at a loss to determine. I do not know whether, on the one hand, you will be shocked by the thought that your words should be imagined to imply so much more than you meant; or, on the other, whether you will be surprised that any one should hesitate to accept language which, with all that it implies, and *because* it implies it, may seem to you the most natural and proper imaginable. Persons like you and me, my lord, trained in different schools, accustomed to look at things from opposite points, to see them under lights and aspects altogether different, and to speak of them in language based on conclusions, assumptions, habits of association, accepted traditions, unquestioned assertions widely apart,—of which, as existing in the other, each may have little knowledge, and can have no sympathy,—why, we, at times, must of necessity use words and convey implications without the consciousness on our part that there is anything in them to surprise other people—any-thing to be objected to in what is said, or questionable or offensive in the opinions or feelings of him that says it.

The different light in which the same thing appears to different persons, from being looked at from opposite stand-points, and under the influence of different church-systems and religious associations, may be illustrated by what your lordship says of the practical efficiency of your proposed scheme. The " terms" on which the " inability" at present felt by your lordship, might " possibly" " at some future time be removed," are described as " indispensable con-ditions," and, on that account, are thus spoken of :—" *With out them there could be no security against the intrusion of even heretical preachers into our pulpits.*"

Now, to us who stand on the outside of the Episcopal Church, and who are accustomed to look not so much to mechanism as to life—not so much to what men subscribe as to what they believe—not to the letter and articles only of an orthodox creed, but to what living men actually teach, and what they *are*—to us the language of your lordship comes with but little force, especially in its bearing on the subject in relation to which it is used, namely, the security of the pulpit against the teachers of error. The stringent and solemn subscriptions of your Church are no security against doctrinal differences in the clergy of the most serious description. " Heretical preachers," is a phrase that may mislead. A Church may have the thing without the name. - " There are many antichrists," we are told by St. John ; and there are many heresies, or forms of error, alike deadly though not marked by the same brand. In the Angelican Church, you have, on the one side, men who are Romanists in everything but the name —who preach the Church, the priesthood, sacramental efficacy, anything but Christ, in the New Testament import of the term ; on the other side, you have men far more than tinctured with Rationalism—men who deny, or explain away, all the essential verities of the Gospel—everything distinctive of Christianity as a redemptive system.

You have no security against these "heretical preachers" in your "orthodox creed." Some of them, when purposely tested by being required to re-sign your articles, sign without hesitation, and then just go on teaching as before. The mere fact of being a clergyman of the Church of England is no security to us that the man would bring with him into ours, if we received him, "the doctrine of Christ;" it is not, therefore, of itself a passport to any of our pulpits. Your lordship will permit me to observe, that I am not objecting, in the abstract, to Church standards ; I am not denying the propriety and importance of professed adherence in ministers to an orthodox creed; I am not one, either, who has no sympathy with the toleration in the clergy of great diversity of opinion ; nor am I questioning, on the other hand, the necessity of "terms" and "conditions," as the basis of such an amalgamation of Churches as your lordship proposes. All that I wish to insist upon is, that the terms and conditions mentioned not only ask too much to secure a small result (the removal of a certain inability), but that *of themselves* they would not necessarily secure the purity of the pulpit in the exercise of the liberty sought.

Setting aside, for the present, the idea of such a union of Churches as would combine all in one great confederacy on certain specified terms and conditions, and which would thus secure a community of labour in pulpit services among the ministers of the different united bodies,—suffer me to offer a word or two on the interchange of pulpits, as distinct from everything else, Churches and Denominations continuing as they are. This is a subject which may be looked at from a ground different from that taken by your lordship. It ought to be contemplated, too, in connexion with the principles and convictions of all parties concerned. Instead of looking to new ecclesiastical arrangements,

either for liberty to act or security in acting, I believe
that an interchange of pulpit services between ministers
of different Churches, is a thing that should rather spring
from and be regulated by their mutual knowledge of and
confidence in each other. If, indeed, the ministers of any
Church are under an interdict, unable to act, *their* inability
will need to be removed by some ecclesiastical change *in
their own body;* but this being done, liberty to act secured
to them, then, I submit, the exercise of that liberty might
safely be left to the men themselves. There is no difficulty
in knowing what bodies of Christians, as such, agree
together substantially in the essential principles of the
evangelical faith. Within these, again, individuals or
classes have affinities and attractions which, without law,
draw them towards each other, and which are far more to
be depended on than any that law could originate or prescribe. Presbyterians, Wesleyans, Baptists, Independents,
thus, as bodies, know each other, and their ministers, as
such, have the ability to interchange pulpits if they please,
and when they please, without their previously adopting,
with a view to that, a common formula of belief. Now, for
the sake of illustration, let us suppose that in each of
these bodies there are schools and sections of "'heretical
preachers," Romanists and Rationalists in everything but
the name—the sound and orthodox portions in any one of
them have already far more security against the introduction into its pulpits of the *un*-sound ministers of the others
than could be conferred by their all agreeing to your lordship's conditions. They have it in spiritual sympathy;
in instincts and feelings belonging to a common inward
life, in addition to their adherence to a common faith,
for there *is* this amongst them though they have not signed
a common formula. By these it is that interchanges are
regulated,—public acts which involve fraternal recognition,
and indicate substantial doctrinal agreement, without
leading to any misapprehension in observers without, or

any clashing of the heterogeneous elements which (by supposition) there may be within.

In this way, and only in this way, does it appear to me that the liberty enjoyed by some denominations might be extended to and participated in by others. The principle hinted at in your lordship's first letter, that ministers of different Churches, waiving all *de jure* discussions, might agree to recognise and regard each other as *de facto* ministers of Christ — this being understood, admitted, and acted upon *on both sides*, all might have the liberty of giving an dreceiving ministerial service, so far as to *preach* for one another; and then, this being secured, everything else might be left, with perfect safety, to the operation of laws far more potent and certain than any verbal agreement in terms and conditions. *They* only would use the liberty who felt they could, and only with those with whom they could. But this, it might be objected, would have the appearance of the action of Churches *within* Churches; to which it would be sufficient to reply, "You have that now —everywhere in a degree, but nowhere to such an extent, among professedly Protestant bodies, as in that Church, which, in the person of your lordship, insists on laying down certain 'indispensable conditions' as a security against it!"

The last paragraph but two of your lordship's letter is this :—" I have now done. The object of my letter to you has been answered. I have drawn attention to the possible future union of Evangelical Churches, but I have found, like another before me, that there are those who, when I speak unto them of peace, make themselves ready to battle." In the last paragraph of all are these words :— " I am content to bide the time, and allow the leaven to ferment." On these statements permit me to say, that I hope your lordship is mistaken in supposing that any, because you have spoken to them of peace, have deliberately made " themselves ready to battle." With the exception of the offensive letter to which you allude, I hardly remember to have seen anything written in an improper spirit. Your words obviously refer to the members of your own Church. But it should be considered that neither your lordship's novel and somewhat startling idea of the "Church of the Future," nor the memorialists' more limited suggestion in respect to the present, could possibly have been put forth without occasioning difference of opinion, and being met by opposition somewhere, especially among the members of a Church so comprehensive, and, therefore, in its communion so mixed, as yours. "The object of your letter," it appears, was "to draw attention to the possible future union of Evangelical Churches." But this "union," in your lordship's scheme becomes (or, at first sight, at least seems to be) fusion, amalgamation—not a fraternization only of existing Churches, but a new "Church of the Future" altogether, involving organic changes in some, and the giving up and altering of much by all; and it is not surprising that the unexpected launching of such an idea should produce something like a ripple in the quiet tide of South Australian life. I really do not think, however, that there was anything like a "making ready to battle." Your lordship feels that your scheme is not likely to be realised at once; that you must "bide your time," and that progress in the public mind with respect to it will not take place without some "fermentation." The fact is, that what your lordship contemplates as an ultimate result—what you require in order to secure it—what you *cannot* do to meet the wish of the memorialists—the ground on which you rest this "inability,"—and a variety of other matters involved in the questions started by your lordship in the suggestions of your first letter, or implied in the language of the second, all these things are at once so grave and so exciting, coming as they do into close contact, if not into collision, with the habits, principles, prejudices, traditions, of *all* Churches, your own and ours alike, that it is not wonderful if the first effect should be somewhat startling. In respect to your lordship's scheme, your own mind has probably become so familiar with it from long and frequent thought, that you cannot realise the impression it produces on those who have it submitted to them for the first time; and in the same way, the principles which underlie your lordship's words in referring to the request of the memorialists, are so essential a part of yourself, have no doubt always appeared to you as so settled and certain, have been so unquestioned in fact, and have seemed so perfectly unquestionable in theory, that it is not possible for your lordship to understand how they appear to those who listen to and look at them from an opposite stand-point. I will not enter into controversy, and I beg that your lordship will do me the justice to believe that, in the remarks which I am about to make, I am neither engaging in battle, nor " getting ready " for it. Your lordship does me the honour to submit to me certain views on the union of Evangelical Churches, and to ask my judgment. To realise these views, or to take the very first step towards them, will involve modifications of opinion and habit on all sides. But it comes out, that your lordship is entrenched in a position, which, so long as it is maintained, will frown upon and forbid the slightest approach to united action between yourself and other Evangelical Churches. Now, it is not my intention to *attack* that position. I will not, as I have said, have any " battle " about it; but I desire to *explain* to your lordship how it looks to us on the outside, and how completely it interposes a preliminary obstacle to approach, conference, union, confraternity, and everything of the sort.

" *My letter*," says your lordship, " *has certainly not bridged the ecclesiastical gap that separates us; on the other hand, I do not think it has widened the breach.*" So far as the " gap " may be said to be personal, something interposed between you and me as Christian men, I can truly say that I care little about it; I don't look at it, or won't see it; it does not affect my feelings of affection or my sentiments of respect. But, *ecclesiastically* speaking, regarded as a barrier, a sunk fence, between different " Evangelical Churches" as such, *that* is another matter. In this respect I do not think your lordship has *widened* the " gap," but I think you have thrown light upon it—you have brought it fully into view—you have reminded us of its width and depth— you have shown it to be of such a nature that it never *can* be " bridged" by any human skill or contrivance.

Disguise the matter as we may—lose sight of it, as we often do amid the courtesies of private life, from personal regard, in social intercourse, or on the platform of religious or philan- thropic societies—hide it from ourselves, keep silent about it, do what we like to cover or conceal it, the fact is, and it is better at once honestly to look at it, that the Episcopalian clergyman *cannot* recognise the " orders" of the ministers of other Evangelical Churches—he cannot regard the men as ministers of Christ, in the full and proper meaning of the words—he cannot admit their official standing, or recognise their official acts. He may respect them as men, love them as Christian men, admire and esteem them as earnest and eloquent advocates of the truth; but to him they are *not* ministers—they have not been Epis- copally ordained, and are therefore not ordained at all; their sacramental acts are invalid; their preaching is without authority—properly speaking, indeed, they cannot " preach," though they may give a " word of exhortation ;" whatever they may be thought by themselves or others, the ministers of Non-episcopal Churches are, in the view of the Anglican clergy, laymen and nothing else. All this necessarily follows from the " tradition of eighteen centu- ries," when, as in the case of your lordship, a man has no doubt of its being an " *apostolic*" tradition, and of " *inspired authority*." The gist of the whole thing lies here. This principle touches and colours all thought—it interposes a bar to all action. Every scheme, plan, proposal for union or co-operation will be wrecked upon this rock, shattered to atoms by the breakers which play around the position your lordship occupies, and from which you look out with such a calm consciousness of perfect security. Or, to take your lordship's own figure, *you* stand on one side of the "gap" or gulf, and all Non-episcopal Churches and ministers on the other; and that gulf, guarded, watched over, kept open by the divine powers that reside in the words "apostolic," "inspired," and such like, how in the world is it ever to be "bridged" by mortal man? It never can be; nor will it ever close to admit the separated parties to come together, till there shall be thrown into it, sent down to the bottom and buried there, a goodly number of the "customs" and "traditions" of past ages. Though I speak thus, I am by no means insensible to the good that there may be in traditions and customs; I am not ignorant, either, how far some Churches may surpass others as to the degree in which they approach the customs and order of apostolic times. I am not indifferent to the questions and consequences involved in or flowing from this; but sure I am, that with the mere hints and germs of things which we have in the New Testament; with the uncertainty which belongs to the first age, the evidence of Jerome and the argument of Chillingworth notwithstanding; with the fact facing us that your orders are as invalid as mine in the view of that Church which, in one sense, is the Mother of us all. On these, and other grounds that might be mentioned, I feel that it is not wise for any Protestant Church whatever, either to assert that it is modelled exactly after an apostolic pattern, or to assume for itself, in relation to its ordinations and orders, such an exclusive validity as, in effect, to unminister all other Protestant ministers. But to this, my lord, your tradition leads—a tradition, with you, "apostolic" as to its age, and of "inspired authority" as to its character and source. Consistently with this, it is impossible for you to recognise the ministerial acts, standing, or office of the clergy of the Non-episcopal " Evangelical Churches ;" and so long as that is the case, you can never co-operate with them, or they with you, on equal terms. I had intended to notice how this principle runs through the whole of your lordship's first letter, tinging its thoughts, modifying its phraseology, hiding from you what lurks in many of its suggestions and proposals, and so reducing the entire fabric to a piece of idealism. But I must defer this to a future opportunity. I had not thought of writing so much in acknowledgment of your second letter, but having done so it precludes my making any reference to the first. I shall still feel it due to your lordship to give that letter my best consideration, but I do not regret that I have been accidentally led to give precedence to the second, since in it the principle on which the other must be interpreted is more distinctly advanced and more explicitly avowed.

Your lordship's concluding allusion to the "watches" and the "clock" reminds me of an illustration of Dr. M'Neil's which I once heard him use with admirable effect. " God," he said, " had, in the Scriptures, set up a sun-dial, by which, as by a Divine standard, the Universal Church was to note and measure the time. In front of this, over, and round about it, Popery had gradually erected a mass of masonry which completely concealed the dial from the public view, and at the same time had set up its own central clock, commanding all men to go by it. The reformers, however, detected and denounced the change; they rose up against it; they pulled down the stone structure that covered the dial, brought it forth to the sun-light, set it up in the sight of all men, made it again what it was intended from the first to be, the inheritance of the people, and thus put it in the power of the church, as a whole, to test the Pope's clock by the true time." Of course every public clock, whether belonging to a parish or a private company, needs to be tested in the same way. The "old church clock," to which your lordship refers, is no exception to this rule. It is very necessary, indeed, to see that it is submitted to it, for it is well known that former rectors, with the mayor and the town-council for the time being, often tampered with it, altering the works and putting the hands backwards and forwards, and back again, as they thought best, a very small change occasionally involving an immense difference.* I do not deny that a clock may tell us the true time, and that it may be very expedient to set our watches by it. While, however, we may use things that are "expedient," we are not to be "brought under their power." "Blessed is the man that condemneth not himself in the thing that he alloweth." Your lordship, I am persuaded, acts conscientiously in going by the "old church clock." You will, I am sure, accord to me like credit in treating all clocks as pieces of man's workmanship—using them where I think they may be used with safety ; but as none of them are of any worth except as they are in harmony with the shadow on the dial, preferring, rather, to go by that; testing and trying by it, as far as I can, whatever sounds from either Church or Conventicle. May we all do this honestly and earnestly, with humility and prayer, and be guided in doing it, that "in *God's* light we may see light !"

I remain, &c.,

T. BINNEY.

---

* Once, for example, the hand of the clock pointed to this :—"Children having been baptized, if they die, are undoubtedly saved, *else not.*" The pointer was put back two seconds, and "else not" disappearing, ceased to rule. But what a mighty difference was made by that little change! Instead of being obliged to hold the positive destruction of all unbaptized infants, the clergy and members of the English Church are allowed to believe in their *possible* salvation. This is all, indeed, for the Church simply affirms nothing, it does not decide, or rule, either way; but even that is a great relief,—the *possibility* of the one thing against the *certainty* of the other!

The Right Reverend the Bishop of Adelaide, to the Rev. T. Binney, in reply to the foregoing.

DEAR AND REVEREND SIR,—When men differ in religion or politics, the sooner they get to understand the principle or supposed principle which divides them, the sooner are they likely either to agree or differ irreconcilably. So far, therefore, from being " offended by the observations" which you have made on my second letter, I am thankful to learn from so competent an authority, " the modes of thought and feeling prevalent in the Non-episcopal Denominations ;" and " the way in which they look at certain ecclesiastical subjects."

In England it always seemed to me impossible to disengage those subjects from the surrounding medium ; to separate them from extraneous matter, so as to look at them simply in the light of God's Word, interpreted by spiritual understanding. In this colony, on the contrary, where the great offence to your co-religionists of a State Church does not exist, I thought religious questions, and among them that of Church union, might be approached from *all* sides clear of that " mirage" which deceives the explorer by exaggerating, or distorting objects. Nevertheless, I have observed from time to time invidious references made to past abuses or present difficulties of the National Established Church of England, as if they were of the essence of Episcopal discipline, and not the accidents of an establishment interwoven with the State for more than one thousand years ; while, on the other hand, the isolation of our clergy from Non-episcopalian ministers, not so much personally as *ministerially,* has not been referred (as you *now* truly do) to its real cause, viz., their *conscientious* holding fast that which they believe to have apostolic and scriptural authority, but to the mere pride of social position, or the domineering spirit of a State-favoured Church, or a Baronial Episcopate.

Had it been all along seen, as *you now* clearly see, that we *cannot* recognise your orders (though we do not take upon ourselves to reject as *ineffectuous* your ministerial acts of baptizing in the name of the Father, Son, and Holy Ghost), I should not have been asked, as I have frequently been, to admit Non-episcopalian ministers to officiate in our churches, burial-grounds, school-rooms, and to co-operate with them in works essential to the prophetical office of the ministry, such as distribution of religious Tracts, missions to the Bush, Sunday-school Teachers' Union, and lately to open *our* pulpits *unconditionally* for their use. The rule, however, on which we act has been plainly laid down for us. We do not *forbid* Non-episcopalian ministers " to cast out devils " by preaching Christ's name and Gospel, *because they follow not us;* but neither on the other hand, do *we* find any warrant for " following" them.

Compelled, then, from time to time to refuse such applications, I was not sorry to seize the opportunity presented by your arrival in South Australia of making it *quite clear,* " *why,*" *and* " *why only,*" we hold ourselves *ministerially* aloof from Non-episcopalian ministers, though as with myself, so with my brethren, our *private* and *personal* " feelings often kick against" our solemn convictions and pledges. I would simply ask you to read the following extracts from the Preface to our Ordination Service, and the twenty-third Article, in order to judge fairly of our position :—

" It is evident unto all men diligently reading the Holy Scripture and ancient authors that from the *Apostles' time* there have been these orders of ministers in Christ's Church—Bishops, Priests, and Deacons; which offices were evermore had in such reverend estimation, that *no man might presume* to execute any of them except he were first called, tried, examined, and known to have such qualities as are requisite for the same; and also by public prayer, with imposition of hands, were approved and admitted thereunto by lawful authority. And, therefore, *to the intent that these orders may be continued*, and reverently used and esteemed *in the United Church of England and Ireland*, no man shall be accounted or taken to be a lawful Bishop, Priest, or Deacon in the United Church of England and Ireland, or *suffered to execute* any of the said functions, except he be called, tried, examined, and admitted thereunto according to the form hereafter following, or *hath had* formerly Episcopal consecration or ordination."

" Article XXIII.—Of Ministering in the Congregation.

" It is not lawful for any man to take upon him the office of public preaching or ministering the sacraments in the congregation, before he be lawfully called and sent to execute the same ; and those we ought to judge lawfully called and sent which be chosen and called to this work by men who have public authority given unto them in the congregation to call and send ministers into the Lord's vineyard."

As a matter of history, it stands recorded that Whittingham was deprived, in 1579, of the deanery of Durham, and Travers of the lectureship of the Temple, because they had received only Presbyterian ordination at the hands of certain ministers on the continent of Europe.

Could I, then, as an *honest* man, invite you to preach in our pulpits ? But as I *could not do so*, I felt " pressed in spirit" to show you how I, and multitudes of others in the Church of England, valued piety, eloquence, and ability in Non-episcopalian ministers; and how much we wished that *they* would *re-consider* those points of discipline which *they* number with " *things indifferent*," but which *we* are *bound in conscience* to hold fast, as being of apostolic origin and possessing scriptural authority. Neither Lutherans, nor Calvinists, nor Wesleyans, nor even " Independent" Independents, like yourself, assert Episcopacy or creeds to be unscriptural or *unlawful*, though they maintain that they are "*not of obligation.*" Non-episco-palians, then, would violate no rule of conscience by adopting either one or the other; *either* a freely-elected Episcopate in its primitive form, or a form of sound words, whereby "*the sunk fence*" of , which you speak, between the Episcopal and more recent denominational Presby-terian Churches, would so far be filled up and disappear.

If it savours of "assumed superiority" on my part in venturing to point out for consideration this condition of union, it is a superiority *forced* upon me, and not of my creating—emanating from former acts of Non-episcopalian bodies. I cannot reverse the history of the Church for eighteen centuries; but I neither "dictated" nor "offered" terms of union; I simply stated what we believe to be our "scriptural and apostolic" rule; and asked Non-episco-palian ministers, in these days of free thought and "inde-pendent" Independency, to consider whether future union of "Evangelical Churches" on certain principles were possible.

I am not sorry that some few eager spirits, who attempted to clear the "sunk fence" at a bound, should have stumbled and fallen therein; or, to adopt your military metaphor, they have not blown in the counterscarp of the ditch, and planted their banners on the breach of a ruined Episco-pacy. That fortress we cannot abandon, because we believe its bulwarks to be of apostolic origin, and to have the sanc-tion of Scripture. And if our Non-episcopalian friends cannot join it and form part of the garrison, let them believe and give us credit for acting "conscientiously" in maintaining our ministerial reserve. Let them cease to talk of "dominant Church," "intolerant hierarchy," &c., as the cause of disunion. We have as much right to *remain* Episcopalians, as they had to become Non-episcopalians. The foxes in the fable were justified in declining to reform themselves by a "fraternal curtailment."

Nor was it merely with a view to remove "the mid-wall of

partition" between the Church of England and those bodies which have dissented from it that I thought the re-adoption of the Episcopate an indispensable preliminary to Church union. If oneness, outward as well as inward, formal as well as spiritual, be the *normal* state of Christ's Church militant as well as triumphant; if we may hope "the Gospel and true Church of God" will finally emerge from Tridentine, Mediæval, or Patristic error, then the "idiosyncracy" also of the Eastern and Greek mind, as well as of Southern Christian Europe, must be taken into some account: and it certainly would be a greater "miracle" to reform those Churches—Greek, Roman, Syrian, Russian— *down* to the *platform* of John Knox—than that you and other evangelical ministers should be willing to sit side by side with Bishops in some Council like that of Jerusalem, when Paul and Barnabas, and Simon Peter, with James presiding, gave forth the decree assented to by the elders and the brethren, condemnatory of a Judaizing Christianity. Whether a more extended "fraternization" might not thus result, not only between the clergy of our Church and Non-episcopalian Dissenting ministers, but Lutheran, Swiss, and French divines; whether an *unscriptural* "denominationalism"—"I am of Paul, and I of Apollos, and I of Cephas"—would not thus help to fill up the "sunk fence" between us, and render access to a Church, catholic *in form* as well as *spirit*, easy on *all* sides; whether Heathen or Mahometan Antichrists, or those within the Church itself, viz., the unbelief which denies the Lord that bought us— the Father and the Son; or that which exalts the creature —sacraments, priest, or saint; so as to keep less in view the Saviour himself (a *will-worship* which He ordained not); whether, I say, such enemies of God and Christ will give way *more readily* if union were rendered possible by the spirit of love leading us "to walk by the same rule, and in honour to prefer one another," I do not presume to decide. I have simply proposed the question for consideration.

But I am reminded by you that something more than identity of Church government, or subscription to the orthodox creed, would be necessary to open your pulpits to the Anglican clergy. I return, then, to this second preliminary condition, viz., subscription to a creed, which you pronounce to be ineffectual to procure doctrinal purity in pulpit ministrations. You describe some clergymen of our Church as Roman in all but name, and others as Rationalists, neither of whom, on any account, would you suffer to preach in your pulpit. Neither would I suffer them to preach in mine.

But I proposed nothing of the sort. That preliminary condition of subscription to a creed might remove an existing barrier, but would *compel* no exchange of pulpits. Liberty might have been gained, but no compulsion introduced. Certain conditions being pre-supposed, it seemed possible that like Peter Martyr and Bucer in the 16th century, so in these days, D'Aubigné or Neander, Chalmers, Cumming, or yourself, might be heard (perhaps to advantage) in St. Paul's or Westminster Abbey—a position for Christian influence which the pastor of the Weigh-House might not altogether despise, though he might think it beneath him to covet.

From the fact, however, that in spite of our Articles there are Romanizing and Rationalist clergymen in our Church, you draw the conclusion that formularies of the faith are useless. You also state, as a matter of fact, that the exchange of pulpits between Non-episcopalian ministers, Congregationalists, Wesleyan, Free Kirk, and Baptist, is far more carefully guarded than is access to those of our Church. Now is it not owing in great measure to the Thirty-nine Articles themselves that these Romanizing and Rationalizing clergymen are *tested and found out?* Your argument, from the abuse of creeds, *proves too much;* for there *are* Unitarians and Papists, despite of the authorised version of the Scriptures and the Latin Vulgate, which led Luther to justification by faith.

If creeds and articles cannot prevent error, neither can the Scriptures! Are the latter, therefore, needless and useless? " The unlearned and unstable wrest St. Paul's Epistles and other Scriptures to their destruction." I do not know that the blame rests with St. Paul for writing his letters to the Churches.

Besides, who commanded the Baptismal creed—belief in the name of the Father, Son, and Holy Ghost, as necessary to salvation? " He that *believeth* and is baptized shall be saved!" Who required belief in *himself* as the *Son of God* before the Eunuch could be baptized? *Why* did St. Paul deliver *first* of all to the Corinthians that which he also had received, that " Christ died for our sins according to the Scriptures; that He was buried and rose again according to the Scriptures?" Why did he tell Timothy to " hold fast the form of sound words ;" and " to commit the same to faithful men who should be able to teach others ?"

Look at the history of Protestantism itself! What Protestant Church did not, at the Reformation, put forth its Confession? · Is that of Augsburg a dead letter? Not *until* the Helvetic Confession of Calvin's Church had been *abrogated* by the Rationalistic Government of Geneva as a test for its State Clergy did a new *evangelical* reformation, inaugurated by D'Aubigné and Malan, become necessary there. Let me further ask, what has become of the orthodoxy of the old Presbyterian Churches in England? What is the faith of the Presbyterian Synod of Antrim? Was it not from the absence of a creed that the Lady Hewly Charity came to be dragged into a court of law? Did the absence of articles prevent the " Rivulet" controversy, and preserve the fountain of Gospel truth pure and undefiled? Not long ago I had the pleasure of receiving from you a sermon, entitled " The Apostles' Creed." Now, if the Apostles had a creed, that is, certain truths indispensable to the Gospel of Salvation, and if *you* have endeavoured to define those truths, surely a *creed* in itself is neither useless nor needless, "yourself being judge."   I might refer also to your friends the Wesleyans, whom you once offended, by plainly telling them "that they must be either Dissenters or Schismatics;" yet *they* have a *creed*, and a tolerably long one too—one, also, of purely uninspired composition, which nevertheless you yourself have morally subscribed before you preached in their Chapel!   I know not whether you are an Arminian or Calvinist, or neither.   But every Wesleyan Minister is bound by Wesley's model trust-deed to preach no " doctrine or practice contrary to what is contained in certain Notes on the New Testament, commonly reputed to be the notes of the said John Wesley, and in the first four volumes of Sermons, commonly reputed to be written and published by him."   Talk of Popery and the Council of Trent, and the infallibility of the Pope!   Those are " motes" not more huge than this Wesleyan *beam*.

I did not ask you, or other Non-episcopalian ministers, to subscribe to the *Thirty-nine Articles and the Book of Homilies* before you could preach in our pulpits, but simply to a creed in accordance with the Nicene Confession.   If this will not secure absolute immunity from doctrinal error, it may do something *towards* it.   I believe in charts and light-houses, although in spite of them some master-mariners contrive to run their ships on shore.

I believe also, as much as you do, that watches, clocks, and even dials must be adjusted to the sun; but the example of adjustment which you have selected, and which you describe as giving " great relief to the clergy and members of the *English Church*," no more affects them than it does you and other Non-episcopalians.   You state that the hand of the clock (that is, from the context, the English Church clock) pointed to this :—" Children having been baptized, if they die, are undoubtedly saved ; *else not*. The pointer was put back two seconds, and ' else not' dis-appearing, ceased to rule.   But what a mighty difference was made by that little change! Instead of *being obliged to* hold the positive destruction of all unbaptized infants, the clergy and members of the English Church are allowed to believe in their *possible* salvation." I am sure it will be a great " relief" to you to learn that this statement, however designed to comfort us, is (so far as the Church of England is concerned) quite unnecessary.

The *first* Liturgy of Edward VI., A.D. 1549, has this rubric in the " Office for Confirmation:"—

" And that no man shall think that any detriment shall come to children by deferring of their confirmation, he shall know for truth that it is certain by God's word that children being baptized (if they depart out of this life in their infancy) are undoubtedly saved."

The words " else not" do not appear in our *first reformed Liturgy*, and therefore could not have been omitted. But to make it quite clear that the doctrine you incorrectly fasten upon the English Church was not held by her leading reformers, take this declaration from the chapter " Concerning Baptism" from the " Reformation of Ecclesiastical Laws;" a treatise drawn up by commissioners appointed in the reigns of Henry VIII. and Edward, of whom Cranmer was the first in rank:—

" Theirs also ought to be considered a scrupulous superstition who so completely tie down the grace of God and the Holy Spirit to the sacramental elements, as explicitly to affirm that no infant of Christian parents can obtain eternal salvation who dies before it can be brought to baptism—*an opinion far different from ours.* 'Quod longe secus habire judicamus.'"

An expression, indeed, which had found its way into the baptismal service of the first Liturgy of Edward VI., 1549, from that of *Luther*, through the Latin reformed service of the Archbishop Herman, of Cologne (1543), was omitted in the *second* Liturgy of Edward VI., in 1552. It is in the prayer before baptism, which ran thus:—" That by this wholesome laver of regeneration, whatsoever sin is in them may be washed clean away: that they, being delivered from Thy wrath, may be received into the ark of Christ's Church, *and so saved from perishing.*"

This prayer is not to be found in the *ancient* offices of the *Church of Rome,* but seems to have been originally composed by *Luther,* though it is not in accordance with his sentiments expressed elsewhere.

"Although infants," he remarks, " bring into the world with them the depravity of their origin, yet it is an important consideration that they have never transgressed the Divine commandments; and since God is merciful, He will not, we may be assured, suffer them to fare the worse because, *without their own fault, they have been. deprived of baptism.*"

So that this chance expression of Luther's—contrary to his own sentiments, and which escaped notice in the baptismal service of our Liturgy from 1549 to 1552, but was then omitted, and which never existed in the *ancient offices* of the Church—is *small* ground enough on which to express your compassion "for the ministers and clergy of the English Church," in the "great relief" they must have experienced.

In conclusion, let me observe, that while minds capacious and independent as yours labour under such misapprehensions in regard to the Church of England and its doctrines, the hope of Church union will remain "ideal." But if Episcopalians and Non-episcopalians will honestly, and in the fear of God, try to learn with accuracy *wherein* they do essentially differ, and *why,* then possibly both may be able eventually, through the grace of God, to adjust their clocks and watches by the sun-dial of His revealed will.

I am, Rev. Sir, yours faithfully and respectfully,

AUGUSTUS ADELAIDE.

NOTE ON THE FOREGOING.

Of the force and relevancy of the above, as a reply to the
letter to which it refers, the competent reader will judge.
Leaving to his own consideration what is said about Episcopacy and creeds, I notice only the closing paragraphs,
as they refer to a matter of fact. The Bishop is at fault
both in fact and argument; he ignores the one, and misapprehends the other. In referring to certain words as
having been once in the Prayer-Book and afterwards left
out, I went on the authority of the Judicial Committee of
the Privy Council. I knew that in their Judgment on
the Gorham case there was this statement:—"In 1536,
the doctrine of the articles is full and positive in respect
to spiritual regeneration in and by baptism. Everything
is asserted that could be possibly claimed for it—insomuch
that infants and children dying in their infancy are declared
to be saved *thereby* and *else not*." So far as the *fact*, then,
is concerned, of such words having once been in the Prayer-
Book, this judicial statement is sufficiently demonstrative.
But the Bishop misapprehends *the argument*. The *point*
was simply this:—"The Church clock" *itself* requires to
be tested, because its hands have been put backwards and
forwards. *Here* is an illustration of that—*here*, in these
two words, which appeared at one time and disappeared
at another. It was a natural passing observation—the
greatness of the change of thought involved in so small a
phrase; but the *gist* of the matter was, not the doctrine
itself that was advanced or withdrawn, but the fact of
successive alterations. His lordship's observations, instead
of disposing of this (the real argument), only confirms it,
for he *proves* that things "found their way" into the book
at one time, and disappeared at another. That "the hands
of the clock" were thus moved and altered was my point;

and that in the illustration I gave, I was not only correct as to a fact, but "fastened no doctrine" on the Church of England but what she once avowed herself, the following words of the Judges already referred to will prove :—

"In respect to the articles, it appears they underwent successive alterations, and expressed on the subject of baptism different shades of opinion, as different opinions as to the sacrament itself were held by successive reformers."

"It is apparent that once, in 1536, two things had been decided, namely, that baptized infants dying before actual sin, were undoubtedly saved *thereby*, and that unbaptized infants were *not* saved."

"In 1543, 'The King's Book' expresses itself in a manner indicative of a change or modification of opinion."

"The articles of 1552 and 1562 differ greatly from those of 1536."

"More especially those of 1562 .... instead of saying that children obtain remission of their sins, &c., by baptism, and dying in their infancy, are saved *thereby*, else *not*, they merely approve infant baptism as a right thing, but they say nothing distinctly as to the salvation of either baptized or unbaptized."

All that was either said or suggested by the letter to which the Bishop refers, is thus fully sustained by the highest authority.

But, so far as the doctrine referred to is concerned, the following evidence may be put in, and will, perhaps, be felt to be weighty. It has been furnished to me by a friend.

"The parties into which the Church was now divided were led by the two Archbishops, and may be ranged in the following order."—(Here follows a list of Cranmer and his party, viz:—Goodrick, Shaxton, Latimer, Fox, Hilsey, and Barlow; and of Lee and his party, viz.:—Stokesby, Tonstal, Gardiner, Longland, Sherburn, and Kite.)

"After much discussion, certain articles, which had been

submitted to them by the King, were agreed upon, and published by the Royal authority; and as they may be deemed the first document of the faith of the Church of England, they cannot be esteemed unworthy of peculiar notice. Their general outline is as follows :—The Bible and the three Creeds are laid down as the basis of our faith. Baptism is declared to be *absolutely necessary*—that is, *that children dying* unbaptized, *cannot be saved*," &c.

The above is an account of the articles of 1536, as given in " Sketch of the History of the Church of England to the Revolution of 1688, by Thomas Vowler Short, D.D., Lord Bishop of St. Asaph." 5th Edit. Parker, 1847.

STATEMENT RESUMED.

The following letter, occasioned by circumstances referred to in it, would have been omitted here, but for the thought, that it may possibly have an interest to some, from what is now occurring amongst us. I refer to facts elsewhere noticed—such as the admission by clergymen of the *schismatical spirit* in which the last revision of the Prayer-Book was conceived and carried out; the singular spectacle of ministers of the Episcopal Church uniting with those of Nonconforming Bodies in preaching to the masses, and in carrying on special religious services; and the manifest tendency of union and co-operation *so far* to abate sectional animosities and promote catholic sentiment.

No. IV.

Rev. T. Binney to the Editor of the " South Australian Register."

CHURCH UNION.

SIR,—Only now and then since I left Adelaide has a *Register* reached me. In those I have seen, there have been occasionally notes and letters on " Church Union," or more properly on the " Pulpit Question." The phrase " Church Union," though signifying less than the Church *amalgamation*, which seemed to be the ultimate object of the Bishop's scheme, implies much more than was contemplated by the first memorialists when asking for an exchange of pulpits. In the first note I sent to you, when it had become necessary to publish the letter addressed to me by the Bishop, I felt it important to point out what such exchange was *not* to involve. Both the clergy and myself, by no act of our own, were called upon to look at a subject which had been started by others. I thought it right, to avoid misconception, to lay down the distinction between simply preaching in a place, or to a congregation, and approving or recognising *all* that the Church which both might belong to, hold. The Episcopalian, for instance, if he preached for me, was not to be supposed to recognise or sanction the peculiarities of opinion or discipline characteristic of Congregationalists; and I, on the other hand, in preaching for him, was not to be understood, by that act, to approve or accept the offices of the English Church, which to me admit of only one construction—a construction involving matters which I do not believe.

Many men, besides the memorialists, have indulged the dream that it might be possible to *begin* advances towards union by a simple exchange of pulpits. They have thought that those ministers of the Church, and those out of it, who are more *one* in faith and feeling than different schools actually within the Church ever can be—they have thought that such, at least, might interchange service; that while thus mutually recognising each other as preachers of the same truth and servants of the same Lord, the act need imply nothing more—thus leaving untouched, as to recognition or approval, many things that might belong to the Churches or denominations of each, as such. I confess I have myself participated in this feeling, but I have done so with another feeling underlying it. Believing, as I do, that *all* parties, Churches, denominations, *have something to learn from each other, and something in themselves to unlearn,* I have been willing to hope that, if some at present separated from each other were brought together in the way proposed, light might be got, and love excited, and reforms and improvements, on both sides, facilitated and secured, till, perhaps, something might be developed that should give promise of a pure and united Church of the Future.

The words of the Bishop of London, in his recent charge, reports of which have just reached us in the last arrivals of English news, are words which embody the deep feelings of many, and are such as can be adopted and echoed by those of other communions :—" Is it not true," he says, " that there is scarcely one of us who does not feel that it is an evil to be separated so much as we are even from those good and earnest Christians who are not members of our own Church?" It *is* an evil; and there are those on both sides who feel and lament it. *How* that gulf of separation is to be bridged, however, is the question. The impression produced on my own mind by observing the course of your Adelaide controversy—or that seems likely to be produced—is this, that nothing can be suggested, no step taken, to bring together those " separated" from one another, without its leading to something which will bring up the original grounds of the separation—throw the mind of the thoughtful back on these—and compel their being looked at, re-stated, and re-examined. It is very obvious that while some men, under the influence of kind and catholic feeling, imagine that they can forget original differences, and, by drawing a little closer together in God's house, be prepared for looking at these by-and-by in such a spirit and under such influences as may make both parties willing to yield something—it is very obvious that at present this is almost as much a dream as the more splendid vision in which my friend, the Bishop of Adelaide, indulged, and which he felt to be so "pleasant" to himself. I cannot refer you to the letters, which, in expressing this opinion, I have in my mind's eye—letters, I mean, which have appeared in the *Register*. I have either mislaid or destroyed the papers, but I may indicate sufficiently what I refer to by saying that one writer advanced something to this effect, that the question was, " whether Dissenters had ceased to be the *schismatics* they were when they separated from the Church ; whether time had so altered things that they could be viewed in a more favourable light ?" Another found a difficulty in the " absolution ;" if Non-episcopal ministers " were not allowed to pronounce it, that might offend *them ;* and if they were, *that* would offend the Church." A third entered largely into the proof that *the Anglican Church regarded the ministers of other denominations as no ministers at all*, and concluded by remarking, with respect to myself, " that though it might be painful to say so, yet so it was, that the Church of England regarded me not only as a layman, but *as a schismatical layman*," and so on.

Now, I find no fault with all this ; I am not offended by it ; nor do I blame others who are determined to adhere to everything in their supposed "primitive and apostolic Church," and who betray something like terror at the thought that anything in its constitution, utterances, or offices should be asserted to be *unscriptural.* Whatever men honestly think and deeply feel, it becomes them to say, and to say with such strength of language as is equal to their convictions. Men, however, who look at things from opposite sides must allow to each other the same liberty of thought and speech. If, therefore, the writers referred to say—" The proposed exchange of pulpits is impossible ; such exchange should be a recognition of the ministers admitted to them and the Churches they represent *in all respects*. But this recognition we cannot give, because we, the Episcopal clergy, regard Nonconformist ministers as no ministers at all, and their Societies not as Churches, but as sinful, because schismatical, confederates." If, I say, gentlemen take this ground, they necessarily drive others to the opposite, and hence the reply of the conscientious Nonconformist will be,—" If by preaching in an Episcopal pulpit, I am to be supposed to recognise the Episcopal Church *in all respects*—not merely to see in the minister of the place a brother in the Lord, with whom I am one in respect to the Gospel, but also to admit everything that is involved in clerical subscription and in the Church *as a whole*—I cannot do it. Exchange of pulpits, if it implies *that*, is impossible; for, in my opinion, the Church was the original schismatic, while certain principles that pervade its formularies are, as I think, unscriptural; though others may so coincide with, or so understand them, as heartily to avow or conscientiously to accept what I am obliged to repudiate and deny."

It strikes me that the way in which the question started by the memorialists has been met must, necessarily, throw the mind of the " dichostasy" back, in this manner, on the original grounds of separation. I shall, probably, have to advert to this in my next letter to the Bishop, though when that will be written I know not, since every hour of my time is so constantly consumed, and likely to be so, by the pressure of other duties. *Without referring, then, to his lordship, or to anything he has written,* I think it may be permitted to me to request the attention of the devout, the conscientious, and the thoughtful among Churchmen, *to some of those things which prevent many from joining the Episcopal Church, who, on various grounds, would willingly do so if they could.* Very few among your readers have ever, perhaps, investigated this subject; and even to some who may have written in your pages, it may not, in its more serious aspects, be familiar. I think it may be worth their while to look at things for a moment from the Nonconformist stand-point, and to try to understand how they must necessarily appear to us. At the present stage of the Adelaide controversy—if controversy it is to be called—

I think this favour may fairly be asked of our friends.
In 1830, twenty years ago, I had occasion to re-examine
the terms on which myself, or any other man, might be
admitted to the ministry of the Church of England. I had
particular reasons for looking more fully and minutely into
the subject than perhaps many clergymen have ever done,
or ever felt that they were called upon to do. I threw my
thoughts into a written form, and read them at the opening
of a place of worship in which a friend of mine, a converted
Jew, was to officiate. They were published at the time.
I have accidentally met in Melbourne with a copy of the
pamphlet, and I should be glad if you could give it to your
readers in four or five successive sections. Your doing so
will put some of my Episcopalian friends (for I will not
regard any man, however he differs from me, as anything
else) in possession of points which may possibly be new to
them; while it will shorten my labour in what I may yet
have to write to their worthy diocesan. There are some
passages in which the language is rather strong; but the
Bishop of Melbourne, with whom I have had much frank
and friendly intercourse, and whom I have learnt greatly
to respect and love, tells me that there is nothing in the piece
to give just offence; at least, he says, it gives no offence to
him, though, not feeling my scruples, he is of course un-
affected by the argument. To show, however, that the
judgment and conscience of others continue to be affected
by what influences mine, and in the same way, I will conclude this long introductory letter (which I have not time
to make shorter) by the following extract from an English
newspaper which has just come to hand :—

" SECESSION OF AN EVANGELICAL CLERGYMAN.—The Rev.
R. M. Milne, B.A. (following the steps of the late Vicar of
Aylesbury), has resigned the vicarage of Youlgreave, Der-
byshire, in consequence of having arrived at the conviction
that various portions of the contents of the Prayer-Book
are not in harmony with the Scriptures; and that it is

wrong to hold a position which involves the continuance of that ' assent' which he gave on entering the ministry, but cannot now give. By this obedience to the voice of conscience and to what he regards as the requirements of truth, Mr. Milne has nobly sacrificed an income of £230 a-year. Mr. Milne's sympathies are still with the Established Church, so far as it favours Evangelical religion ; and, like the great bulk of the Evangelical clergy, he holds what are called moderately Calvinistic opinions."

I am, Sir, &c.,
T. BINNEY.

St. Kilda, Melbourne, February 11, 1859.

P.S.—The Bishop of Melbourne, in a letter now lying before me, arising out of the Adelaide question, very justly says :—" Certain Congregations, or Churches, upon conscientious objections to its doctrine or constitution, separated themselves from the communion of the Church of England. If these objections are well founded, then the matters to which they relate are the real barriers to a union. If they are groundless, then the mistaken views of the separatists are the barrier." This is well put ; and it would seem to follow from it, that, if any movement towards union is made (not merely exchange of pulpits), it must begin by the sifting of the objections referred to, in order to determine whether the " barrier" lie in the " matters" themselves, or in the " mistaken views" entertained about them. The sections, or chapters, which are to follow this letter* touch on some of these " matters" and on certain " views" respecting them. It is for the reader to say which he thinks wrong—the " matters" or the " views.   If all could only come to see alike as to this question—*one way or the other*—that would be the beginning of the end.   The subject is one of great interest, especially

---

* Instead of the piece thus referred to being given in sections in the newspaper, it was published as a whole in a pamphlet, under its original title, " Conscientious Clerical Nonconformity."

to those who, in the words of the *second* memorial, " earnestly desire and await *the reduction of every profession of Christianity into the bosom of one communion.*"

The following letters and extracts are given, as they bear on the above, and are elsewhere referred to.

No. V.

Correspondence published, with the Sanction of the Bishop of Adelaide, in a pamphlet issued by some of the leading Counter-memorialists.

1.

Gilbert-street, Adelaide, 9th September, 1858.

My Lord,—I have the honour, by the direction of the Committee of the South Australian Sunday-school Teachers' Union, to inquire if your lordship is willing to receive a deputation from the Committee, and if so, to request an appointment for that purpose of a time and place convenient to your lordship.

The deputation named, consists of Mr. Samuel Bakewell, one of the Vice-presidents of the Union ; Mr. Martin, and myself. Its object, is to obtain the consent of your lordship to preside at a Lecture to be delivered on *behalf of this Institution*, by the Rev. Thomas Binney of London.

If agreeable to your lordship, the deputation would be glad to fulfil its duty on Saturday next, the 11th instant, at 3 p.m.

Requesting the favour of an early reply, I have the honour to be,

My lord,

Your most obedient Servant,

(Signed) J. S. WAY, Hon. Sec.

The Right Rev. the Lord Bishop of Adelaide.

2.

Bishop's Court, September 10th, 1858.

SIR,—I am sensible of the compliment paid me, whether personally or officially, by the Committee of the South Australian Sunday-school Teachers' Union, in offering to depute some of its members to request me to preside at a Lecture about to be delivered by the Rev. Thomas Binney, on behalf of this Institution.

Allow me to assure the Committee, that as a powerful advocate of Orthodox Evangelical Christianity, I respect Mr. Binney; a respect which a slight personal acquaintance has tended to increase.

Had it in my view been consistent with the acknowledged principles of the Church of England, and an honest adherence to them, I should have hastened to invite Mr. Binney to preach to our congregations ; but such is not the case, and I can only wish that the work to which he and others believe him to be duly called, may prosper in his hands.

For a like reason I have felt it to be beyond my power to join the Sunday-school Teachers' Union. The congregations to which those teachers belong, have separated in times past from the Church of England, on some not unimportant points of doctrine and discipline. They still differ in their views and teaching respecting the Sacraments and Ministry ; I can only make "common" ground with them, by abandoning or ignoring the practice and principles of the Church over which I have been called to be an overseer. It would be inconsistent and not of " faith" in me to do so ; nor can I sanction in others what I disapprove in regard to myself.

For these reasons, I regret to be obliged to decline receiving a deputation from the Committee, not being prepared to join the Union, for the special benefit of which Mr. Binney has been invited to lecture.

I remain, Sir, yours very faithfully,

AUGUSTUS ADELAIDE.

J. S. Way, Esq.

Extracts from Two Letters:—the one from the Rev. T. Binney to the Right Reverend the Bishop of Adelaide; the other from his Lordship in reply.

1.

St. Kilda, February 11th, 1859.

*　　*　　*　　*　　*　　*

I have this week received from a friend a pamphlet. In glancing through it, I observe there is a correspondence given between your lordship and Mr. J. S. Way, in which I am referred to. This correspondence was, I presume, furnished by your lordship. *　*　*　*

I send some MS. to Adelaide by this mail, which may or may not see the light. It does not refer to your lordship's letter, nor is it addressed to you. It bears on that aspect of things which the Adelaide question, as it seems to me, *has now assumed*, namely, the nature, the sufficiency or insufficiency, of the reasons which *compel some of us* to occupy such an ecclesiastical position that, in the language of a writer in the *Register*, the Church of England feels authorized to regard me as " not only a layman, but a SCHISMATICAL LAYMAN."

To the Right Rev. the Lord Bishop of Adelaide.

———

2.

Bishop's Court, Adelaide, February 22, 1859.

*　　*　　*　　*　　*　　*

My letter to Mr. Way was shown to Mr. ——, and made public at his request, because it placed my intentions unmistakeably before the Church at large. The meaning of my letter *to you* had been misrepresented, my object misunderstood, and finally my sincerity called in question. That letter, *if published at the time*, would have cleared up the whole matter. Somewhat unaccountably to me it was

R

never adverted to, and never saw the light. In *self-defence*, therefore, and *to re-assure the Counter-memorialists*, it was inserted by the Editors in the pamphlet. I do not hold myself pledged on that account to sanction all that pamphlet may contain.

*　　*　　*　　*　　*　　*

I accept the Bishop of Melbourne's statement of the question. " Certain Congregations or Churches, upon conscientious objections to its doctrine, or constitution, separated themselves from the communion of the Church of England. If these objections are well founded, then the *matters* to which they relate are the real barriers to a union. If they are groundless, then the mistaken *views* of the separatists are the barrier." This is precisely the point of discussion which I desired to raise in my letter to you, except that it is *unnecessarily narrowed* to the differences between the Church of England and those *denominations* which have dissented from it. I would include the Lutheran and Reformed Churches of Europe, together with the various sections of the Presbyterian communion in Scotland, in the description. The re-unions of individuals holding in common Evangelical views, called " Evangelical Unions," seem to make no nearer approach to a *Catholic Unity of Reformed Evangelical Churches;* but a step will have been gained, if they or other seriously disposed Christians will prayerfully consider what are the Evangelical truths, apostolic constitution of Churches, and ecclesiastical practices, which would once more unite the Evangelical communions. The basis of such union appeared to me to be a Common Creed, a Common Liturgy, and a Common Church Government. I wait to learn whether such union is deemed by Non-episcopalian bodies unnecessary or inexpedient; or, if not, what are the difficulties and objections, which, if not removable, would form an insuperable barrier to a complete fellowship of the Churches in the Gospel of Christ.

Whatever be the result, a dispassionate consideration of the question cannot be unprofitable or uninteresting, either as regards the evangelization of the heathen world, now thrown entirely open to Christian missionaries, or the maintenance and diffusion in Christendom of the faith once delivered to the saints. Meanwhile, I cordially subscribe to the following words of the present Bishop of London, in a sermon preached before the University of Oxford, February 2nd, 1845,—" The most ardent attachment to our holy forms, the most full appreciation of their efficiency in guiding our own souls in the way of life ; nay, a conviction that under Providence our own Church seems more likely than any other to be our Lord's instrument in spreading a pure and enlightened and orderly Christianity throughout the world—our conviction of all this can have no natural connexion with any uncharitable feelings towards those who are not able to agree with us."

I am, my dear Sir,

Yours truly,

Augustus Adelaide.

Rev. T. Binney.

P.S.—It occurs to me that Mr. Way, the Honorary Secretary of the South Australian Sunday-school Teachers' Union, may possibly not have preserved my answer to the application of the Committee. Nor do I assent to the statement of a writer in the *Register* that the Church of England feels authorized to regard you, " as not only a layman, but a schismatical layman." It is a different thing to pronounce, with the Church of Rome, your orders *null and void*, and your ministrations schismatical and invalid; and to say, as the Church of England appears to me to say, that they lack that apostolic traditionary authority which, not being at variance with Scripture, she retained at the Reformation, for those who should minister in her congregations. I am not aware that she would unchurch the Lutheran or other Protestant Evangelical Churches in Europe. She may lament their loss of that primitive Church Government, which she was providentially permitted to preserve. With regard to the Nonconformist bodies in England, while she stands in the old paths, and condemns the spirit which seems to perpetuate and sanction endless division; rejecting for herself as being *irregular* the ministrations which result from it; the hope is still cherished, that past *mutual* injuries may be put out of ' remembrance; and existing defects or blemishes removed, so that the wise and good among those bodies may be able eventually to find a spiritual home within her pale.

The three following notes require no special remark. They illustrate certain references in the " Address."

No. VI.

STATE-AID.

The Bishop of Melbourne—The Bishop of Victoria, Hong Kong—The Wesleyans.

The following are illustrations of the statements in the text. A public breakfast was given in Sydney to the above-named prelates, a report of which appeared in the Sydney *Morning Herald*, of June 27th. The report states that " the Chairman, Sir W. Burton, alluded in condemnatory terms to the proposed withdrawal of STATE-AID."

Referring, in the course of his speech, to that subject, the Bishop of Melbourne's words were :—" State-support had, undoubtedly, been very useful, but he could not advocate a system which equally favoured truth and error."

The Bishop of Victoria, Hong Kong, spoke more at length in alluding to the topic, and in a tone which must rather have taken the Chairman by surprise. Addressing the company he said, " God grant that your metropolitan diocese of Sydney—the eldest Australian daughter of Britain's Colonial Church—may long hold forth the lamp of pure unadulterated Christian truth in these lands ; that the holy zeal of her Bishops, the self-denying labours of her parochial clergy, the liberal and disinterested munifi- cence of her laity, may ever render her independent of the uncertain and insecure props of State-aid and political support, and also prove her to possess within herself the power of self-extension, and the inherent elements of life and strength ; that at a distance from the traditionary helps and prescriptive influences of our fatherland, Austra- lia's Church may remember her chosen national motto, ' Advance,' and go forward hopefully on her errand of mercy and mission of love, adorned and beautified with the presence of her great Divine Head, free, unimpeded, and unfettered by the disabilities and restraints of the Church at home, and endued with the power of self-adapta- tion to the varying circumstances, anomalies, and wants of a new country. Thus lengthening her cords and strengthen- ing her stakes, may she enlarge her sphere of evangelistic work over the isles of the sea, and become to generations of Britain's emigrant children yet unborn, a resting-place and a bulwark of truth amid the vicissitudes, the shocks, and the storms, which may imperil the ark of Christ, and agitate the Church of the living God."

A Meeting of the " Wesleyan *Church Extension and Sus- tentation Society*," Sydney, was held on Monday evening, June 4th, 1859, from the printed report of which the fol- lowing passage is extracted :—

" The Rev. G. Hurst referred to the probable speedy termination of the present system of State-aid, and amid considerable applause exclaimed, ' The sooner the better.

Methodism wants no State-aid. It has had none in our fatherland, where it has obtained so high and honourable a position; it has had no State-aid in America, and yet it is the largest Protestant Church in that country; and, I verily believe, that when State-aid shall cease in this country, Methodism and true religion will advance with far more rapid strides than they hitherto have.'"

<hr>

No. VII.

Part of a Conversation between Judges and Members of the Bar, on Colonial Ecclesiastical Law.

The following extract is taken from Swainson's " New Zealand and its Colonization." It is described by him as " an amusing illustration of the ignorance of the highest legal authorities as to the power and *status* of a Colonial Bishop." It is, however, more than that; it is deeply suggestive;—especially by the admission it contains, that an unlicensed clergyman " may preach wherever he can find hearers,"—without, I presume, affecting his position in England beyond what is supposed in those passages of the preceding Address to which this note refers. A clergyman in a neighbouring colony has *offered* to preach for one of our ministers; but the offer has hitherto been declined from a reluctance to accept what, however well and kindly meant, might possibly damage him who rendered it. It *might* here,—but it is at least questionable whether it would affect, in the slightest degree, his position in or relation to the Church at home. The subjoined colloquy took place in the Queen's Bench—*The Attorney-General* v. *the Provost and College of Eton* (May, 1857).

Lord Campbell said it was difficult to know *what a Colonial Bishop was;* he has not the ordinary *status* of a Bishop of the English Church. What could such a Bishop do *in invitos?*   He might have the title of Bishop.

The Attorney-General.—He might excommunicate.

Lord Campbell.—What would follow from that?

The Attorney-General.—That would depend on the mind of the object of the excommunication.

Mr. Justice Coleridge.—Such a power had been exercised.

The Attorney-General.—He might degrade a clergyman, and he would not be entitled to hold a benefice.

Lord Campbell said that not the smallest effect could be given to such a degradation.   Like the Scottish Bishops, his authority would be merely voluntary to those who chose to submit to it.

Mr. Justice Coleridge thought it would be more than that. When the Crown created a diocese in the colony, it could not divide it without the consent of the Bishop.   A Colonial Bishop had power to exercise episcopal authority in the district.

*   *   *   *   *   *

Lord Campbell.—What power has such a Bishop more than a Roman Catholic Bishop in the same place?   What jurisdiction has he?   He might give his advice to those who chose to submit to him: but those who were unwilling would not be bound.

*   *   *   *   *   *

The Attorney-General said that a Bishop of the English Church received direct authority over the clergy in his diocese; he instituted, ordained, visited, and revoked.

Lord Campbell.—Is not that all voluntary?   The Roman Catholic does the same.

Sir F. Thesiger said, a Colonial Bishop could not hold Courts; he could only exercise his influence as Bishop: and that Colonial Bishops were titular Bishops.

Lord Campbell said that they were true successors of the Apostles.＊

The Attorney-General said they had the power of ordaining.

Lord Campbell.—A Bishop *in partibus* could do that.

The Attorney-General said, though the ecclesiastical jurisdiction was not aided by the temporal sword, the ecclesiastical jurisdiction was complete.

Lord Campbell said it was good for all those who chose to respect it: but who was to enforce it?

The Attorney-General.—The Bishop might revoke his licence.

Lord Campbell.—But suppose he preaches: *quid tum?*

The Attorney-General.—*He may preach wherever he can find hearers.*

Lord Campbell.—*But in England he cannot,* as was shown in Shore's case.

＊   ＊   ＊   ＊   ＊   ＊

No. VIII.

The Three Bishops.

The statement, in the Address, respecting the principle of interpretation adopted by the Bishops of Melbourne and Sydney, is made by me on the following grounds. In relation to the first, on the authority of his printed declaration of opinion; and in relation to the second, from having myself heard his lordship, at a confirmation, address the candidates, in relation to the service, on the principle referred to, namely, that " the compilers of the Liturgy" meant their words to be understood " not categorically, but

＊ Does this mean that Colonial Bishops are " true successors of the Apostles," because they can only exert official " influence," not being able to hold " Courts," and not having their " Ecclesiastical jurisdiction aided by the temporal sword?"

hypothetically." In opposition to the judgment of the Bishop of Tasmania, it appears to me, that clergymen are legally warranted so to interpret the Prayer-Book, although I do not feel that I could so interpret it myself. I could admit that the baptismal service *for adults*, might be so interpreted and used; we are all in the habit of using hypothetical language, with or without conditional explanatory terms, in respect to those who make a personal profession of their faith. I feel a great difficulty in interpreting the service *for infants* on this hypothetical principle, as I certainly could not use it as if it was so meant. I know it is said, that as the service for adults must be used with the implication referred to, the other service ought, in conformity with that, to be regarded in the same light. It so happens, however, that the Prayer-Book did not, at first, contain any service for adults, so that the interpretation of the other *in conformity with that* could then have no place. Whatever principle of interpretation may be possible, or may be admitted now, I fear that when "the compilers of the Liturgy" adopted, or arranged, the baptismal service for infants, they *intended* the words to be understood to *mean*, "*categorically*," what they *said*.

In respect to the judgment of the Judicial Committee of the Privy Council on the Gorham Case, to which reference is made also in the Address, I had once intended to give, pretty fully, my reasons for coinciding with the Bishop of Tasmania in my views of it, *theologically* considered. I find, however, that I cannot do this now. The following very rapid and imperfect enumeration of particular points must suffice.

The Judges interpret the Prayer-Book as they would an Act of Parliament,—which of itself is repugnant to religious feeling, though the proper and only course which men in their position could pursue. They state that the Book is "to have applied to it the same rules of interpretation which are *by law* applicable to all written instruments." As no "rules of interpretation" are "by law" made applicable to biblical exegesis or theological controversy, the statement must be understood as referring to such "written instruments" as Acts of Parliament. Advancing to their task, they begin by uttering several complaints, expressive of the difficulties with which they are surrounded. They complain of the Bishop of Exeter,—and of Mr. Gorham,—and even of the Prayer-Book itself! The accusation is not clear,—the defence is not clear,—the Prayer-Book is not clear. The Bishop's "questions" to Mr. Gorham, are described as "perplexing," "entangling," "many of them not admitting of distinct and explicit answers." The "answers" are described, as "not given plainly and directly," but "with the apparent view of escaping from some apprehended consequence of plain and direct answers." Of the "articles" in the Prayer-Book, it is said, "they do not determine what is signified by right reception" [of baptism]; and "they do not particularly declare what is the distinct meaning and effect of the grace of regeneration." In attempting to interpret the baptismal service, they intimate that, in consequence of the circumstances surrounding the administration of the rite, the mind of the officiating minister is raised into a high state of feeling and faith, and that, as it is *"during the continuance* of the same persuasion, and the same undoubting confidence" that he has to speak, " he is directed" to express himself in the most positive and unqualified terms; forgetting, apparently, that *the catechism* cannot be so interpreted, and that children, in repeating it, are the farthest possible from a state of excitement or enthusiasm !

Then again, their lordships greatly *under*state Mr. Gorham's doctrine, while Mr. Gorham himself *over*states it. They say, that Mr. Gorham believes that " in no case is regeneration in baptism unconditional," and Mr. Gorham says, that " he does not *deny* that infants are made in baptism members of Christ, and the children of God, and inheri-

tors of the kingdom of heaven ;" but Mr. Gorham's *system*
is, that children must first be regenerated "by an act
of grace, *prevenient* to baptism, to make them *worthy recipients of that sacrament;*" Mr. Gorham's doctrine is,
that regeneration *is* unconditional, **but that** *it* is the
condition for the reception of *baptismal* **grace**, which,
with him, is *not* the grace of regeneration at all. **It is**
absurd to say that *the same thing* is at once the condition
for baptism, and the blessing or grace which *in* baptism is
conferred on *some other condition,*—and yet this is what Mr.
Gorham and their lordships make out between them ! The
fact is, that his Judges fail to distinguish between Mr.
Gorham's regenerating prevenient grace, and his grace of
baptism, which is something else ; and Mr. Gorham himself, by his contradictory affirmations and denials, contri-
butes to the confusion and mystification. Finally : their
lordships appear to admit that,—or at least they decline
saying whether or not,—" other opinions opposite to Mr.
Gorham's may not be held with *equal* or *even greater reason*
by learned and pious ministers of the Church ;" they speak
of Mr. Gorham's views, as not being repugnant to the " declared doctrine" of the Church of England, and yet, on
their own " principles of interpretation," they might easily
construct *another* argument to prove that teaching the very
contrary to his, was not only not repugnant to that "declared
doctrine," but might even be held with " greater reason ;"
while, all the time, they really cannot themselves tell what
the doctrine of the Church actually is, although they speak
of it as " *declared !*" The whole thing is a " mull." It
would seem, that two opposite things are neither of them
repugnant to a third thing standing between them, and yet
what that third thing itself is, nobody can tell !—at any
rate, I defy any one to make it out from the elaborate
argument of the Judicial Committee of the Privy Council.

I do not wonder, then, at the Bishop of Tasmania
holding the judgment of their lordships very cheap. If

I at all understand the matter, (and I tried very hard to do so at the time the judgment was delivered,) it would have no more effect on my individual conscience, than if they had declared that servants, in asserting "categorically" that their masters or mistresses were "not at home," were to be understood as only saying so "hypothetically," or on an implied "condition." Nevertheless, apart from the reasoning of their lordships' argument, their judgment itself is a legal decision. It is that of the Queen as the Head of the Church,—for the Queen is only the representative of the Majesty of the Law. Through her Judges, She and the Law speak; in whatever way it is at any time constitutionally determined, that a supreme authoritative decision shall be arrived at and uttered, *that* is final. In the case before us, the judgment at once confers a legal liberty on those who can receive it, and *binds* those who, by continuing in the Church, continue and repeat their clerical subscription to the three articles of the 36th canon. The first may be thought by the second bad members of "the Church of the Prayer-Book;" but, most assuredly, the second may be regarded by the first, as very questionable members of "the Church of England."*

* If any one cares about verifying the statements of the above note, they may do so by referring to the volume before-mentioned, entitled "The Great Gorham Case." The view of the Queen's Ecclesiastical Supremacy as at present understood, with which the note concludes, is rather more than countenanced by the following words of a high legal authority:—

"Let them," (the Parliament,) said the Attorney-General, Sir Richard Bethel, "discuss the law if they would; but when they had arrived at the conclusion that it ought to be the law of the land, let them require, without a moment's hesitation, on the part of the clergy, obedience to that law."—*Swainson's New Zealand.*

*_** When an English edition of this Work was acceded to, it was decided to omit in the "Appendix," everything but what was more or less *referred to* in the "Address." It is thought, however, that "THE LIGHTS AND SHADOWS" furnished by the following matter ought not to be excluded.

Sir R. G. MacDonnell to the Rev. T. Binney.

Glenelg, October 16, 1858.

My DEAR SIR,—I herewith return the Bishop's letter of the 22nd ult., on the " Union of Protestant Evangelical Churches." I have long felt deep interest in this subject, and as a more than usually healthy feeling in connexion therewith seems to prevail here at present, I am well pleased that it has been thus prominently brought forward by the Bishop. Moreover, whilst the moment for this step seems well chosen, the truly catholic spirit in which the subject is treated by his lordship is, in my judgment, matter of congratulation to us all.

2. As, however, you have asked what I think of the suggestions in his lordship's letter, I shall give you my opinion, but only in such imperfect manner as the little time at my disposal permits.

3. I have no doubt we both admire the eloquent and forcible manner in which his lordship dwells on the numerous fundamental principles of agreement in doctrine between the various Protestant Evangelical sections of the Church of Christ. We must both also deplore with his lordship the great injury sustained by that Church in the inherent and inevitable weakness engendered therein by the absence of any systematized and united action available for the expansion of its limits, and the diffusion of the really vital principles of faith and doctrine common to all its sections.

4. Nevertheless, I do not find that the Bishop, when he

treats of "the principles and conditions on which a union of the Protestant Evangelical Churches should be effected" —either professes to devise a remedy *in presenti* for that deficiency, or speaks hopefully of accomplishing such union hereafter. His suggestions seem to be aimed too high in pointing to a " Church for the Future, which is to conciliate all affections and unite all diversities." Nevertheless, the willingness of the Bishop—as representing the Anglican Church here—to recognise for certain mission purposes, the *de facto* ministers of Evangelical congregations—to give up a State Episcopacy—to modify the compulsory uniformity of Divine worship, and to omit portions of the offices for the administration of sacraments and conferring of holy orders—evinces the tolerance of an enlightened Christian, and breathes a spirit, in which, if we were all to meet one another, there would soon be but one section of the Reformed Church of Christ.

5. Looking, however, to the practical expediency of his suggestions, and having regard to human nature as it is, I do not see—even here, where the ground is comparatively cleared for the erection of such a structure by the abolition of all State-aid—that there is much immediate prospect of establishing a general Protestant Church holding by one set of articles, however few, or by any fixed form of Liturgy, however curtailed—especially if its bishops be not elected by all denominations, placed for that purpose on terms of equality.

6. I admit that such a Church, with its affairs administered by bishops or overseers elected by the general body of the Church (which, however, does not appear to be altogether his lordship's meaning), and with its bishops, aided by representatives of the whole Church assembled in synod, would be a Church well adapted to the spiritual wants of mankind, and eminently apostolical in its constitution: Yet, although, as the Bishop truly says, we " *might* thus exercise the great privilege of spiritual men—that is, com-

bine freedom with submission to law, and general order with specific distinctions"—the main difficulty would still exist, and the real question would only be begged, not solved; for there would still be a law—a rule, in which, as the Bishop says—"we should walk, and by it steadfastly abide." Now, whatever be the rule, it would be difficult to induce the various Protestant sections of Christ's Church simultaneously to adopt it, or *afterwards abide by it.* Men had, in the first century, the teaching of Christ Himself; they had the apostles for their ministers and bishops; they had the recent evidence of Christ's miracles, and yet schism even then arose. It would do so again, even if a United Protestant Church were for a space to gather within its fold all the evangelical denominations of the Reformed Church in this province, and in Great Britain also.

7. It may be, however—indeed it is our belief and hope —that such a consummation will yet be witnessed in the fulness of time; but meanwhile I sincerely hope that what the Bishop himself calls " the pleasantness of this dream" will not divert us from more immediate and practicable exertions, which, without disturbing the existing internal organization of the various sections of the Reformed Church, may yet eliminate, if they do not find ready to our hand, some, if not all, the elements for united action, when pursuing the main objects of all Christian Protestant action, viz., the diffusion and application of the broad vital doctrines of the Protestant faith.

8. And herein I do not see why we might not at least prepare for such united action, without waiting to break and fuse all varieties of Protestant worship and organization for the purpose of recasting them in a uniform shape from one mould. For my part, though I much prefer the forms of my own Church, I do not object to the organization or practice of the Baptists, the Independents, the Wesleyans, or many other denominations of Protestant Christians. It might perhaps be better if they were all to form one deno-

mination; but I have doubts on that point; whilst it would come nearly to the same thing, if we could but fully regard one another truly as brethren; and if we felt bound to help one another in all that might develope the pure principles of our common faith, whilst we illustrated them in our practice by works of mutual charity and help.

9. I would, therefore, suggest that we should test the sincerity of our mutual advances either towards union or alliance, by *at once* commencing a more intimate and brotherly intercourse with one another in our schools, our pulpits, and our missions; and that we should thus prepare the way for such a further mutual understanding as may, with God's blessing, fit us hereafter to discuss the question of fusing into one denomination all the various evangelical sections of Christ's Reformed Church.

10. I would ask, are we to have for ever merely a community of faith, and not a community of labour in all good works; a brotherhood of doctrine, but not of action? If the Bible be the foundation of our faith, why should any intelligent, pure-minded, and approved Protestant expounder of that Bible be excluded by an ecclesiastical rule or tradition from preaching the doctrines of any Church in one of its places of worship, if invited to do so by the special minister of the building? Is such a union of Christians impossible in carrying on Christian duties? Whenever such interchange of pulpits is permitted, under no restrictions but those which are desirable to ensure fitness of education and character, as well as soundness of doctrine (and I trust a high standard in all those respects will ever be maintained), it will be time enough to meditate on a still more general fusion, in approved ecclesiastical form, of the Protestantism of this and other lands.

11. I do not, however, perceive that the Bishop suggests any immediate step in this direction, although his lordship thinks he might have invited you to exhort the Church of

England congregations here " without violating any ecclesiastical law in force in this diocese or province." I am only surprised that he did not use this power, when he gives so many reasons why it might have been wisely and usefully exerted in your favour. Those reasons, however, are so well stated by the Bishop, that he cannot long resist the conclusion to which they point. Indeed, I consider it fortunate on the whole that you did not arrive here till men's minds, having become reconciled to the abolition of State-aid to religion, had begun to feel the necessity and probable advantage of a very different aid, viz., that which might be derived from greater unity of action amongst themselves. It is no small sign of progress that the Bishop should have stated the case so forcibly, even though he has not yet availed himself of his own argument.

12. I also think it fortunate that neither in public opinion, nor perhaps in his own, is any clergyman of the Anglican Church in this province regarded as more powerful or truthful in expounding the faith held by that Church than yourself. It makes the fact all the more remarkable, that a large portion of this community, as belonging to the Anglican Church, should agree in your doctrines and be anxious to benefit by your teaching, and yet be deprived of the opportunity of hearing you in any pulpit of their Church, simply because you hold no licence from their Bishop, and are not officially, therefore, regarded in this diocese as a *de jure* minister of the Gospel, the preaching and illustration of which form, nevertheless, at once the labour and glory of your life.

13. I rejoice, therefore, that your visit has made people ponder on such a pernicious—I would almost say un-Christian—distinction of man's device without a spiritual difference. I sincerely hope the application of such a rule to yourself may produce results useful to us all, and end in throwing open God's work to all who may be worthy of the labour.

14. It is, I hope, unnecessary that I should here guard against the possibility of being supposed to imply that the occasional interchange of pulpits which I advocate should be allowed to prejudice the usages or internal discipline of any denomination. Thus, if a Wesleyan minister were to exchange services for a day with our Dean, he could not expect to conduct the service at Trinity Church as he would at Pirie-street Chapel; nor could the Dean conduct the service at Pirie-street Chapel otherwise than according to the usage of the congregation there. Therefore I do not contemplate any such interchange of pulpits as possible, except where there might be a previously existing common belief in the great and vital truths of the Protestant faith, and a comparative indifference to the details of ritual service and discipline in use amongst the various congregations of that faith.

15. I would add that, whilst this first step seems to disturb no Church organization now existing, my own feelings convince me that an advance in this direction must be far more agreeable to many thousand others than an attempt to form a common Church by the sacrifice of services and customs to which I and they are personally attached. More especially would I protest against a sacrifice of the greater portion of the Liturgy, as suggested by the Bishop. I have reverently listened in my childhood to those prayers and words of solemn beauty. They have often been the consolation of manhood. They are fraught to me with a thousand hallowed memories and aspirations; and I would fain hope they will be amongst the latest sounds which may soothe my ear. With such feelings I not merely protest against such a concession to the prejudice of others; but my own reluctance to accede to this teaches me to deal gently with all who may refuse similar concessions to my prejudices.

16. I therefore own that I am not much troubled at present to give a theoretical uniformity of outward structure

to the Reformed Church. I would rather look to the foundation before roofing the Temple. The details of discipline and practice—if there be no wilful or marked violation of any scriptural command or leading truth necessary to our spiritual welfare—may be left safely to the various congregations who are most affected by them. Such things need not, and ought not, to be any bar to the most unreserved spiritual intercourse and community of labour amongst Christians of Christ's Church.

17. My life has been hitherto so much more one of action than of theorising, that, hoping to be more useful by practically doing something to effect what I recommend than by writing about it, immediately on reading the Bishop's letter, which I did not peruse till this day, I took the first step towards realizing my suggestion. As a communicant of the Anglican Church, I have signed a memorial to the Bishop requesting his lordship to invite you to preach at one of our Churches. It is clear that some one must take this first step, and that the objections thereto are no more forcible now than they would be if I were to defer that step for years. The right hand of fellowship, moreover, ought, in my opinion, to be offered first by the Anglican Church, as that which has hitherto been the most exclusive and exacting in such matters. I have, however, taken care that the memorial should express the conviction of those signing it, that they are thereby assisting to develope his lordship's own views — a point which it is difficult to doubt, after perusing his very interesting and eloquent letter.

18. I know not how far these views, which are entirely my own, and as yet communicated to none but yourself, may coincide with your own opinion. I am, however, certain that if you think you can usefully exert yourself in removing prejudices which narrow the sphere of usefulness of Christ's ministers you will not fail to do so.

19. To assist in establishing a greater unity of action

amongst the ministers and congregations and various sections of the Reformed Church would be indeed a noble
vocation. I earnestly desire that your exertions in that
respect here, where the field is more open than elsewhere,
may yet produce results to which you will gladly recur
hereafter as amongst the happiest mementoes of your trip
to Australia.

Believe me to be, my dear Sir,

Most sincerely yours,

RICHARD GRAVES MACDONNELL.

No. II.

The Rev. Canon Russell to the Rev. T. Binney.

St. John's Parsonage, Adelaide, October 21, 1858.

REV. AND DEAR SIR,—Forgive the liberty I take in
troubling you with a few lines in reference to the most important part of your speech of yesterday. I felt thankful
that, in reference to a subject surrounded with difficulties,
you were enabled to speak such calm and wise words. On
the part of many who listened to you, there would have
been a great dread of any amalgamation of Churches: there
would be, in our own Church, the strongest feeling against
any tampering with the Prayer-Book; there would have
ensued a convulsion which could have ended in nothing
short of dissolution, from any general attempt to accommo-
date our ecclesiastical polity to that of other Christian
communities.

Let me explain my own position. Not born and bred
in the Church of England; not fettered by any early prejudices on the subject; but having heartily embraced the
doctrine and order of the Church of England, as soon as

I was old enough to think and choose on such a subject—
I confess that I should yet have strongly shared in the
above apprehensions. When a man born in the·midst of
Scotch Presbyterianism, thrown during early youth into
close association with the adherents of English Congrega-
tionalism, and brought in various ways into friendly contact
with men of the widest variety of view in reference to
theology and ecclesiastical polity—when a man who has
had a history of this kind embraces the Church of England
system, he does it with his whole heart. Its distinctive
peculiarities he cannot bear to part with; for they are
among the things which attracted his love. The chances are
that if he be a man of ordinary generosity of mind, he will be
able to think of the men of other communions, in a spirit at
once more intelligent and just, with a fuller understanding
both of the strength and weakness of their position, than if
he had been trained in the midst of Church of England
traditions; but the very fact that he has, on unworldly
principles, chosen his place in the Church of England, would
lead one to expect that he will embrace all her peculiarities (if I may so express myself) with that sort of romantic
reverence and depth of attachment with which a man falls
in love for the first and last time in his life. I was thankful, therefore, beyond expression, to hear you distinctly
declare your own feeling, that any mutual recognition of
Protestant Churches should be one in which the respective
polity and constitution of the said Churches would be preserved in their integrity. Will you, then, suffer me to
point out what, in my opinion, must not be attempted in
order to the desired recognition ?

It seems to me that you must keep clear of the two points
around which most of the controversies of Christendom
have been found to turn. 1. What constitutes fitness for
the position of a member of the Church? 2. What constitutes fitness to minister in the congregation ?

1. The Anglican and Congregationalist theories of Church

membership are not only in fact widely different, but essentially irreconcilable. Mr. Stow, in an address before the Melbourne Conference in 1855, has explicitly declared this. He says:—" Our principle of admission to the Church is personal piety, avowed and evidenced to the satisfaction of the Church. . . . . . . There are other Churches, containing vast numbers of truly pious persons; but that they should be such is not the condition of admission. . . . . . A certificate, then, from such a Church is not a certificate of spiritual character; it is simply a certificate of membership. It is not, then, a certificate which meets our rule." Here, then, is a preliminary difficulty with respect to fitness for communion, and terms of communion, which, when adequately discussed, must raise very important questions on which different individuals and Churches will arrive at very different conclusions, and the preliminary discussion of which would b exceedingly likely to set us permanently by the ears. I am, on the contrary, in the habit of speaking of *baptism* as verily and truly membership of the Church, and of protesting against the bad life of some of our people on that express ground. We may discuss for ever what constitutes membership, and what should lawfully admit to full communion, without arriving at a common point of agreement.

I am strongly of opinion, then, that you must not make common communion at the same table of the Lord—beautiful and desirable as the idea is—a condition of the Christian union to be attempted.

2. It is not only, however, that there is difficulty as to terms of communion. There are difficulties as to the officiating persons. It may appear to some an evil thing, but it is the fact, that even in our own Church all ministers are not allowed to administer the Sacrament of the Lord's Supper. A duly ordained minister, if only in the order of a deacon, may preach; he cannot minister the Holy Communion. If, then, even a minister of our Church may not,

until he has attained to the position of a presbyter, it is quite hopeless to expect the adherents to our system to consent to any arrangement by which ministers of other Churches may perform an act from which certain of our own ministers are excluded. You, who do not propose to amalgamate Churches, would not attempt to force us from a position which we have deliberately taken, and which belongs properly and logically to the constitution of the Church, and the relative position in it of bishop, priest, or deacon. I ask you, then, not to aim, in the name of Christian union, at what will render the likelihood of any visible union among the Protestant Churches more remote than ever.

That union must clearly respect all that is essential to the integrity of our polity. Now, according to that polity, there are within our Church three orders of ministers to whom, respectively, peculiar functions are assigned. In so far as certain of these functions are restricted to these several orders, they must prove undoubtedly, however unavoidably, obstacles to visible union—obstacles, however, not arising out of illiberality of sentiment, but out of the necessities of our Church-life. But on the other hand, is there any function of the Christian ministry *common to all* these orders, and exercised by the ministers of other Protestant Churches? *I think there is* ONE. It is in some sense the greatest, the most responsible, and the most influential of all: that which most stirs the heart to great actions, arouses the soul out of sensual slumbers, and arms the spirit of man for the battle of life, and in the exercise of which the minister of God finds the freest scope for all his faculties. It is the preaching of the Word of God. In the Church of Rome, even, there were preaching orders with their peculiar discipline, and not restricted to the general rule of the Church. I, for one, would not be without hope that the general Church of England might be led to adopt a system by which, the Liturgy being left untouched, and the ecclesiastical polity being left untouched, the great body of preachers in all Protestant Churches might at least be *empowered* to exercise their gift for the edification of all.

In order to the adoption of such a system, however, there must necessarily be a doctrinal basis, but it should be one containing as few dogmatical statements as possible, and limited to the great central facts of Christianity. I should be content with these three:—The Bible, the Rule of Faith; the Trinity in Unity; the Incarnation and Sacrifice of Jesus Christ our Lord.

Allow me, however, to say most unequivocally that, after careful inquiry, I am satisfied that the laws of our Church would not at present admit of the preaching, in any of our Churches, of any minister but a bishop, priest, or deacon, in our understanding of these words. I am sure we ought not to break existing laws. If they appear to need alteration, the alteration must be attempted in a constitutional manner.

Now we, in these colonies, happily enjoy the normal action of the Church. There are Diocesan Synods: there must, ere long, be a Provincial Synod. The change can be arrived at only in this way:—1st. Until a Provincial Synod exists, by declaratory resolutions in the several Diocesan Synods, which would declare the mind of the Church on the question. 2nd. By ecclesiastical legislation on the basis of such resolutions, so soon as there is a Provincial Synod.

There can be no question that it must add greatly to the strength and dignity of every Church, to be able from time to time to call into action the services of the great apologists of Christianity, wherever they may be found ; provided all reasonable securities have been taken for soundness in the old catholic faith of Scripture and the Primitive Church.

In this hasty letter, I have endeavoured to fix upon the

one function of the Christian ministry, in the exercise of which I see the only hope of successfully aiming at visible union. I do not see that the question of liturgical forms need embarrass the inquiry. Public preaching, apart from public devotion, ought not to be a new thing to a Church in which the memory of Latimer and Paul's Cross are still revered.

Begging you to accept this letter in the spirit in which it is intended,

I am, Rev. and dear Sir,

Your faithful Servant,

ALEX. R. RUSSELL,
Minister of St. John's, and Rural Dean.

P.S.—You may make what use of this letter, either here or in England, you may think desirable.

[This letter very much expresses my own views; for, though I have been in the habit of uniting in my aspirations after Christian union, the mutual recognition of Churches and their meeting in sacramental fellowship, as well as ministerial recognition and exchange of pulpits, I am sensible of so many difficulties in respect to the former of these, that I feel the latter is the *only* thing that is at all possible as a first step. Personally, I have no difficulty when visiting with Episcopalian friends, attendants on an Evangelical ministry, in communing with them. I have done so; though I am well aware that both among my Dissenting brethren and the clergy of the Church there are those who would wonder at the act. But I have also had clergymen remain and commune in the Lord's Supper in my own place of worship, which is something, I suppose, more extraordinary still. These, however, were individual and personal acts, and involved nothing more; and I don't know that my views, however strongly put in the form of popular writing or speech, have really gone much beyond this, as a beginning. Certainly, I never thought of the Nonconformist and the Episcopal minister exchanging places as the *officiating* persons, at the table or the altar, but only of the one being free and willing *to unite with the other* in the act of communion, as in the cases first mentioned. There are many points in Mr. Russell's letter, which might invite a word or two of remark, but I must not allow myself to go on, lest I should write a dissertation. The clear and well-defined way in which Mr. Russell puts the ONE point on which he insists is worthy of notice: so also is his view of the freedom to act which he attributes to colonial Churches. I differ from him as to any *special* "doctrinal basis," being required for such action as is contemplated, since I assume the interchange to take place on the ground of personal knowledge and public reputation, between ministers who already have their standing in the general Church on the ground of their Evangelical faith.]

No. III.

The Diocesan Synod of South Australia on Church Union.

(Abridged from the South Australian Advertiser of June 3rd.)

On Thursday, 2nd June, a meeting of the Synod was held at White's Rooms. There was an unusually large attendance, great interest being felt in some resolutions of which His Excellency the Governor had given notice.

These resolutions, which, after he had "tabled," His Excellency received permission to amend, were submitted to the Synod in the following form:—

"1. That in the opinion of this Synod the time has arrived for promoting Christianity and the spread of Evangelical truth in South Australia, by a closer alliance between the branch of Christ's Church which this Synod represents, and the other Protestant Evangelical denominations in this colony.

"2. That the most expedient course for usefully effecting such alliance appears to be a prompt and hearty recognition on terms of equality of our Protestant Christian Evangelical brethren, whether originally sprung from the Anglican Church or not, as being all members of the General Reformed Church of Christ—with whom, therefore, we may safely and usefully ally ourselves in all good works."

His Excellency, in rising to propose the resolutions of which he had given notice, but which were amended, as he had stated, said, "that although he had not had much time to devote to the subject of these resolutions, he could see and gather from the tone of that assembly, and from circumstances which had occurred, both inside and outside, that a very strong interest existed upon the subject. He felt, therefore, that he had taken upon himself a great responsibility in bringing the resolutions forward; but had that responsibility been ten times as great, or had he stood alone in supporting the resolutions, he should have felt it his duty to do so, a great Christian principle being involved. He felt very much interested in the resolutions, and was the more sorry that circumstances over which he could exercise no control, had prevented him from giving them that amount of attention which would have enabled him to treat them in a more complete manner. He should have liked to have laid before the Synod a greater amount of information bearing upon the questions, and have supported the resolutions with a greater amount of well-considered arguments than he felt he would be enabled to do. It was his belief, however, that so clear a principle was laid down in the resolutions, that when these resolutions were clearly understood, he did not despair of finding the support which they would receive much greater than had been supposed. He thought it better to state at once what was the gist of the resolutions, which was not, as some persons imagined, to attack any fundamental principle of the Church, or ecclesiastical discipline, but simply to require the brethren of the Church to look beyond the pale of their own, and see the large Churches outside holding on every essential point of belief the same doctrine as our own; and to consider whether, where there was notoriously a common field for religious exertion, a greater amount of religious life could not be obtained by uniting than by standing aloof. The alliance proposed might be, in fact, nothing more than an alliance of good works, such, for instance, as the Bible Society, Sunday-school teaching, bush missions, missionary efforts, &c.; still it appeared to him there was little doubt that by united efforts they would be enabled to accomplish very much more, even in those matters, than by the separate and divided efforts of those whom it was proposed to unite. Suppose there were two separate states, with races speaking different languages and of different descent, still alliances could be made between them without compromising their independence, or sacrificing their institutions, and even so means might be found by which alliances could be made with Protestant brethren without sacrificing ecclesiastical discipline, or that subordination which was due to the Church at home. He should be sorry to propose a resolution which he believed could possibly bring about such a disastrous result. On reading the resolutions, he thought any one would be sadly puzzled to determine how, if carried into effect, they could possibly produce such a result, merely expressing, as they did, an opinion that the time had arrived for promoting Christianity and the spread of Evangelical truth in South Australia, by a closer alliance between the branch of Christ's Church which the Synod represented, and the other Protestant Evangelical denominations in the colony. How such a course could militate against the interests of the Church he was at a loss to make out. The second proposition was, that the most expedient course for effecting such alliance was to give a prompt and hearty recognition to our Protestant Christian Evangelical brethren, no matter what was the origin of such bodies, if in the essential doctrines of salvation they held the same belief as ourselves. He would ask the Synod to determine whether the time had or had not arrived for promoting Christianity and the spread of Evangelical truth in South Australia. Those who opposed the resolution would declare that the time had not arrived. It should be remembered that we had in some instances driven those parties with whom he now proposed an alliance out of our Church ; and in those cases, at least, it became our duty to offer alliance. A motion had been carried with the view of constituting a General Synod, and it had been suggested that they should wait until this General Synod had been constituted ; but if they were to wait till that were constituted, they might wait for twenty years, and he would rather that they who were disposed to vote for such delay, should vote against the resolution. It appeared to him that to wait till the constitution of that Synod would be an adjournment of the question *sine die.* He believed that the time had arrived for such alliance, and that the question might be argued upon broad grounds, without reference to recent events here. When he gave notice of the resolutions, he believed that on the part of the clergy and the laity there was a strong desire to give some sign of goodwill to the various Protestant bodies throughout the colony ; and if the result of that day's proceedings showed that he had been mistaken, he could only regret it. In attempting to lift the question from the point at which it had been left, he only hoped that they would give credit to him for the same desire to do his duty that he was willing to accord to others. The opposition generally likely to be made to such alliance exhibited great disregard of facts, and a forgetfulness that certain Christian bodies had not been separated from the Church of their own free-will ; they had been driven out, in fact, and then we asked them why they left us. Those who had left had thriven, and God's Word had been promulgated over the world in consequence. It was impossible to ignore the existence of other great Protestant bodies ; and to show that the time had arrived when such alliances as those which he proposed should be made, he had only to read an abstract of the Ecclesiastical return for 1858, in connexion with this colony, by which it would be seen that of the Protestant denominations, for the Church of England there was church accommodation for 6,333, whilst the attendance was 4,500 : for the Congregationalists the accommodations amounted to 6,000 ; for the Methodists the accommodations were 16,261, and the attendances 17,300 ; the whole average of congregations were 34,816, the Church of England being one-eighth, the Congregationalists one-tenth, and the Methodists one-half. Those returns were, he thought, sufficient to convince them of a fact which no one a hundred years ago would have ventured to prophesy. The Church of England, with all its old associations and prestige, only numbered as its members one-eighth, whilst the Congregationalists were a tenth, and the Methodists one-half. He trusted that friends of other denominations would not be offended when he said that though he moved these resolutions with a catholic feeling, he did so more especially in the interests of his own Church ; because he felt that the comparatively slow and diminishing progress of the Church arose from the position which had been assumed in reference to Protestant brethren of other denominations. He believed that if the Church had been freed from some few usages and traditions which isolated her here, her progress would have been far greater. It was impossible that any person, by standing in the middle of a landscape and shutting his eyes, could remove the mountains and other objects which presented themselves; they would be there, though he did not see them; and it would be well with us if, instead of shutting our eyes, we observed the progress made by other denominations. That progress would continue, though we shut our eyes to it. He referred particularly to the Methodists, having had particular means of ascertaining the progress which they had made, and which had been greater than that of any other Evangelical Christians. Upon looking to a return published in England in 1851, he found that on 'Census Sunday,' the congregations of their Church numbered 2,300,000, and the Wesleyans, 1,000,000. According to a rule in the Wesleyan Church, every member called a full member was a communicant, so that there were more such in proportion in the 1,000,000 than in the 2,300,000, the number at that time being computed at 400,000. Here the Bishop had informed him that only one in ten was a communicant. Looking to America, we found the Wesleyan communicants, whose quality we refused to recognize, numbering 2,500,000, with Church accommodation for 4,500,000, and Church property valued at £3,000,000. It was with great satisfaction he found such great Churches springing from the loins of the English Church. He did so with the pride which a great empire looked upon her prosperous and numerous colonies. There was nothing to regret in the advances which had been made, but much to rejoice at. When they looked at the present position of the Church, and their decrease of numbers, compared with the spread of other denominations, some ideas must present themselves suggestive of what the future might be. If it were thought better that they should

T

remain in *statu quo*, of course it would be better that they should take no steps in the matter ; but he must confess, he did not envy the feeling or the reasoning by which such a conclusion was arrived at. He could not conceive any opposition to the resolution which he had proposed, unless from an unfounded fear that it struck at some fundamental rule in our discipline. The resolution merely affirmed that in all good works there should be alliance, but did not dogmatically assert that this or that course should be adopted. It would be left to the Committee to determine and report whether such alliance was desirable or not, and then it would be for the Synod to consider that report."

After a debate in which both clergy and laity joined, in the course of which the " previous question" was moved as an amendment, his lordship put the question—" Shall the resolutions now be put ?" which was negatived, the votes on a division being, Ayes, 13 ; Noes, 17. The clergy were equally divided, nine to nine. The Archdeacon did not vote, but handed in a Protest. His lordship did not vote on the occasion.

TWO HUNDRED YEARS AGO;

THEN AND NOW.

Illustrative Clerical Testimony.*

* See Preliminary Chapter, pp. xxxvi., xxxvii.

TWO HUNDRED YEARS AGO.

"After an interval of exactly two centuries, the country is presented with a new Act of Uniformity. Mr. Henry Seymour and Lord Fermoy have prepared a Bill ' to enforce uniformity in the use of ecclesiastical vestments by Priests and Deacons of the United Church of England and Ireland.' . . . . But would the words of the Act be sufficient to secure the uniformity desired ? We think not. . . . . The Bill would confine clergymen to black and white." But "the *dimensions* or *cut* of the robe might be made to symbolize opinions with as much ease as the colour. . . . . . To be effectual, it ought to prescribe the minutest particulars of costume. . . . . Even then, there would be room for difference, and difference would infallibly show itself. These varieties of costume are but symbols of deeper divergencies, and the shadows could never be suppressed while the substance remained. . . . . To cut the matter short, *the subject is not one for Parliamentary legislation.*"

Such are some of the sentences of a leader in the *Times* of the day on which I sit down to put together the materials of this tract (March 7th). The last words express what will probably turn out to be the opinion of Parliament, so that the matters in question will still be allowed to take their own course. In a large community like the Church of England, there must inevitably be comprehended men of great variety of sentiment; this will show itself in some way or other; minute enactments as to external manifestations of it, will only produce either a bitterness of feeling from the sense of constraint, or contumacy and disobedience to assert liberty. All Church-legislation—if legislation there must be, and every thing *national* must be subject to that—should be distinguished by tolerance. By avoiding minute and vexatious prescription, it should allow as much scope as possible to the exercise and expression of free thought.

But Parliament has always dealt, and will always deal, with the National Church. Convocations may resolve, and royal commissioners recommend, but the suggestions, I suppose, of either one or the other must be ratified by Parliament. Or Parliament may originate, discuss, and pass, what the Church, as an Establishment, must accept. The Prayer-Book itself was treated by the Judicial Committee of the Privy Council, in deciding on the Gorham case, as an Act of Parliament. The Church of England is not the Church of Christ. The national institution may have a true Church within it, but, in itself, it is the creature of law, and by law has often been subjected to modification. If Parliament were to enact what conscientious men within the Establishment could not submit to, which demanded either professions or acts which violated their convictions, they might say, in the words of the Rev. Walter Blunt, " It is time for us to divest ourselves of much that is beautifying and elevating, and even to carry our holy rites, if necessary, to cellars, and sheds, and caves, substituting for their lost magnificence a comeliness of penitential tears, and greater earnestness and humility, and rejoicing in the presence of Christ amongst us, though veiled in manger garb." Supposing they did that,—ceasing to be comprehended within the National Institute, where many, however, might consent to remain,—they would not cease to be comprehended within Christ's own Church. If their Bishops went with them, they would be a Church, even in the view of those who require for that apostolic succession and valid orders; but if they did not, *Protestant* principles would sustain and justify their claim. However broken, marred, deficient, in respect to form, their external arrangements might be, their adherence to vital truth (for that is supposed) would, to the Divine eye, make them one " with God's holy Church, throughout all the world."

I propose, in this paper, to go back to the time when that act of " Parliamentary legislation " took place, which gave to the Church of England its present form,—the time when it received its last great modification, and became what it now is. But I must introduce the subject by showing its connexion with my Australian reminiscences.

II.

When I arrived in Australia, in March, 1858, I had no thoughts of anything, as has been seen, but of quietly moving among my co-religionists. In August of that year, when I arrived in Adelaide, I had never uttered a word about the Church of England, nor done any thing—except that I had refused to preach on behalf of a Free Episcopal Church, because I would not intermeddle with ecclesiastical disputes, nor presume to sanction what, for anything I knew, might be a schismatical proceeding. There was nothing wrong, surely, in that,—unless it be, as some may think, that I suffered a desire for peace and quietness to prevent my investigation of what *might* have turned out to be justifiable and deserving of support. The first thing that occurred soon after I got to Adelaide was this. Having consented to deliver a lecture on behalf of the Sunday-School Teachers' Union, an institution including, I should have thought, the teachers of schools belonging to the Episcopal as well as other Churches,—the Committee requested the Bishop to oblige them by presiding. His reply, declining their request, while speaking most kindly and respectfully of myself personally, spoke of my being regarded *by others* as " duly called " to the ministry; and with respect to the " Union," he could not recognize it, as the teachers belonged to congregations which had " *separated in times past from the Church of England.*" To me, there was nothing offensive in this, nor surprising. It is right in every man to decline doing what, to himself, may seem to sanction what *he* thinks wrong. The second thing, however, that occurred *did* occasion surprise,—that was, the receipt of the Bishop's letter, referred to in the preceding pages, which was written a few days after the above-mentioned note. The first impression was bewildering. Properly understood, the two documents were not really inconsistent; because the letter, while breathing a most loving and catholic spirit, *began* by telling me that my " orders were irregular, and my mission the offspring of division," and *ended* by proposing that all Nonconformist and Non-episcopal bodies should accept the recognition and rule of the English Bishops. Then came, one after another, as has been already referred to, various utterances, charging all the " schism," " separation," " division," &c., on us, which, with the necessity of complying with the Bishop's request, occasioned, to my own special inconvenience, the writing, delivery, expansion, and publication of the preceding " Charge."

Now, being myself more of a religious Nonconformist to the Church of the Prayer-Book than anything else—having no great objection to moderate Episcopacy, or liturgical forms; and knowing, moreover, that *the two points* which I was called upon to touch in my Australian apology for Nonconformity, will be objected to as springing from dissenting inaccuracy and dissenting misconception; I mean here, like the Bishop of Tasmania, to justify my statements by calling into court two clerical witnesses to give *their* testimony on the points mooted. Of the *first* point—what occurred " in times past," (two hundred years ago)—it will be said, it *is* said, that *the fault was ours, the separation causeless*, the result to *us* schism and sin. Of the *second* point—the meaning of the Offices—it will be said, *it often has been*, (I speak, now, only of one party,) that we do not understand the peculiar language of the Offices, or will not; that we mistake or ignore the proper mode of interpretation. I propose that we listen to what *Churchmen* have to say on both these points. But this, it may be objected, will only be individual opinion. True; that, however, in such men, men environed as they are, is quite sufficient to excuse or justify other men, differently positioned, for thinking like them.

III.

We begin with the Rev. Isaac Taylor ; and before we receive his testimony on the precise point on which he is to deliver it, he shall speak a few words bearing upon a matter briefly referred to in our " preliminary chapter."

" While many moderate Churchmen will probably be of opinion that prudence may well dictate some timely liturgical concession, they will stoutly refuse to admit that the Dissenters themselves have any right or title to demand the smallest change. It will be said, that though the adoption of conciliatory measures is a matter of vital consequence to the Church, yet that our opponents have no *locus standi* in the revision of the liturgical forms of a Church from whose teaching they have withdrawn themselves. This would be a valid argument, did it relate only to two *sects*, both on an equal footing. Thus the Baptists have no imaginable right or title to exercise any interference, direct or indirect, with the devotional practices or the doctrinal teaching of the Independents.

" But the Church of England is not a sect. She enjoys the prerogatives of her connexion with the State, and she must submit to the bondage thence ensuing.* She is the *National* Church. Her connexion with the State is most intimate. The Sovereign has an ecclesiastical supremacy, unexampled save in Utah, or in the Papal States. The Bishops of our Church are Peers of Parliament. The edifices of the Church are national property, maintained by a national impost, and built, some of them, by a Parliamentary grant. More than half of the Church patronage attaches, directly or indirectly, to the Crown. The formularies of the Church have a Parliamentary sanction. Her offices all Englishmen can legally claim as their birthright. Her revenues, for the most part,

" * It is perhaps needless to point out that higher grounds are here inadmissible. The argument relates to the Church of England, not to the Church of Christ. To assume that the Church of England is, in England, the sole and divinely appointed conservatrix of truth, would be to beg the whole question ; or at least to argue it on premises which nine-tenths of Englishmen would refuse to admit."

are not private foundations, like the endowments of Dissenters, but are national property, and are, and have been, controlled by Parliament, in a manner which would be utterly inappropriate and unjustifiable in the case of the revenues of any body of Dissenters whatsoever.

" So long, then, as the Church continues her connexion with the State, so long is she a national institution ; so long every citizen of the State has a beneficial interest in her endowments, and a personal concern in the teaching of her formularies.

" If the teaching of the National Church is in such discord with the conscientious convictions of any man that he is compelled to withdraw himself from her pale, he has an ostensible grievance ; and it is his right and duty, by the use of those means which the Constitution has provided, to endeavour to obtain the redress of this grievance, and to strive to produce a conformity between the teaching of the National Church and what he conceives to be the true doctrinal and ritualistic standards. . . . . .

" The Dissenters hold firmly to the great fundamental doctrines of the Reformation, as embodied in the Articles.   In the Prayer-Book, as it came from the hands of the Reformers in 1552, they would find comparatively little to which they could object. But since the time of the Reformation the Prayer-Book has undergone most material alterations. It has been subject to no less than three re-actionary revisions. The first, in 1559, was made with the politic object of facilitating the conformity of the Romanists, who were then a numerous and formidable body. The revisions of 1604 and 1662 were carried out under the auspices of the High-Church party, with the object of over-riding and crushing the Puritans, and rendering their conformity distasteful or impossible. The modern Nonconformists are the theological and ecclesiastical representatives of those Puritans who, in the course of the seventeenth century, were, by these aggressive revisions of the Prayer-Book, driven out against their will from their national and ancestral Church.

" The fact that the Prayer-Book was reduced to its present form with the express purpose of being unacceptable to those holding opinions analogous to those which the Dissenters hold, gives them, in these days of theological calmness and moderation, a strong claim to be heard anent this question of Liturgical Revision.

" Strong as is the constitutional right of the Dissenters to a voice in the revision of the National Liturgy—formidable as is their numerical claim upon our consideration—yet *their historical claim* can be urged with even greater force on men of calm and catholic temper."

The last statement carries us from principles to facts, and thus naturally introduces the subject of inquiry,—namely, what took place *two hundred years ago*. As an appropriate heading to Mr. Taylor's testimony, we may place over it the opinion of a very eminent man, who, on looking back to the period in question, thus spoke of what occurred

THEN.

" All hope of union was blasted by that second most disastrous, most tyrannical, and *schismatical* Act of Uniformity, the authors of which, it is plain, were not seeking unity, but division."

ARCHDEACON HARE.

It is not, of course, my intention to quote every thing in Mr. Taylor's pamphlet which bears on the point before us; I merely wish to take what will be sufficient to satisfy those into whose hands the work is not likely to fall, and to encourage others to obtain it for themselves. As our object is to listen to what the witness has to say, the extracts may be given almost without comment.

" The story of the rise of the Dissenting bodies is indeed a lamentable and a shameful one. At first driven out from that Church, with which they would fain have remained in communion, then utterly alienated by fierce persecution, beggared by ruinous and repeated fines, and embittered by long imprisonments, they were ultimately called into numerical equiponderance with the Church by the rigidity of her liturgical and ecclesiastical system, by the criminal apathy of many of her ministers, and the fatal sluggishness of her gigantic organism in providing for the spiritual destitution of the masses. . . . . .

" In fact, as will presently appear, this revision seems to have been conducted with the express object of making the Prayer-Book as distasteful as possible to the Puritans, and so of preventing any extensive conformity from taking place. In this unwise and unchristian spirit the Prayer-Book was systematically revised— obnoxious ceremonies were not only retained, but were fortified by auxiliary rubrics :—almost every incidental word or phrase in the Liturgy, which the Puritans valued as being favourable to their own ecclesiastical theories, or their doctrinal views, was now carefully excised, and such words and such phrases were substituted as were known to be specially offensive to their prejudices. Those matters, about which the Puritans scrupled, were now made more prominent ; and a coherence and a systematic consistency were now for the first time given to those sacerdotal and sacramental theories, which had previously existed in the Prayer-Book only in an embryotic condition ; and certain dogmas, which, by the moderation of the Reformers, had been couched in vague and general terms, were now expressed in ample and emphatic phraseology."

After stating that about six hundred alterations were at this time made in the Prayer-Book, most of them minute in themselves, but many being indicative of a certain " intention ;" and after saying that they may be divided into two classes, the *first* consisting of alterations which were undoubtedly improvements ; Mr. Taylor proceeds :—

" The alterations of the *second* class are of a re-actionary character, and seem to have been introduced with two chief objects. A few alterations, mostly rubrical, seem to have been made, *with no other assignable object than that of rendering the Prayer-Book distasteful to the Puritans, and so preventing any probable or possible conformity.* There are, also, doctrinal alterations of a very insidious character. *They* seem to have been introduced with the purpose *of bringing the Prayer-Book into a more systematic harmony with the sacerdotal and sacramental theories* then held by Gunning and his coadjutors, and so destroying the balance which the Prayer-Book hitherto had held between the two parties —Puritans and Romanizers."

Many of the changes referred to are considered in detail. Some are selected from the *first* class, showing— how, in spite of remonstrance, additional lessons were added from the Apocrypha, and the discretional liberty previously possessed of changing such lessons for others, was taken away;—how, in the words of Hallam, "the Puritans, having always objected to the number of saints' days, *the Bishops added a few more,*—more than sixty of the mythical or semi-historical heroes of monkish legends," and, for the charitable purpose of annoying those who objected to all commemorations of the kind, *the names of a few Popes* were considerately included in the list:—how, because it was desired "that parents might be allowed to present their own children at the font, and to dispense with the intervention of other sponsors, *to render that impossible* a rubric was now first added to enjoin *three* godparents for every child;"—how, the Puritans wishing the word "priest" to be changed to "minister," the words "pastor" and "minister" *were changed into "priest,"* with other offensive alterations that could not but have been designed. The following paragraphs are then added:—

"These changes, trifling and indifferent as perhaps they seem at the present time, struck with a deadly malignity at points which, to the Puritans, seemed vital points. The Puritans held that a bishop was only '*primus inter pares:*' that is, that the difference between bishops and presbyters was a difference of *degree*, not a difference of *order:* or, to use the words of Cranmer, that 'they were both one office in the beginning of Christ's religion.'

"In the reigns of Edward and Elizabeth the Church of England, by statute as well as in practice, had recognised Presbyterian ordination. At the close of the sixteenth century 'scores, if not hundreds' of clergymen were officiating in the Church of England who had been ordained by presbyters in Scotland, or on the Continent.

"*Now*, however, a clause was inserted in the preface to the Ordinal, asserting the necessity of Episcopalian ordination, and consequently denying the validity of the orders of all those who had been ordained during the last fifteen or twenty years.

"This liturgical change was not suffered to remain a dead letter. The Act of Uniformity *deprived of their ministerial character all those who had received Presbyterian ordination,* unless, by consenting to Episcopal rè-ordination, they would agree virtually to confess the nullity of their previous ministrations.

" But while the leaders of the High-Church party were devising liturgical innovations, which they well knew would drive their antagonists out of the Church, at the same time, with an almost blasphemous irony, they inserted in the Litany a petition *for deliverance from that* ' SCHISM' *which* THEY WERE THEMSELVES INTENTIONALLY BRINGING ABOUT *by their own high-handed and intolerant conduct.*"

IV.

Mr. Taylor, after having thus noticed "the changes which, though not without doctrinal import, appear to have been primarily introduced for the purpose of rendering the Prayer-Book as distasteful as possible to the Puritans," proceeds to refer to those " which seem to have been mainly effected for the purpose of giving consistency to the doctrinal position of the High-Church party." " These alterations," it is observed, "must of course be chiefly in the Offices." Two or three pages then follow on the Communion, Baptismal and Burial Services; after which come a variety of observations and remarks which bear more on the present time than the past. As the past, however, is that in respect to which the witness has been called, we confine his utterances to *it.* The following passages are all for which we can find further room :—

"A modern High-Church writer, while speaking in approving terms of the results of this revision, asserts, that 'to compare the Communion Service, as it now stands, especially its rubrics, with the form in which we find it previously to that transaction, will be to discover, that without any change of features which could cause alarm, a new spirit was then breathed into our Communion Service.' . . . .

"At the Savoy Conference, the Puritans had objected to the mention of the sanctification of the waters of Jordan, or any waters, by reason of Christ having been baptized therein. The Bishops, in 1662, not only retained the obnoxious allusion, but *introduced a still more obnoxious petition for the sanctification of the water in the font.* The semi-Popish Office of 1549 contained a similar petition, which had been struck out in 1552, in deference to the strong representations of Bucer. He thought that 'such blessings and consecrations would create in people's minds the notion of magic and conjuration.'

"This consecrating clause was probably introduced partly to disgust the Puritans, and partly to render tenable *that magical theory of baptismal regeneration*, which was held by the High-Church party at the time. . . . .

"Such, then, was the character of this revision of 1662. *It was re-actionary in its theology, unconciliatory in its temper*, short-sighted in its policy, but was eminently successful in bringing about *the desired result.* ' What was the result which was desired, is not a mere inference from the character of the alterations which were made, but is established on independent evidence. Bishop Burnet says: 'The Presbyterians laid their complaints before the King; but little regard was had to them. And now all the concern that seemed to employ the bishops' thoughts was, not only to make no alteration on that account, but to make the terms of conformity much stricter than they had been before the war.'

"Extensive and disastrous as was the schism *which was produced by this high-handed revision*, even this did not satisfy the framers of the Act of Uniformity, or come up to their expectations.

"When the Lord Chamberlain Manchester told the King, while the Act of Uniformity was under debate, ' that he was afraid the terms of it were so rigid that many of the ministers would not comply with it,' Bishop Sheldon replied, ' I am afraid they will.' Nay, 'tis credibly reported he should say, ' Now we know their minds, we'll make them all *knaves, if they conform.*'"

The candid and straightforward way in which Mr. Taylor gives his evidence is worthy of high praise, but a parting caution may not be amiss. Such language as " dealing a deadly blow to the prosperity of Dissenters" is not in good taste; and the frequent somewhat intemperate reference to " political Dissenters" is unwise. The one makes people think of godly Dissenting ancestors, who might have held, with Doddridge, that " Dissent was not only the cause of rational liberty, but in a great measure that of serious piety too." The other may provoke the remark, that if there was not a political Church, there *could not be* political dissent. The first begets the second, and it is really too bad for the Parent to disparage his own Child.

NOW.

I.

Mr. Taylor having thus given us his views about the last revision of the Liturgy, (two hundred years ago,) the spirit in which it was conducted, its aim and purpose, its successful result in the rupture that followed, and the rise of a power *without* the Church, we proceed to call our second witness, that we may hear from him something about what, at the present time, is passing *within*,—the thoughts and feelings which are stirring and throbbing in the minds and hearts of many of the clergy of the present day, as they look at their Church formularies, and realise their ecclesiastical position. The Rev. Philip Gell has put forth his "THOUGHTS ON THE LITURGY;" his object is to acknowledge and set forth "*the difficulties of an honest and conscientious use of the Book of Common Prayer.*" With some men, these difficulties are the grounds of their "conscientious clerical nonconformity." With Mr. Gell, they are consistently considered as a "*loud and reasonable call to the only remedy—*REVISION." He expresses himself sometimes very strongly, but always seriously, earnestly, calmly, and like a man of honest purpose, uprightness of mind, and depth of feeling, *burdened* by a weight which he sighs to have removed.

The following extract from his preface has received increased significancy by the events of the last few weeks, and hence, also, a new interest.

"Observe how Convocation declares against all doctrinal improvement of the Liturgy. True it is that some Bishops have not shunned to express their wish that salutary changes might be made, but their SYMPATHY, as a principle of action, appears to be less with those who feel *hurt and forced* in conscience by expres-

sions in the Services, than with those who do *not* so feel. . . . .
We go mourning under the difficulties of the Book we use, but no
comfort do our venerated Fathers seek for us. . . . . To speak of
a reformed Convocation, and bid us wait for a revised Liturgy by
means of it, is but to trifle with our hopes or our credulity. This
is far out of sight."

In the first section, entitled " Opening Statement of the
Subject," Mr. Gell begins by referring to the fact, that "four
leading heresies" have for some time been forcing themselves on public attention.—" *Confession*, with *priestly absolution;*" " The power of Episcopal hands *to give the Holy
Ghost to every ordained priest*, perpetuating thereby what is
called apostolical succession, and imparting Divine powers to
men in sacramental administrations;" "The *real presence*,
maintained in a way which eludes ecclesiastical jurisdiction;"
" Absolute *baptismal regeneration*, preached in most of the
Churches of the land." After some remarks on the way
in which these " grievous and alarming corruptions" have
recently sprung up amongst us, comes the following
passage :—

" Now, whatever fault may be chargeable upon MEN in the
revival. and earnest propagation of these offences, it cannot well
be denied that our ecclesiastical FORMULARIES *are the real ground
from which their origin has been derived.* Would any person have
originated one of them without believing confidently that he had
liturgical authority to stand upon? Does he not point to, and
plead, THE VERY WORDS IN THE PRAYER-BOOK, on which he thinks
himself required to teach and act; and has he not ostensible *reason
in those words*, understood most naturally, and at first sight, for so
doing ?"

Section II. is " On the Difficulties occasioned by the Lan-
guage concerning the Absolution of the Sick." The most
of the clergy of any moderation give up this, but, like
Dr. Robinson, many persuade themselves that the words
" I absolve thee," only mean " I declare thee absolved."
Even that is offensive, and liable to serious objection ; but
Mr. Gell believes that the subterfuge is utterly imaginary,

and, by a reference to the views of Cranmer, and other arguments, he makes good his position. The Bishop of Melbourne said to me in a letter, " I regret the expression used in the Visitation of the Sick, thinking it calculated to mislead." Mr. Gell says, when looking at the most favourable side of the question :—

" Even when we have done all we possibly can to modify such an expression, is it worth the labour ? Is it not at least too bad to keep, considering the trouble it gives?

" The fact is, our best apology is honestly to confess our delinquency, accept the consequence, and labour to remove both the words and their apologetic interpretation as soon as possible."

Whatever may be the low and modified sense which some of the clergy attach to the absolution in question, and however others may constantly, and of design, abstain from the use of it, I imagine that in many quarters it is viewed as of great importance, and much suspended upon its being received, from the idea that some mystic virtue clothes and accompanies the words of him to whom " Jesus Christ has given power and authority to pronounce it." It is very natural that this should be the case. Indeed, if such a feeling is not to be indulged, the whole thing, the claim asserted and the act done, is a useless impertinence, and something more.

One day, as I was walking leisurely down a street in Sydney, a young man came hastily up to me in a state of considerable agitation, and said, " Sir, are you—are you—a clergyman in full orders?" Knowing his meaning, and seeing his distress, I could only meet the question in his sense of it, and state that I was not what he sought. I then said, " But are not you a clergyman ?" " Yes ; but I am not in full orders, and I want one *immediately* who is ;" and away he started, in hurry and distress, in search of a qualified person to administer, as I supposed, to some dying mortal, that absolution which the priest only, not the deacon, is able to pronounce. I looked after him, and then turned away to ponder on the evil and danger of superstitious dependence on priestly acts, and the encouragement of this by priestly pretensions; and I could not help asking myself whether something of the sort might not be lurking in all Churches, from the importance attached by the sick and dying to the mere fact of having "a minister to pray by them." Who can tell, I thought, but some of us, who lay no claim to the power of absolution, by our want of faithfulness, or the perfunctory performance of the visitation of the sick, may stand exposed to the sarcastic rebuke of the prophet, "*and so they wrap it up?*"

II.

In Section III., "On the words of Consecration and Ordination," Mr. Gell, as I think, demonstrates that the words of the Bishop, "receive the Holy Ghost, &c.," must be understood in the sense of imparting the Divine gift, and not as a prayer that it may be received. "That the donative sense stands immoveable is evident," he says, from the considerations, reasonings, and facts to which he refers. The book must be read for the argument to be appreciated, for it is long and elaborate. The following words, coming from a Churchman, have a solemn significance:—

"If it may be believed that through a solemn declaration and imposition of hands the Holy Ghost is actually given to every one episcopally ordained, the same gift having been transmitted from one Bishop and Presbytery to another, from the Apostles, and Christ himself,—it is concluded, with apparent reason, that all the endowments of authority and power belonging to a true ministry are conferred upon every individual thus ordained, be his real character and qualifications what they may; nay, even the endowments of true ministers are surpassed by some pretended to be *super*-ordinary, seeing that such 'priests' give the body of Christ to His people, really baptize with the Holy Ghost, deliver Divine pardons upon confession; and again, when consecrated bishops with another donation of the same Spirit, themselves give Him in their ordinations, as they received Him. Thus dead professors assume to be living ministers of Christ, and are let into the sanctuary of God, pretending to exercise Divine powers, but destroying innumerable souls, instead of saving them, by their false ministrations."

Mr. Gell treats only of the consecration of persons; but there is the consecration of *places*. I know not exactly how much this is supposed to include, but that some extraordinary sanctity is imparted by it, and continues indelibly attached to the consecrated edifice, would seem to be understood. Any place where "two or three" habitually meet to worship, and where, according to the Divine word, Christ will be spiritually present in the midst of them, is to me hallowed. I enter with a feeling of reverence into the meanest little "Bethel" or "Ebenezer" under that sentiment; just as I never go into a Church, especially an old one, without awe,—not from thinking of its ceremonial consecration, but because in it are lifted towards heaven the thoughts of earth, in such words as "Thou art the King of Glory, O Christ." When a Church, in a large town in the north, was opened with great pomp, the newspapers, I remember, reported what seemed to me a somewhat irreverent and ostentatious display, intended to show how the clergy regarded the approaching rite. After the people were assembled, but before the service began, they walked about the Church in a careless sort of way, and *with their hats on;* they did so, it was said, purposely to express how the building was as yet "common and unclean," but that after consecration it would be felt to be "holy," and such an indecency would never be repeated.

One day, walking in a small town in one of the Australian colonies, where houses, streets, public buildings, &c., were in a very imperfect and incipient condition, though it had been settled some years, I was struck by observing what looked like a *ruin*. "That is singular," I said to my companion, "a ruin in a new country! —of something, too, which seems to have had architectural solidity and pretensions; what is it?" "It is the old Episcopal place of worship: there is a new Church, you see, rising on the hill. This was a pretty little building, and its destruction is much regretted. The people wished to have kept it for their school, but that could not be allowed, because it had been consecrated." "I wonder at that; especially as the education would have been religious, carrying on what had been begun in the children at their baptism within its walls." "We thought so; but such a use of it could not be sanctioned or permitted by the Bishop. It was ordered to be taken down, but with the proviso that the stones should be used in the walls of the new Church." "And that is being done?" "As far as possible; but the materials cannot all be made available; some have been disposed of, and in one case, have been used in completing a public-house." The speaker seemed puzzled by the prohibition, and scandalized by the result. I explained to him what I took to be the theory of the thing, which, if correct, I thought would in some measure alleviate the mystery. "Consecration," I said, "was an act which separated and set apart to sacred uses *an edifice,* as such: it did not probably confer any sanctity on the stones, individually, though it did, I believed, on the ground on which a Church stood, and which it covered. It was seemly, however, in the present instance, to work the materials of the one Church into the other, and unfortunate that any of them should have been apparently desecrated." At the same time, I could not but acknowledge, that it might have been better to appropriate the building to a school, instead of incurring the risk of any of its parts becoming devoted to worse purposes; to providing facilities, as in the case mentioned, for the morning "nip" or the mid-day "nobbler."

To return to Mr. Gell. His fourth section is headed, "On the Indications of the Presence of the Body and

Blood of Christ in the Lord's Supper, and of the Holy Ghost causing new birth in baptism, *which are taught in the Catechism.*" From this, the following passages may be taken.

"But there is worse in the Catechism than this, for it teaches correctly in one answer, that a sacrament is ONE thing, the outward sign of another; but in another answer it teaches that a sacrament is *two* things,—a sign, and *also the thing* of which it is a sign. In the Lord's Supper, it is bread and wine received by the mouth, and ALSO the body of Christ received by faith; and in Baptism it is a washing in water, and ALSO a vivifying or new birth by the Holy Ghost. This is *confusion!* There is no holy discerning of the Lord's body from the material symbols of bread and wine; no discerning of the baptism of the Spirit from the symbolical baptism of water. And so the minister has got the possession, and command, and distribution, both of Christ and of the Holy Ghost, the pride and ambition of pretending to which has given rise to the confusion under the *old* instigation, ' Ye shall be as Gods.' And throwing into the sacraments the very *realities* of heavenly things, even of God himself and his Almighty operations in the salvation of men (of which, in truth, they are only the edifying representative celebrations), people are fatally deceived with the idea, that when they participate in the celebration, they most properly receive the reality also. . . . . .

"Pity it is that human blindness and superstition should ever have conceived the idea of taking the representation for the reality, and imposing it as such upon multitudes, to the eternal destruction of their souls ! . . . . .

"How many of our most valuable Christian teachers have often to explain away the misleading errors of our old Catechism, with a secret sadness that it should be necessary for them to do so; how many are conscious that their attachment to it is but very questionable, though still they use it; how many have almost given over teaching it; how many are troubled that it should exist at all, misleading multitudes of poor children, who receive the teaching without any antidote !"

III.

From the next section, "On the Difficulties attending the *Ministration* of Baptism," we might quote largely, and we must be somewhat liberal, though we will confine ourselves to as few as possible of the more striking utterances. We meet, near the commencement, with the following statement of the writer's opinion :—

"Taking the words of this service *in their plain and literal meaning*, we should be clearly unjust if we did not agree to the following general proposition, as to the principle on which it is constructed, namely, that

" *The Baptismal Service of the Church of England is formed on the supposition that the baptism or birth of water, and the baptism or birth of the Spirit, are both administered in one and the same ordinance.*"

After stating certain grounds on which many thoughtful men in the Church feel compelled to put a meaning on the words different to this obvious and natural one, Mr. Gell says :—

"These considerations are thought strongly to prove that we ought to put an interpretation upon our service more consistent with facts, and to reject the natural sense as illegitimate ; in other words, that when we read, *this child is regenerate*, or, *it hath pleased thee to regenerate this infant*, (absolute and dogmatical assertions, concerning which it might very well be asked, How can you speak so certainly?) we should say, ' Oh, we *suppose* it to be so,'—we mean, *this child*, AS WE HOPE, *is regenerate ;* or, *it hath pleased thee*, AS WE HOPE, *to regenerate this infant;*—distinctively charitable suppositions, meaning something quite different from those dogmatical assertions ;—notwithstanding which, *it is held to be better thus to say one thing and mean another, at the risk of being continually misunderstood, than to disturb the old forms and make corrections, so as to say what we mean unmistakably.* Surely, this is barbarous !"

The hypothetical theory, referred to in the preceding Address, which was strongly held and advocated by some of my clerical friends in Australia, is then submitted to a full examination. We have only to do with the result—the fixed shape which our friend's thoughts have taken, in the form of a settled opinion respecting it, and which comes out in sentences like these :—

"The positive and absolute meaning of the words, as they stand, is altogether banished, and supplanted by another of hypothesis and hope. The words are not to mean what at first they did mean, and *naturally ever will* mean: they may say one thing, but they *must* mean another. And, instead of 'This child *is* regenerate,' our *thoughts* are to be, ' *We hope* this child is regenerate.' . . . .

"We have to hold and fearlessly assert that is means *we hope is*, and IT HATH PLEASED THEE means *it hath pleased thee, as we hope*, and CHRIST HATH PROMISED means *Christ, we hope, hath promised*, just as I ABSOLVE THEE is held to mean, *I declare thee absolved;* and it matters little, to our shame and sorrow be it spoken, that we have solemnly subscribed to the Prayer-Book, as containing in it nothing contrary to the Word of God, at the very time that conscience obliges us to reject the natural sense as un-scriptural, and to invent another; and that we have declared that we will use the form in the said book *prescribed*, and no other, when, fictitiously and covertly, we *are* using another all the while, and rejecting this. . . . .

"To proceed in this way of duplicity before God must be wrong in a very high degree, whatever excuses may be made for it. . . .

"There is *no authority or leave given us for this* superinduced meaning *in the Ritual itself*—not the slightest expression of such a charitable hypothesis or hope from one end of the service to the other, as it now stands. . . . .

" The very idea of a mere hope is unnatural to them [the whole three baptismal services]. Let them only speak, let them be heard, and they give the same certain sound everywhere. But this we drown by imposing the hypothetical sense, and, while they plainly *say* one thing, insist upon their *meaning* another! *   .

" In all this, whatever research or adroitness of argument may be shown in endeavouring to prove, from the principles and writings of our Reformers, that such an hypothetical meaning ought to be imposed, we are sanctioning falsehood *while we keep the words as they are*, and perplexing many by our sophistical explanations. We are leaving plain people to stumble upon the dark mountains of a mistakable Liturgy, interpreted in a way of

"* The honest 2000 clergy, ejected in 1662, could not do this. Not the shadow of an idea had they that those who took the natural sense were fools, and ought to drown their folly in the hypothetical, which was the true and intended sense. If this had been then conscientiously dis-coverable, would not those martyrs have seen it ?   (See ' Moore's Gorham Case,' Dr. Adams's Argt., p. 334.)"

rare expediency, and not of truth, when all ought to be so plain that 'the wayfaring man, though a fool, shall not err therein.' And to leave men to take baptism for regeneration, what can be worse?

" To rest contented under such a state of things can indicate no very safe state of conscience : to confess oneself honestly to be uneasy under it, and to be seeking complete deliverance, may give us hope concerning ourselves.

" In fact, the theory is wholly unsatisfactory as a relief of conscience before God, though it serves, as it were, to keep us afloat in the difficulties of our condition. To go on in this way much longer we shall be ill content."

From section sixth, " On Confirmation," we confine ourselves to one extract. The words directed to be said by the Bishop, it will be remembered, describe the candidates, in positive language, as regenerated and pardoned.

" It being impossible, however," Mr. Gell remarks, " to speak of the regeneration of these persons, and the forgiveness of their sins, as generally or in all cases certain," it becomes requisite, for the same reasons as in the case of baptism, to give to the language the meaning only of hope and supposition. He then goes on to say—

"We feel, indeed, that it cannot possibly be true that they are all really regenerate, and have all their sins forgiven them ; and it is unspeakably painful to the conscience to hear it so said by a Bishop of the Church of Christ. . . . . .

" The Bishop himself, to his distress in some instances, cannot use the words in their literal meaning ; and, if accused of solemnly affirming what is not true, he would, most probably, rejoin, 'It is so, *as we hope.*' But then, why not so *say ?* Why not speak in honest and conscientious language, giving pain to no one, and admitting of no objection ?"

An illustration of what is here said came before me in Australia, occasioning, at the moment, *the mental utterance of the very words which are here used.* When on a visit at some little distance from Sydney, there was to be, we were informed, one morning, a confirmation at the Church. Some of the family were going to attend the service, and I availed myself of the opportunity to go with them and witness the ceremony. It had many points about it of great interest. The most of the candidates were young women, household servants or the daughters of small tradesmen. They had all white veils over their heads, and, though in some cases there was a marked contrariety between the appearance of the person and the ornamental robe, the sight was, on the whole, both picturesque and affecting. It was preferred, I was informed, that the head *should* have some covering upon or over it at such a time,— though this could not be so in the case of youths, of whom there were four or five. The service was becomingly conducted. The Bishop, in his bearing, was kind and paternal. The address he delivered to the candidates after the administration of the rite, was exceedingly good ; plain, familiar, serious ; full of important and wise counsels ; well adapted to guard the young against the moral and spiritual dangers to which they might be exposed, and to direct them in respect to the course they should pursue, and the habits they should cultivate, to preserve and advance the religious life. But I could not help something like a shock going right through me, by one thing I heard and saw. The Bishop, kneeling at the altar, distinctly uttered the solemn words,—"Almighty and everlasting God, *who hast vouchsafed to regenerate these thy servants with water and the Holy Ghost, and hast given unto them forgiveness of all their sins ;*"—rising up he came forward, and, in the course of the service, told those of whom he had thus spoken, that they were not to believe it ! They were not to take the words they had heard as meaning what they seemed to say. They had been described as " regenerated" and " forgiven ;" this did not mean that they *were*, but that they ought to be, might be, or might be hoped to be that. The question immediately rose within me—Then, *why not say so ?* Why retain words so likely to deceive, and which, I suppose, many Bishops never take the trouble to explain when they use them? Why employ language, and that, too, in addressing God, which expresses exactly what you do *not* mean? It would surely be possible, without detracting from the solemnity of the service, to find forms of speech which would be more consistent with outward facts, and more in harmony with inward conviction.

IV.

The fact is, that the Church of the Prayer-Book is the ideal, not only of a spiritual, but of a supernatural, community. All its Bishops are successors of the Apostles, possessing something like a Divine prerogative, the ability to confer or convey Divine gifts; all its ministers are " moved by the Holy Ghost," the second order having a distinct qualification for giving to sacramental administrations a mystic virtue; all its members are regenerated in baptism, and recognized in confirmation as having received the forgiveness of their sins; and, at last, all are buried as " the blessed dead," who " die in the Lord," and " enter into joy and felicity." Now, let it be granted that all this is nothing but the proper idea of the Church *of Christ;* that it is just what His true, spiritual Church *is,* and what the professing visible Church *ought to be.* Still, there are two objections to the Anglican theory, especially as realised in the National Establishment. The first is, that all the supernatural influences and results, just spoken of, are linked and tied to the action *of rites,* through which what is Divine flows, by which the spiritual is effectuated. The second is, that the official formularies not only identify the visible with the spiritual Church, but, worse than this,— by the Church of the Prayer-Book becoming the Church *of England,* she becomes identified with " the world," properly so called, if there be one; she gives the whole people a legal right to have her high spiritual and supernatural utterances applied to them; she accepts the obligation of including and comprehending the masses within herself, and of so speaking and so acting as consciously to throw her divine pearls in such broad-cast fashion over the land, as not only cannot enrich the multitudes, but—by being unfit to be handled by them, being to large numbers, in the higher classes as well as the lower, only what material diamonds would be to savages—to secure their being looked upon with mere ignorant wonder, thrown to the winds, or trampled in the dirt.

The sects, I think, have erred in many of their attempts to separate the true from the professing Church ; to make the external, visible fellowship to be exclusively that of the faithful. True, it is only God's spiritual priesthood that can, properly speaking, *worship ;* on that principle public Divine service must, in a great measure, proceed. Still, it is important to keep in view the mixed character of an audience, and even in worship to remind it of the sug- gestive fact. The Church *of England*, as such, takes the high ideal of the spiritual Church, and, practically at least, applies it generally. In its offices and formularies, its language recognizes alike congregations and individuals as being all the actual recipients of spiritual grace. The Church is worse than the sects in two ways ; it goes far higher in theory and pretension—it goes much lower in actual fact, in promiscuous recognition and mixed com- munion. If there must be fixed forms for public worship and the administration of the sacraments, surely it is pos- sible so to construct them, that they shall neither be a pres- sure on the clergy nor a peril to the people. A few sen- tences of Mr. Gell's work, embodying his views on this matter, may be added here :—

" It is said by some that the Prayer-Book is so worded as to be specially applicable, not only to true Christians, but to true Chris- tians of the most excellent and certain character : not merely to such as are Christians in hope and by supposition, but to those who are really and undoubtedly so. And this is asserted to be the principle on which it is constructed, taking the words in their primary, natural, and grammatical meaning.

" No sooner, however, do we enter into the *general* use of the service, than this principle is, to a great extent, ignored, and the words are required to be applied in a sense of hope and supposition contrary to it, to the great trouble and perplexity of conscientious minds. . . . . In *congregational* worship, where the presence of some true Christians may and ought to be relied upon, the principle may be sustained and rightly acted on ; but, in an office of *individual* application . . . . it is impossible.

" But if so, why should we have such an individual form at all as is rarely, if ever, known for certain to be realised, and is always, in practice, to be used with a sense of charitable supposition, and nothing more ? Why, therefore, should not the form be expressly suited to true Christians *in hope*, according to facts, rather than remain a transcendental form, above all ordinary attainment and use ? Why not *say*, we hope, we assume, we suppose? Why not *speak as we mean* with a unity, and not a duplicity, between our words and our meaning ? Why not worship before the Lord in the language of truth and honesty ? . . . . How much more happily would the consciences of true, but ordinary, Christians be consulted, without any injury to those of the highest, if natural words were given them for the expression of their devout affections! The Christianity need not be lowered, much less discarded. . . . .

" The inference, then, is clear and irresistible—that we are shut up to REVISION as our only real deliverance."

There is something at once so startling and affecting in the following statement, that, though we have already far exceeded the ordinary limits of quotation, we venture to give it. The extract will close Mr. Gell's evidence. After telling us, that " he has been moved to speak because so many refrain from doing so, who would nevertheless most heartily rejoice if such, or nearly such, revision could be achieved without the difficulties they are afraid of," he adds · —

" I claim to speak because of many—
" 1. Who, though able, are only *almost* ready, to speak far better for it than myself:
" 2. Many, who persuade themselves that the Prayer-Book is,

on the whole, 'well enough as it is, though it *might* be improved:'

" 3. Many, who desire nothing so much as peace in their own
time, whatever may come after:

" 4. Many, who do not allow conscience to complain of faint,
but true, misgivings within their own minds:

" 5. Some, who think and fear that they should lose their influence (a sacrifice for which they would gain no equivalent), if
they said what they think:

" 6. Some, who are too much swayed by thoughts about their
patrons and preferments to act independently:

" 7. Some, who go heavily and despondingly, under the want of
sympathy in those who are ' in place of authority,'—too heavily to
say anything but ' No man careth for my soul ! my often wounded
soul !'

" 8. Others, who are so inured to their oppression, that they only
desire that nothing may be moved, lest their chains should gall
their sores if they be disturbed."

The enumeration continues. 9. Refers to those who
fear encounters and heartburnings. 10. To Nonconformists. 11. To those who think that God having vouchsafed to bless them, His will is that they should rest in the
enjoyment of what they have. The passage then concludes :—

" 12. Many, who will not plough by reason of present cold, and
have no faith in things unseen as yet, and recollect not how God
works by the patient and reiterated efforts of His servants, and
will have men ready for the time, as the work of the time requires
them:

" 13. Many, who think too little of the incalculable amount of
good involved in the measure ; the amount of comfort to innumerable consciences ; the extent and stability of pacification in the
Church at large ; the purity of doctrine attained and confirmed ;
missionary preaching and ministration invigorated by consistency
in the rites administered ; our war with Antichrist delivered from
occasions for counter-accusations ; and confidence and power
increased in spreading Christianity everywhere, through the
harmony of our worship with the truth of God, and the assurance
of His blessing :—all this amount of good, and very much more,
involved in the revision, is far less thought of, I think, than it

ought to be, wherefore many are silent, *and I cannot forbear to speak.*"

V.

Nor can *I* forbear to speak ;—although I am quite aware that many will be of opinion, that I have given to an unprofitable and irritating subject, time and labour which might have been better bestowed on other themes. I have spoken—although I had hoped to speak on such matters no more, and certainly with the resolution of never speaking on them again. I say this in spite of the declaration of Dr. Robinson, that nothing " is to be compared to Church questions in the magnitude of their issues ;" as " they are questions for the wisest statesmen to ponder well, for theologians of all schools impartially to discuss, and on which the highest intellects may be most profitably engaged." It may be so; but I candidly confess I was never drawn into anything so contrary to my wishes, and never wrote anything under such a sense of compulsion and constraint, as this book. I accepted the imposed duty, however, at first, and I have further and more fully discharged it now, in the hope that both Truth and Charity may accept the service. Like Mr. Gell, I claim to speak, because many, who could have spoken much better, will not; for some who are not aware of the necessity for speaking; or who shrink from doing it, though they may not be sorry that it is done for them. Many Dissenters take no interest in " Church questions ;" they regard them as belonging only to Churchmen, ignorant of the fact that some of them are discussed with a special reference to themselves. It seems to me that when Churchmen take the trouble to sketch schemes of " comprehension" and " union," or to put forth "practical methods" for " the revision of the Liturgy," *with a view* " to the restoration of Dissenters to the Church," it is at least becoming for some one to notice them, and to do so in some other way than by a few lines in a newspaper or a review.

Our clerical friends cannot, of course, be aware how things look from the Dissenting stand-point; how utterly insufficient to satisfy most Nonconformists are many of the liturgical alterations they suggest; and with what incredulity some would read the complacent statement that " no Dissenter will deny the essential correspondency of the Church of England with the Apostolic Church in doctrine, ministry, sacraments, and prayers." Instead of merely smiling at the efforts of good men to effect—I will not say, in the Australian dialect, " the subjection of all denominations to the dominion of one Church," but—the " restoration" of the English Nonconformists, the Church of Scotland, other Presbyterian varieties, Wesleyans, and Baptists, " to the communion of the Apostolic Church" under Episcopal authority,—it seems better to look at the overtures thus made, and to say whether or not they are likely to be successful. I quite admit that it is not graceful or wise to advance to us holding the overtures in one hand, and brandishing a flaming sword in the other; saying, in effect, " Your concurrence or your life;—accept, submit, or,—a warfare that shall seek your extermination and make terrible havoc upon your strongholds;" still, since the proposals are well intended, and, on the one side of the world or the other, are the result of a wish to attain a good object, and seek this according to what is natural to men occupying a certain ground, it is only proper to explain, why, whether right or wrong in their views, Dissenters may be expected to say, that, unable to acquiesce in what is proposed to them, they must be content to yield to the " terrible" alternative.

I am as tired as any man of mere Sect-life : of this and the other portion of the body becoming a separated limb; men combining together on this and the other point or points, one or five as the case may be,—taking some idea as to " ministry," or " fellowship," or the form of a Church, fixing upon that, rallying round it, taking a name from it, segregating themselves from all other Christians, refusing recognition, acknowledgment, intercourse, surrounding themselves with a cordon which is exclusive and forbidding on both sides. " Now Jericho *was straitly shut up; none went out, and none came in.*" I am tired of all this, and have long been so, whether practised by large communities or small. We are all too fond of our bits of " testimony," what we " witness for;" far too anxious to fix and fashion the minutest particulars of creed and discipline, and then to say, like the King to the çlergy, " From this we will not endure any varying or departing in the least degree." In addition to this, we are all too apt to think we have the keeping of other people's consciences, or at least we are afraid in the smallest thing to *seem* to countenance what we regard as wrong; to appear in any way to have fellowship with it, lest we should take upon ourselves our neighbour's responsibility, and become "partakers of other men's sins." Unquestionably, there is a great truth, a cardinal moral principle, in all this; but it seems sometimes to be too sensitively felt, and to be carried out till the feelings displayed become rather the symptom of disease than health. In the preceding Address, having in some degree to speak for others, I spoke according to what I know to be their views, with which, of course, to a large extent, I myself sympathize; but I am free to admit that I could personally see comprehended in the same religious community a far greater difference of opinion, and far greater varieties of ministry, association, form, service, *in companies that should yet be one with the whole,* than some people would deem it right to tolerate. There would be a Church-life in this, a generally diffused vital sympathy, instead of so many separate bits of Sect-life. I have no hope, however, of this being realised by the " restoration" of the sects—*all other " Evangelical denominations"*—to " the Church," that is, " *the Church of England.*" What might have prevented much which took place two hundred years ago, would not be enough now to restore and to re-unite. No " practical method" has yet been suggested, likely to bring about this result speedily, and on a large scale. The first and great thing is for every Church to do what is right, because it is right. To alter and amend whatever needs to be altered or amended, not with the aim of attracting others, but from the desire to be in harmony with truth. At the same time, let all cultivate unity of *spirit*, mutual sympathy; let none refuse to " fraternize" where there is no fundamental error to forbid; and then, in the first place, something like the sense of a wide, catholic Church-life would be felt through the action of this very " spirit;" and, in the second place, one and another of the distinct members might come to coalesce; dislocations might be reduced, and limbs set by the force of an internal *vis medicatrix*, which never would have submitted to external bandages or mechanical manipulation.

Not that this second result is to be regarded as so very necessary. A blessed and exalted feeling would exist, if the first were realised, and was hearty and general. I believe it does exist to a much larger extent than many imagine. A vast mass of Christianity, of true spiritual life, exists in denominations bounded by Episcopacy on the one hand, and Brethrenism on the other. As denominations, they are unrecognized on both sides; for different reasons no communion can be held with them. But they can recognize each other, and do so; they can have intercourse with each other, and to a great degree have it, though they might have more; and thus, by the culture of religious large-heartedness, wide sympathies, loving thoughts, and brotherly action, they rise beyond the low level of Sect-life to the higher region of Church-life. For my part, I strive to pass, in spirit, the guarded limits on both sides. If neither Episcopacy nor Brethrenism will love me, they cannot debar me from loving them. I see no reason why there should not be both;—only, let neither think that itself is every thing. I could live a Christian life under either, and have no quarrel with those who do so; I think they might be willing to act towards others in the same way, even though they did not feel as they do. As for the objections to the " one man system," and the constant discharge by the same individual of the public ministry, why, no one, I suppose, would more enjoy, as a spiritual luxury, the quiet meeting of a few individuals for mutual edification, than the preacher of a large Dissenting Church, or the over-done incumbent of a poor, extensive, and populous parish. It may be all very well, and I doubt not is exceedingly comfortable and refreshing, to assemble with a number of congenial minds in an upper room, to read, and pray, and edify each other, free from the heavy obligations of public effort. I see no objection to such meetings, but they are obviously for the few, not the many. The masses must be cared for, as well as ourselves. Those, of every church, whose life is a constant toil, because " necessity is laid upon them," as they think, and who are obliged to forego personal enjoyment for general usefulness, are fairly entitled to more consideration than they sometimes meet with from the spiritual *élite*. We have all need to take care of identifying the " ministry," " fellowship," and outward form of the primitive Churches with our own peculiarities, and especially not to unchurch other " brethren" because they " follow not with us." " *Grace be with* ALL them who love the Lord Jesus Christ in sincerity."

VI.

When I was in Australia, and had to plead for the Colonial Missionary Societies connected with our Churches, I always took the double ground of their *denominational* character, and their *general relations*. We were there because it was England transferred to the antipodes ; among the emigrants were of necessity many, who had been brought up in the forms and habits of our Denominational-life; who

were attached to our modes of worship, accustomed to our
" service of song ;" and who would welcome in town or bush
the preaching and ordinances they had enjoyed at home,
and which were deeply interwoven with all their early and
home associations.   But we were there also as a part of the
great Christian Household, with a Gospel to preach, and a
mission to fulfil, and a work to do for society at large ; to
seek the spiritual benefit of the community generally, that
it might be kept from sinking into negligence and indifference,—be called from ungodliness and sin ; that, with
our land's language, laws, literature, institutions, might be
propagated and preserved her Evangelical Protestant Christianity.   But this work was not ours alone, nor did we claim
or pretend that we must do it all.   It belonged to the
different Churches in common.   We had our share of it to
accomplish, our sphere in which to work ; but we advanced
to the high service, rejoicing in the presence and zeal of
other communions ; willing to feel as " fellow-workers" with
them ; wishing them success, not doubting that posterity
would reap an advantage from the action of various instruments, so far, at least, as our sectional peculiarities
interfered not with the truths of " the common salvation."

I don't see why Churchmen, especially · Evangelical
Churchmen, might not take a ground and use language
like this, without any letting down of the dignity of the
Church, or any disloyalty to its scriptural claims.   I am
sure they would be the better for the cultivation of wider
Protestant sympathies, and the hearty recognition of the
services of those who, in the words of the Bishop of
Adelaide, " are pledged to the same cause" with themselves, " rejoice in the same hope, and are devoted
to the same duty of preaching Christ and Him crucified to
a dark and fallen world."   Attending, one Sunday morning,
at the Church which serves at present as the Cathedral at
Hobart Town, I heard a reputedly evangelical clergyman

address the congregation (in a way remarked by others) as
THE REPRESENTATIVES *of British Christianity in the colony ;*—
as if there were none but themselves ; utterly ignoring the
existence, the labours and services of all other Protestant
bodies whatsoever. True, he was not called upon to do
more. It is not usual, even in the colonies, for the Church
to be conscious of the existence of the sects. Be it
so ; but neither was he called upon to talk to that
mixed congregation about the virtue of " HOLY BAPTISM,
*wherein they were all made children of God, members of Christ,
and inheritors of the kingdom of heaven ;*"—in a diocese, too,
where, of all others in Australia, it is necessary to warn the
people against a doctrine—or the abuse of it—with its
consecutive ramifications, which, as we have seen, is enforced by the Bishop with terrible emphasis ; a thing which
cannot be without effect (as I know it is not) on the habitual
teaching of some of his clergy, or without influence as to
the class which he honours and prefers. Very naturally
and properly so, according to his lordship's honest convictions ; but that class is the antipodes of the one with which
our clerical friend was understood to rank.

It is very sad, this ecclesiastical exclusiveness,—this
refusing to be cognizant of the existence, or to admit the
worth or usefulness of any but ourselves. The evil spirit,
of which it is the manifestation, no doubt lurks among the
sects as well as anywhere else, and finds for itself some
appropriate mode of development and utterance ; but it is
more noticeable at times in that " Apostolic Church," (the
privilege of communion with which is so urged upon us by
some,) when, as it sometimes happens, the denominations ignored agree more in fundamental truth with
a given Bishop, than that Bishop agrees with another.
The present Bishop of London, I believe, is of the
Broad Church, having sympathetic tendrils coming out
of him, and touching more or less all parties on all sides.
That seems to me a very right thing for one of his

order. The Bishop of such a mixed body as the Church
of England has always been in fact, and is now authorized
to be by law, ought as far as possible to feel and act in
accordance with this. It is just as wrong for an Evangelical
Bishop to make his diocese too hot for the Anglican, as it
is for the high Anglican to hunt out of *his* all in whom he
sniffs the taint of low Evangelicism. But even the Bishop
of London has no bowels for any but Churchmen. In his
speech at the Mansion House to encourage and aid the
Bishop of Brisbane, he is reported to have said, that if *they*
did not take possession of the land, and establish the Church
in it, and sustain their preaching and ordinances, the
Romanists and Dissenters would not be idle,—by one or
other of whom the work would be done;—or something to
that effect. Now, without reminding his lordship that
the colonial Government pays for the support of Popery, it
may be asked, why should not other Protestant bodies
besides the Church of England aid in the work of evangeliz-
ing Australia? And, since they hold the great essentials of
Christian truth, not only without any approach to Romanist
perversions, but *without countenancing Romanism by drawing money with it from a common treasury*, why should
not their zealous and disinterested efforts be recognized as
something good as far as they go, and worthy of being
thought of and spoken about as at least better than nothing?
" If we don't do it, they will." My lord, they *have* done it.
I have been in the diocese of Brisbane. There are
Wesleyan congregations, Baptist, Independent, Presbyterian, which (without reckoning the Catholics) together
far outnumber, I imagine, at least in Brisbane and
Ipswich, the attendants on the English Episcopal worship. Now, I do not say that these Nonconformist congregations have arisen from the negligence of the Church
of England,—for the Bishop of Newcastle, in whose diocese
Queensland has hitherto been included, is a most laborious
and pains-taking prelate,—but from the existence in the

population of the religious element in its several Dissenting forms, which naturally craved to be met, and from the presence in the respective denominations of some interest in the work which all Churches have committed to them. The Bishop of Brisbane, however, is going out, I believe, very much in the spirit of a Christian Evangelist, and I can cordially and sincerely wish him, as such, all success,—the more so, as his system might be made to adapt itself more easily than some others to the necessities of the scattered dwellers in the bush. The ministers of the different bodies, as far as they can, go out for a month or so, and visit the far-separated stations, where every one coming as a Christian minister is sure of a welcome. The sturdy Presbyterian will receive the Episcopal minister, and both give him a couch and get him a congregation ; and the Churchman will welcome the Methodist or Independent, and do the same. It will be a pity for such a state of things to be discouraged. At the same time, if any one Body possesses a special power for doing a particular work, or can be easily adapted to it, by all means let it be undertaken, and may God abundantly bless and prosper it !

The folly in the colonies of ignoring all Christian communities and Christian efforts but our own, is sometimes made manifest in a way that might provoke laughter, if it was not far too sad and mournful for that. In one of the Australian colonies, I found it stated that the Episcopal Church has for some years been diminishing. Of course, I can only speak of this on the authority of others ; but they put the proof of the fact in the form of figures taken from authentic Government statistics. The result is shown to be this :—At a specified time the Episcopalians are one-fifth of the Protestant population ; a little time after, some of the other bodies are found to have doubled, while the Church has gone back, and yet, during that period, the Immigration Reports show that the accessions to it, according to the tabular classification of arrivals in the colony, *exceeded*, by nearly a hundred per cent., those received by all the other Evangelical denominations put together. Now, what strikes me is this, that while other denominations are thus active and zealous,—so much so, that they have devolved upon them the charge of feeding and tending the scattered sheep of the Episcopal fold,—there is a silly party in that body, who, on the one hand, talk superciliously of those who do their neglected work, as Schismatics and Dissenters, and, on the other, like a set of boys, play at being the Catholic Church! High, exclusive ecclesiastical language is ever on their tongue, and in their monthly paper there is a Calendar of the Church's services for the month,—fasts, festivals, and saints' days,—in which are given the Scriptures to be read at—*when*, think you?—" MATINS" and "EVENSONG!" Nero fiddled when Rome was burning. How much better than this child's play is the irregular zeal of Methodist, Dissenter, Bible-Christian, Schismatic, or any one else intent on *work* and achieving something ! " *Waiting* for the reduction of every profession of Christianity into the bosom of one communion"—"our own Apostolic branch of the holy Catholic Church!" As things go, some people, it would seem, will have to wait long enough for that. One Churchman said to me, " The fact is, if something is not done, the whole thing will die out." And another asks, " Is it the Church of England in this colony that dissents from the great majority of orthodox Protestants, or is it the majority of Protestants who dissent from the minority, as represented by the Church?" I don't myself put truth to the vote, and decide by the majority where it is; but I do think that the facts stated, looked at in connexion with the airs and graces of the gradually diminishing catholic sect, suggest something as to the un-wisdom of feeling and talking as if we alone were the " temple of the Lord," and all other Christians little better than publicans and sinners.

O Lord God ! Father of all on whom the name of Christ

is named; in whose sight outward distinctions avail nothing; who hast taught us that what thou requirest is a new creature, vital union with thy Son through faith, that inward life which is love; send down on thy Church universally the spirit of wisdom and understanding, of charity and zeal. Burn up our mutual prejudices, our low selfishness, our unbrotherly thoughts. Help us so to live, and work, and worship, that love in the heart becoming light in the reason, we may be more and more brought to unity in the Faith, and fellowship in the Church, through the guidance of thy Holy Spirit. Amen.

P.S.—After writing the foregoing, I read two articles on Liturgical Reform and kindred subjects, in the February and March Numbers of "*Evangelical Christendom*," which had been mentioned to me by Dr. Steane. I read them with much interest, not only because they referred, as I found, to the very publications, among others, which I had been myself noticing, but on account of the ability by which they are distinguished. I do not feel called upon to make any remarks on these papers. As, however, the writer looks at things from the *inside* of the Church, it may be well, I think, for the reader to use his statements as a set-off against the prejudice, ignorance, or mistake, which no doubt colours what I say who speak from the *outside*. In one of the papers are two rather remarkable letters, from Dr. McNeile and Canon Stowell respectively, in reply to an application for their signatures to a petition against Liturgical Reform. I had once thought of remarking on the movement out of which this application has gone forth throughout the land. There must be some deep significancy in the united action of persons so diverse that, if they were not nominally one, the way in which some of them speak and write of the others would make us believe that they are *two*,—or twenty. I could have wished, too, to have made some use of Canon Wodehouse's letter on withdrawing from the Church,—the views it contains and advocates, and the light it lets in on what has been for years the writer's inward life. But these, and many other things besides, I must leave.

I trust, however, I shall not be violating any principle of courtesy or propriety if I put on the last page of this book an extract from a letter which I received along with the proof of the last sheet. It is from a clergyman of whom I have no personal knowledge, but who has written to me, from a distance, on questions which interest us both, but on which we cannot be supposed to see exactly alike. He refers to having read some of " The Adelaide Correspondence" published in the newspapers here; but *he knows nothing of my having delivered the preceding " Address " in Australia, or of my being now employed in preparing this publication.*

·Keeping in mind this fact, the reader, I think, will peruse the following passage with some interest. That I should have received it when I did, is to me a singular circumstance.

* * * * * " I have determined by God's help to write a treatise on the Church of the Future, and to go as fully as He shall enable me into the whole matter. As Mr. Gell, of Derby, and Mr. Fisher, of the Middle Temple, have fairly stated what I conceive to be the views of Dissenters generally on the revision of the Liturgy, yea, and of many of the Evangelicals in the Church, I shall try to give an equally fair statement of the objections of spiritually-minded Churchmen to the proposed alterations. I could never consent to the rationalizing of Christianity, for which the parties I have named are the avowed advocates. I am convinced that you have suggested the first right practical step towards unity, namely, the abolition of the restricting

system. Let there be an exchange of pulpits, voluntarily, for the single purpose of preaching the Gospel. At the same time, every publication which brings out the deep spirituality of our Liturgy will lessen prejudice and obviate objections by enlarging the views of those who have had but too good grounds for prejudice and objection. For our Liturgy, in the hands of unconverted men, is undoubtedly chargeable as the fruitful parent of formalism, and as furnishing materials for a disguised Romanism."

Having given this extract, it seems but fair to give another; one on a different subject, indeed, and from a different quarter, but the more on that account illustrative and significant, as showing how thoughtful men, the antipodes of each other (in more senses than one), are at present looking at "Church Questions." A letter just received from a ministerial brother in Australia contains the following passage :—

* * * "Mr. —— has been talking of going home for a year, but it is not easy to get a supply, and from the peculiar circumstances of the case there would be a risk of his finding disorganization on his return. How much our congregations and churches in these colonies are dependent on mere personal attachment to the minister! In some cases, removal or death would cause extended dissolution or dispersion ; the successor, or successors, would have to build up again almost from the foundation. I often think it would be so, in some measure, even in the old country. Is not this one of the many indications we have of the radical unsoundness of much in our modern Independency? And the evils in the colonies, where there is little of local attachment and fixed association, such as you have in England, are proportionally greater. I see no remedy for it, except our going back to the old plan of making the Church, so to speak, a municipality. One town—one Church, with as many places of worship as they like, but

with a plurality of presbyters, who, however, shall be officers of the one society, and not of each separate congregation."

These words are but the echo from afar of the thoughts of many here, which find occasional utterance in conversation and correspondence. If on all sides we were more honest and open, admitting what we feel to be defective in the working of our respective systems, perhaps in time we should arrive at, or this itself might be, *the beginning of the end.*

POSTSCRIPT TO THE SECOND EDITION.

WHEN intimating my purpose (*Ante*, p. 111, Appendix) of speaking no more on ecclesiastical questions, I did not intend to preclude myself from an occasional utterance through magazine or review; I was thinking more especially of such tasks as the one I was then completing. I felt quite at liberty, therefore, to accede to the request of the proprietors of the *Patriot* newspaper to furnish them with an article on one which had appeared in *Macmillan's Magazine*, in which the Rev. F. D. Maurice had put forth his views on Liturgical Reform. Soon after the appearance of what I was led to write, I was favoured with a letter from Mr. Maurice, containing a further exposition of his views. This letter he forwarded to me with the liberty to make any use of it I thought fitting. I don't know that I can do better than submit both Article and Letter to the readers of this book. Those who are interested in it, will be interested in them. I think, also, that it may be due to Mr. Maurice himself, and I am sure it will be acceptable to some of the readers of his paper in *Macmillan*, for it to be seen how he meets that objection to his theory which naturally occurred to me, and which would occur, I imagine, to most persons reading the Prayer-Book as I do, whether themselves within the Church or outside of it.

I.

The Rev. F. D. Maurice and Liturgical Reform.

(*From the "Patriot," Thursday, April* 26.)

The Revision of the Liturgy is gradually becoming one of the questions of the day. It may be true that it is only interesting to certain minds, or to certain classes, and that the bulk of the people care nothing about it. It is, however, also true that the subject is capable of being put in a popular form, and that there are points in it which affect laymen as well as ecclesiastics. Indeed, with our conviction that the people are the *Church*, not the clergy (or rather neither exclusively, but both combined), and with our belief that the nation, as such, has a right to interfere with and a duty to discharge towards whatever is national, we think it likely that the subject will become, as it certainly ought, one of deep interest to " all sorts and conditions of men." " Some may desire," it has been said, " that only clergymen should suggest improvements in the book which they are obliged to use." Is it nothing to the laity what their spiritual guides consent to accept and have habitually to " use?" Do the laity themselves not use the book? Is it not used for them, over them, in relation to themselves and their children, and have they no interest in that in which they are made to live, and move, and have their being? The Prayer-Book besets them on every side; it is about their path and about their bed, encompassing all their ways; it lays its hand upon them as soon as they breathe, and keeps it there till they breathe no more; it goes further than that,—for it not only touches them at every step from the cradle to the grave, but it has a theory about them before they are born and after they are buried! Into all this the laity have surely a right to look. If they show no interest in it, *that*, we fear, will be found to arise from their secret disbelief of the theory itself on which the book is built,—a state of mind which makes them utterly careless as to what becomes of it, or which leads them to regard all talk about reform or revision with hopeless scepticism or silent scorn.

In respect to the Prayer-Book and the subject in question, there is *doctrinal* revision, and there is *non*-doctrinal, —the one would remove or modify certain expressions of belief; the other seeks only a shortening or re-arrangement of the services. Some schemes are . put forth by writers who seek relief for themselves ; others are advocated with a more especial view to the conciliation of Dissenters. It is not our intention to go into these topics ; our present purpose is to limit our remarks to one article, in which the writer deprecates all revision, and urges adherence to the Prayer-Book as it is ; and we further propose to confine attention, as much as possible, to one point in relation to that article.

We refer to the paper " On the Revision of the Liturgy and the Act of Uniformity," by the Rev. F. D. Maurice, which stands first in *Macmillan's Magazine* for the present month. No one who has the least personal knowledge of Mr. Maurice, or the most superficial acquaintance with his writings, can for one moment doubt his earnestness and sincerity, his devout feeling, his simplicity of purpose, the strength of conviction with which he holds his religious theories, or the perfect conscientiousness with which he retains his position in the Church. For Mr. Maurice, personally, we entertain great respect, although we hesitate not to say that we deem his theology seriously defective, and his style of writing singularly unsatisfactory. As to some of his pet theories and favourite forms of thought, we candidly confess that we don't understand them; or, if we do, that it surpasses our ability (though, of course, not his) to harmonise them with adherence to the teaching of the Prayer-Book, or the consistent retention of the position of a clergyman.

In another part of this paper will be found a short analysis of Mr. Maurice's article. This, by giving our readers a general view of the whole of its contents, leaves us more at liberty to fix attention on the one thing which we wish to notice. That one thing is the advantage which Mr. Maurice thinks he enjoys over the sects, by the way in which the Liturgy teaches him to regard all mankind. Its spirit, tone, language,—everything about it,—breathes towards humanity a Divine benevolence. The nation, the race, men as men, are regarded by it in a way which Mr. Maurice dreads to think of as modified by some suggested doctrinal alterations. We shall first, however, do Mr. Maurice the justice to let him put his thoughts forth in his own words. Having given the extracts from his article which will do this, we shall then candidly state how they strike us, standing, as we do, on the outside of the Church of the Prayer-Book.

As it is not our purpose to enter into Mr. Maurice's argument with Mr. Taylor, but only to look at one thought which runs through it, and which is capable of being detached from it without injury to itself, we omit, in making our extracts, whatever would interfere with the simple object we have in view. The following sentences, if not all that might be given, will be sufficient as the basis of our subsequent observations :—" We have had the daring *to tell our children* that *they are members of Christ, children of God,* inheritors of the kingdom of heaven." This Mr. Maurice says in his own person. In reply to the suggestion of altering the Baptismal Service on the ground that all that is asked for is a consent to the *modified* assertion, or the less obtrusive exhibition of certain theological and ecclesiastical theories, he puts the following words into the mouth of a Dissenter :—" Certain theological and ecclesiastical theories ! What, you do not think it is a practical question, then, *whether a child is the child of the Devil or of God !* You think you may go on, age after age, *proclaiming that as a fact which we deny to be a fact*, and then suddenly make a less obtrusive exhibition of your creed, lest you should endanger the Establishment." Mr. Maurice proceeds to state that he thinks the Dissenter will further say,—"Is this which you propose to omit an isolated statement? Can it be? Must it not go through the whole Prayer-Book? . . . . Is not this what you mean when you address all the motley crowd in your churches as *Dearly beloved brethren*,—when you call them all to address an *Almighty, most merciful Father*, not in some vague sense, but in *Christ Jesus our Lord*, in whom *Thou hast made promises to mankind?* Is not this the reason why you repeat the Lord's Prayer so often? Is not this what excuses your general thanksgiving *for the redemption of the world;* your eucharistic acknowledgment of a *full, perfect, and sufficient sacrifice, oblation and satisfaction for the sins of the whole world?* Are you not cheating us in saying you will strike out certain offensive lines, when your services from beginning to end are redolent of the same offence?"

Such must be the feeling of a Dissenter, Mr. Maurice thinks, arguing the question from without. He cannot believe that it is a dispute about a word which may have a dozen different significations. " It is nothing less than a question *how we are to think of children, of grown men of the human race; on what ground we are to place our education of children, our appeals to the consciences of Englishmen* who do or do not frequent our Churches, *our missions to the nations of the earth.*" Mr. Maurice goes on to say, that " he dare not urge the Dissenter to think less seriously than he does of the error and sin we have committed, *if our hypothesis is wrong.*" His reason is, " For then I believe that when he comes into our Churches and joins in our worship—however much natural revolting it may cause him at first—he will begin to ask himself whether *the hypothesis* may not be right?" The way in which "the hypothesis" is brought out,—in which, as felt and apprehended by the Dissenter from the impression made upon him by the Liturgy, it is explained and put forth,—is on this wise :—" There is a kind of universality in the petitions, which appears to him very strange, and somehow—opposed as it is to his habitual notions—very attractive. 'May it not be true,' [he is supposed to say,] ' that the God who made heaven and earth *is really claiming* all the persons in this crowd, who are gathered about me, as His children?   I should like to think so, wrong as it would be.   If I *could* think so, much that I read in the Bible would certainly look a little plainer.   I should be able to take the words literally about a kingdom of heaven having come to men. . . . . Is not the old Jewish doctrine, that his nation was a righteous society, and that the unrighteous members of it, however numerous, must be looked upon as departing from their true state, a doctrine which commends itself to reason, and which explains the course of the Old Testament history?   Is not the doctrine which some find in the New Testament, of *a human family redeemed in the Son of Man,* that which justifies it for each particular nation?   Does not the Prayer-Book embody this, and apply it directly to our own land?' "

The idea which runs through these passages is set forth again and again in many others.   " If you take away from us the right to speak *to our countrymen* as members of a Divine family ; if you tell us, that at any rate you must hold that only as a pious opinion ; we shall inflict upon you all our stupid talk about regeneration ; we shall treat that word as one of life and death ; we shall try to force as many as we can into harmony with our notions upon it. Such reasonings and such attempts do infinite harm.   They produce a general sensation in practical English minds, of indifference and disgust, as if we had nothing to tell men which concerned their business and bosoms, but would only argue about terms and definitions. . . . . The Gorham controversy was a curse to the land . . . . . the decision was a blessing; . . . . but it left the Liturgy as it was, to be interpreted as men could conscientiously interpret it. If you alter it in a certain sense, if you hinder us from teaching children and men as we have been wont to teach them, you open that sore again, and drive us back to our scholastic talk." " If our sermons were more in accordance with the Prayer-Book; if we did address *men* as sons of God, and tell them *what right they have* to call themselves so—why they have no right to call themselves by any lower name ; Dissenters would not be listening to a thrice-told tale; our words would have the force and charm of freshness, old as they are; they would meet a want in their minds which had not been met. To reform the Liturgy according to the standard of the sermons, would be Mr. Taylor's scheme of reformation. *To reform the sermons according to the standard of the Liturgy would be mine.*"

Such are the expressions, or some of them, in Mr. Maurice's article, which most powerfully arrest our attention. We are not sure that we quite understand their exact import. What is really meant by the " hypothesis " to which Mr. Maurice refers? Whatever it be, it is emphatically, it seems, the hypothesis of the Church of England : it is something quite foreign to Dissenting conceptions ;—thought to be wrong, but, hearing the Liturgy, and being subdued by it, the Dissenter is so affected as to be led into deep searchings of heart ; he begins to suspect himself, to doubt, to inquire—" after all, *may* not the hypothesis be right ? " What, then, *is* this hypothesis ?

If we understand the meaning of Mr. Maurice's words as lying before us in the foregoing extracts, the hypothesis itself, with some of its immediate practical issues, might be exhibited in this way :—" Men, as men, are the sons of God, because humanity was redeemed in the Son of Man ; the race being thus all claimed by God as His children, any particular portion of them, existing as a nation, is a

Divine family; children, therefore, are to be told that they are God's children, and on this their education is to be based; men are to be addressed as the sons of God—they have a right to call themselves so, no right to call themselves anything else. This ground is to be taken in addressing our countrymen as such, in appealing to the consciences of Englishmen, whether they attend Church or not; and on this ground are to be placed missions to the nations of the earth. On this hypothesis of a human family redeemed in the Son of Man, which now justifies for each particular nation, the world over, a position like that of the Jewish formerly, any number of persons have a ground for uniting in worship; using the Lord's Prayer; being called dearly beloved brethren; addressing God as a merciful Father, who, in Christ, has given promises to mankind; giving Him thanks for the redemption of the world, and joining in the recognition and acknowledgment of a full, perfect, and sufficient sacrifice and oblation for the sins of the whole world. The hypothesis conducts to a solemn, practical issue; the question comes to be nothing less than this—A child—the child of a redeemed humanity —is it a child of the Devil or of God?"

If we have succeeded in rightly apprehending the import of Mr. Maurice's statements, this is what he means—this is the " hypothesis" which he announces and advocates. We may possibly say something about it on another occasion. There is matter in it for much remark :—how far it is scriptural; what is the proportion of truth in it, what of error; in what sense, or in what degree, it may be foreign, or familiar, to the Dissenting mind; on what grounds Dissenters place and conduct a religious education—urge on their countrymen the "claims" of God—believe and rejoice in the redemption of the world—and conduct their missions to the nations of the earth. These topics, however, and many others suggested by the subject, we altogether waive at present. We confine ourselves to one remark. We may be mistaken in what we are about to say; we may be looking at things through a false medium—judging according to educational and inveterate prejudice. We cannot help it, though we try to do so. We can only speak according to the way in which things appear to us from where we stand outside the Church—a standing adopted or retained *because* things did and do so appear. According to our views, impressions, and beliefs, then, right or wrong as they may happen to be, we are constrained to say respecting the foregoing system of opinion, that—it may be the hypothesis of Mr. Maurice, but it is NOT *the hypothesis of the Church of England.*

We do not wish to inflict on our readers any " stupid talk about regeneration ;" but we beg to say that a grave subject is not to be got rid of by an expression like that. Things must be looked at as they really are, not as they are set in the brilliant hues of an eloquent exposition, which so glorifies them as to dazzle the eye of the observer, and which might prevent his noticing the foundation-fact on which everything rests, if he is not observant, especially as of that nothing is said. Mr. Maurice's view of the Liturgy—the *super*-services, if we may so call them—may be touching and beautiful, awakening emotion and winning the heart ; but properly understood (at least, as we think), they are not what he represents,—they do not flow from his parent thought,—they are not the product of *his* " hypothesis." If the Church is to be allowed to explain herself,—if she is to be understood to mean what she says, and is to be believed, —the " hypothesis" on which *she* rests everything is this : —" Forasmuch as all men are conceived and born in sin, none can enter into the kingdom of God except he be regenerate and born anew of water, and of the Holy Ghost." . . . . " This child, being born in sin, and *in the wrath of God*, is now, by the laver of regeneration in baptism, *received into the number of the children of God*, and heirs of everlasting life." Everything in the Prayer-Book is built up from *this;* everything harmonises with it. It appears to us an entirely different thing from Mr. Maurice's redeemed humanity; his *man—mankind*—all, *as such,* God's children; his appeals to the conscience, and missions to the heathen *on that ground.* " We have had the daring to tell our children that they are members of Christ, children of God." No; you have had the daring to tell them that " in baptism they were *made* that!" " If we did but address *men* as sons of God, and tell them *what right* they have to call themselves so." Well, according to the Prayer-Book, their *right* rests on what was done for them by the Church, not simply on Christ's redemption. The whole thing is a great fundamental practical question, it seems, " whether a child is a child of the Devil or of God?" Very true. But what is the answer of the Church to the question? What is *its* " hypothesis?" *This:*—a child, *quoad* child, is "*in the wrath of God;*" a baptized child *has been made* a member of Christ. Mr. Maurice may be very èloquent in describing his own hypothesis as we conceive of it; it is quite capable of being put forth in a manner highly attractive. But whenever he baptises a child, he has to use language which, in our view, is directly in the teeth of all his speculations. Mr. Maurice, we have no doubt, perfectly understands, as he fully believes in, himself. We, however, must confess that we really do not understand him when he says :—" Our baptism is the simplest and fullest witness of a redemption which covers and comprehends those who are not baptised." It may be so; but we do not see it. The Gorham controversy Mr. Maurice " holds was a curse to the land." He deprecates being driven back again into " scholastic talk." He wants to speak to men, not about " terms and definitions," but of " what concerns their business and bosoms." Quite right. But as long as the Prayer-Book remains as it is, especially in respect to the Baptismal " hypothesis," we shall always be in danger of some " stupid talk about regeneration," seeing that there will be men, both in the Church and out of it, who will persist in thinking that what the Prayer-Book actually says and means is of *some* weight in judging of its teaching,—of Church and Dissent, and Liturgical Revision, and kindred things. Without going at present into other topics, we shall close this paper by quoting from an article which appeared ten years ago, when the Gorham controversy was raging, a passage which would seem to have some bearing on the "hypothesis" of the Prayer-Book, and,—as the words of a Dissenter,—some relation, too, to what may be the *Dissenting* hypothesis :—

"The two theories (the Exeter and Gorham theory of baptism) alike proceed on the assumed fact, that in spite of God's 'inestimable love in the redemption of the world by Jesus Christ;' in spite of the mediatorial work of the Redeemer, and the gracious constitution of things in Him, through which humanity is born under mercy, and continually in contact with spiritual influences ; in spite of the declaration of Jesus (in whom we see the Father) in relation to children, that ' of such is the kingdom of heaven ;' in spite of the asserted ' holiness' (whatever sense may be attached to the word) of the offspring of a union where even only *one* of the parents was a Christian ; in spite of the instincts of nature, the authority of the heart, and the Fatherhood of God ; in spite of all this, and far more, the foundation-fact of both theories is, that every babe drops from the womb, and falls into the loving arms of its mother, in a condition, spiritually, *fit for hell !*—that it actually *is* under God's ' wrath' and curse ; and that whatever joy may kindle in the soul, brighten in the eye, and tremble on the tongue —joy, full, infinite, irrepressible—' because a new man is born into the world,' must be dashed and darkened by thoughts of God's wrath, hell, and the Devil, until ' holy baptism,' or ' prevenient grace,' has benevolently interposed, and snatched the guilty but unconscious immortal from the ' terrible pit.' . . . Gloss, disguise, modify, extenuate it, as they may, this is the naked and simple truth ; both parties hold and avow it, and they do so consistently, for the Prayer-Book expressly teaches the doctrine."—*The Great Gorham Case.*

II.

The Rev. F. D. Maurice to the Rev. T. Binney.

5, Russell Square, May 14.

MY DEAR SIR,—A number of the *Patriot* newspaper, containing an article which is signed (in ink) with your name, has been sent to me. I beg to thank you heartily for the kindness with which you have spoken in it of me. I appreciate that kindness the more, because I know how difficult you must have found it to give me credit for an honest purpose, whilst you believed I was straining words, which I professed to value, in a dishonest way. And you had a perfect right to suppose that I was so straining words; I do not see how, looking at the subject from your point of view, you could suppose otherwise. I should scarcely feel myself justified in spending your time in an attempt to remove that impression—for a man's character is, after all, not worth much to any one except himself, and if he cannot trust it to God, he has not much chance of getting it cleared, suppose it were worth anything—but I have a sort of hope that while I am explaining my own thoughts, I may illustrate one or two truths, which are equally important whether I am false or not.

Before I speak of any points in which I differ from the most earnest of the orthodox Dissenters, I should wish to tell you wherein I agree with them. 1. No expressions which any of them (say, for example, Bunyan) have used to describe the evil of man in himself, apart from Christ, seem to me exaggerated. None can go beyond St. Paul's, "*In me, that is, in my flesh, dwelleth no good thing;*" and to that statement, undiluted and unsoftened, my inmost conscience responds. 2. Nothing that they have said about the impossibility of rising out of subjection to this evil nature, except by faith in a Redeemer, seems to me exaggerated. 3. Nothing that they have said—even the most ultra-Calvinistic of them—about the impossibility of exercising this faith, unless there had been a previous calling and adoption of God in Christ and an action of His Spirit seems to me exaggerated. I regard the tendency in our day to substitute a weak, semi-Pelagian theory of human nature for these statements as a dangerous tendency. But I think it is an inevitable one, unless another side of the Pauline doctrine, which has been kept in the back-ground, is brought forth into the same prominence with that side of it to which I have referred. Where this experimental process ends, his Gospel, it seems to me, begins. He starts from the will of a righteous God, not from the sin of a rebellious man. He sets forth that will as perfectly manifested in Jesus Christ, the Son of God. 'He sets forth Christ as the true Head of every man,—who has been made of a woman, made under a law, that He might redeem them who were under the law, and give them the adoption of sons. He sets forth the Spirit as coming forth to claim men as spiritual creatures, to convince them of their sin against the Father, to convince them of the righteousness they have in Christ, to convince them of the judgment which shall separate righteousness and evil for ever. This state of redemption, this state of the new birth, this state in the Son of God, he proclaims, it seems to me, as our true human state; the departure from this as the inhuman, anomalous, monstrous condition, into which each man must sink, who will follow nature instead of living under grace; into which each of us does fall and feel himself at every moment tempted to fall; but which is not the true state of any man whatsoever, and which men are to be told is not their true state.

To proclaim the kingdom of God, the kingdom of the Father, the Son, and the Spirit, to announce this name as that great and holy and loving name, of which all partial names of God, so far as they have presented Him as good and gracious have been aspects, so far as they have been dark and evil have been contradictions; to tell men that they are living, moving, having their being in this God, that He is not far from any one of them, that He is seeking to embrace them in His covenant of mercy and love; to declare that to resist Him and to follow our own evil nature, to suppose ourselves merely citizens of this earth, to set up a false and dark power instead of Him, is to destroy ourselves; to set forth the wonderful Atonement of mankind to God in Christ, how He reconciled this world to Himself in His Son, not imputing their trespasses unto them; to declare how every day He puts away sins, and brings back man to Himself,—this I hold to be the function of the Christian preacher, whether he is speaking to the members of his own nation, or to the heathens.

Now, baptism into the name of the Father, the Son, and the Holy Ghost has been, as I hold, the great witness and assurance of this kingdom to men. Claiming it for themselves and their children, they claim that men shall be regarded, not as they are after the flesh, not as they are outside of God, but as they are redeemed, justified, adopted by God in His well-beloved Son. That which is the true, human, reasonable state, the state which God has intended for them, they assert as theirs; they solemnly renounce the world, the flesh and the Devil, as not their masters, but as powers which are striving with them, and with which they must have not a less but a more deadly conflict, because they have claimed to be members of Christ, and children of God, and heirs of the kingdom of heaven.

Now I find a Society in my land which teaches that men, being by nature born in sin, and heirs of wrath, are in baptism made children of grace. I find it telling the poorest sons and daughters of this land that they have received a name which assures them that they have been made in baptism members of Christ, children of God, heirs of the kingdom of heaven. I find it grounding its education upon this announcement, and upon the fact consequent upon this, that the child will all its life through have to maintain a conflict with the world, the flesh and the Devil. Certainly, at the first look, there is something here which corresponds to that lesson which I think I have been learning from the Bible. Here is a state—not a natural, fleshly, animal state, but a spiritual state, affirmed to be the state on which our life is grounded. But I am told "it is impossible *you* can accept those words; for *you* say that men as men are redeemed by Christ, that men are claimed as members of Christ, and children of God; whereas *here* we are told those who are naturally sinful are in baptism made children of grace." I have admitted that to *you* (as a Dissenter) this contradiction must seem as of the grossest kind. For you have been wont to start from the notion of men as merely natural creatures ; to assume, that certain men are raised by faith out of the natural condition, and that those who are made saints are brought into a condition altogether different from that which belongs to ordinary men. You have another thought which struggles with this in your mind, which oftentimes becomes uppermost. You tell people that they are doing a strange, monstrous thing in not believing, in not claiming their rights as children of God. You tell them this, even though you know, or think you know, they are not leading godly lives. You tell it them because they are not leading godly lives. But theologically your habit and tradition would lead you to speak the other language. Now, surely, if I have been led deliberately and by the strongest conviction to assume the ground constantly which you assume occasionally—if I must always speak to every man as having the rights of a citizen of the kingdom of God—knowing at the same time that he, like me, has in himself, that is, in his flesh, no good thing; that he, like me, so far as he separates himself from God— so far as he stands upon his own notions—only does and thinks what is not good—such words *cannot* involve a contradiction for me. Living in this day when the habit of contemplating mankind from this evil ground has become so general,—when consequently the words seem to numbers as if they intimated that a certain ceremony, by a magical process, translates an evil thing into a good,—I more commonly talk of baptism as *affirming* or *declaring* men to be sons of God. Probably, if left to my own fancy, I might have put these words into the Catechism. But I solemnly believe that they would, on the whole, convey less truth, and deliver from less falsehood than the words which I have not chosen, and which have been given me. Those import more distinctly that our spiritual state is distinct from our natural or fleshly state; that one is opposed to the other; that the spiritual state is that into which God adopts us; that it is as spiritual beings that we are sons of God.

If the words are open to the interpretation you put upon them, so are the words of Scripture from which they are derived. If people do put that interpretation upon them, I appeal to the context of the Catechism for the refutation of it. If a child is made from a bad thing into a good by the act of baptism, what means the conflict into which it is told that it has entered, and in which it must be engaged all its life through? What has this transmuted thing to do with a conflict? Does not this imply that it carries within it just the same nature as every heathen carries about with him? And if you say, "Yes, but not that it is raised to a state which may be proclaimed to all heathens as their state;" then I refer you to the exposition of the creed in the Catechism. Why is Christ said to have redeemed me and all mankind, if this is not so? Am not I, a poor, miserable, individual beggar, taken into that glorious condition of *mankind?* Has not Christ claimed me, not as a separate creature, but as one of a race of which He is the Head? (*The Head of every man is Christ*, are not *my* words, not the expression of *my* " hypothesis," or *my* " crotchet.") I appeal to the Catechism against those who would pervert the Catechism. I say it does not attempt to limit the Father, the Son, and the Holy Ghost. It does announce a covenant of which baptism is the blessed sign and witness, but which no ceremony can define; which is higher than heaven, deeper than hell.

If you say to me, " But if the words are open to this misconception, why not alter the words?" My answer in part has been given already. I know no words which are not liable to misconception. Those which I could imagine for myself I believe would be liable to more misconception than those which I should abandon. I add now: If these words are taken in that very grovelling, narrow sense which you suppose, it is needful to bear testimony that this is not the sense which has upheld the faith and the national life of generations of Englishmen; that there must have been another deeper than that, however it may have been encrusted with sectarian notions and opinions. If it is true that there is only a " misty," "muddy" thinker, like me —a person who has a very wicked meaning but does not well understand it himself—to bear this testimony, I am sure that God will raise up some to bear it who are not misty or muddy, whose meaning is not wicked, and who do understand it themselves. And I feel this necessity the more, because this controversy and even, if I may venture to say so, your own article, interesting and able as it is, leaves the impression upon my mind that there is a craving abroad for some statement on this subject which shall admit the Fatherhood of God, *in a certain sense*, but not in the sense in which alone it seems to me to have any practical worth, or to be connected with the revelation of Jesus Christ; as if we were God's children, because we are His creatures; as if we were His children, and yet not members of Jesus Christ, not subjects of the teaching of His Spirit. These middle senses, or half senses, I dread more than I can express. I am sure they destroy the strength of each of the parties which they try to reconcile, and, after all, form no real bond between them, rather an excuse for perpetual discontent and repulsion. I think I long for unity as much as most men ; but it must be unity which involves no sacrifice of my opponent's convictions any more than my own ; which does not reduce the acid and the alkali to a neutral salt, but retains each in its fullest vigour. When I speak of the name of the Father, the Son, and the Holy Ghost, the one God blessed for ever, I speak of that which I believe contains the secret and pledge of all unity. I wish to force the profession of that Name on no man. I wish that every one should state all the difficulties which he finds in receiving it, or any doctrine or fact which is connected with it; I wish that each man should express just as much as he can express, and no more. And then I feel confident that the everlasting unity which is embracing him and me, will more and more reveal itself to him, and to me, and to all of us. I am afraid of no discussion, no opposition. I am only afraid of substituting material interests for moral, an Establishment for a National Church, a dead compromise for a living fellowship.

I have addressed these words to you, not to the editors of the *Patriot*, because I am not in the habit of writing to religious newspapers of any school. I should expect quite as much courtesy from the Dissenting journal as from any of those which represent High Church, Low Church, or (if there be such a ridiculous anomaly) Broad Church parties. But I have not the least objection that you should make any use of my words which you think fitting. I have said nothing which I wish to conceal. The *Patriot* and the *Guardian* are quite right that in their sense of the word I have no " following ;" if the words I speak have no force in themselves, they will gain only weakness from their association with my name. Nevertheless, I always do associate them with my name, because they are unpopular, and because it is not good for any man to shrink from unpopularity, or to pass off his opinions for more than they are worth by pretending that they belong to any one but himself.

Believe me, my dear Sir, very respectfully yours,

F. D. MAURICE.

No one can read this letter without being interested by the warmth of heart displayed in it, or without being impressed by the manifest sincerity and earnestness of the writer. It is most obvious that he is deeply convinced not only of the truth, but of the importance of his views; and that to himself it is logically demonstrable not only that they may be allowed in one using the Offices of the Prayer-Book, but that they are the just and proper interpretation of its teaching. For myself, I beg to say, that I hold Mr. Maurice, and have always held him, to be perfectly conscientious and upright in all he says. I have no " difficulty in giving him credit for an honest purpose." I don't believe that he seeks to " strain " anything " in a dishonest way;" or has any " wicked meaning " under-lying his words. At the same time, I candidly acknow-ledge that, while thus entertaining, and feeling myself at liberty to express, the highest moral estimate of Mr. Maurice, my mind is so constituted, logically, that very often I cannot see the connexion between his premises and his conclusions, and many a time have inwardly to confess that I am *not* satisfied, even when he seems most fully to have satisfied himself.

It is not my intention at present to enter into all the questions opened or suggested by the foregoing letter. That which alone authorises the insertion in this book either of it or of the paper which precedes it, is its connexion with the question of Liturgical Reform; and the only thing

to be looked at *here* is the one point which is raised
in my remarks, and met by Mr. Maurice. Whether "the
hypothesis," or theological system, call it what you please,
which Mr. Maurice advocates, is Pauline and Scriptural,—
whether it be true that Humanity is redeemed in Christ *in
such a sense* that men universally are born justified, adopted,
and so on,—is not the question. The real and only
question between Mr. Maurice and myself is, whether this
hypothesis is that of the Prayer-Book,—that on which its
Offices are based, on which they proceed, and by which
they are to be explained? Allowing Mr. Maurice's exposition of the spiritual condition of humanity to be correct,
and that baptism, properly understood, is the "affirming"
and "declaring" what men *are*, the question still returns—
Is that what the Prayer-Book says and means? Is it its
intention to express that, when it says, "this child being
born in sin, and in the wrath of God, is, *now*—by the laver
of regeneration in baptism—*received* into the number of the
children of God?" The doctrine of pre-baptismal regeneration may be often met with, as in the sermons of the late
Mr. Robertson of Brighton, who likens baptism to a coro-
nation—the ceremony not making a man a king, but only
recognizing and declaring the fact that he is one already.
I have reason to think that these views are being adopted
by some of the younger clergy. They may be perfectly
just and scriptural, but the question is, are they those of
the Church of the Prayer-Book? I enter into no further
argument on this point. I submit it to the judgment of
the reader, and leave him to say how far Mr. Maurice meets
and disposes of *the one thing* with which I dealt. Many
of his observations and statements respecting it might call
for remark, but I prefer leaving myself and him, as represented by our respective papers, in the hands of those

who may care to look into this book and this post-
script.

With respect to what I must be allowed to regard as Mr.
Maurice's " hypothesis," or system, I may say, as I have
already said, that there is doubtless much in it worthy of
serious consideration. It certainly *is* a question of great practical moment, whether a child is the child of the Devil or of
God? Believing, as is expressed in the extract with which
my paper concludes, that the gracious constitution of things
in Christ is such that "humanity is born under mercy and
continually in contact with spiritual influences," I have
always felt repelled by the Prayer-Book *because* of its being
based—as it seemed to me to be in its primary or baptismal
office—on the wrath-and-devil hypothesis, not on the
redemptive and the divine . . . It is an important practical
matter, also, on what principle the education of children
is to be conducted,—a question of very difficult solution
indeed on the hypothesis that what may be called the
natural history of the rise and progress of the religious
life in an adult gentile of the apostolic age, must be
experienced, as to its successive stages, in exactly the same
order of development, in those born of Christian parents
and "brought up in the nurture and admonition of the
Lord."* . . . It is also true, as Mr. Maurice hints, that there
is a craving abroad for some definite conception of the
Fatherhood of God,—something which shall not be an un-
reality and a mockery. These and several other matters
touched upon in Mr. Maurice's letter open questions of
grave importance, on which much might be said if this
were the proper place. I have occasionally spoken on
some of them, and may again,—*here* I am precluded from

* EDUCATION: Two Addresses delivered at Mill Hill School by the
Author.

attempting it. Other and more appropriate occasions will, I dare say, occur; and if not, there will be nothing to regret, for many are speaking, and many will be led to speak, on these great questions, who are able to do so far better than I.

GEORGE UNWIN, GRESHAM STEAM PRESS, BUCKLERSBURY, LONDON, E.C.

WORKS BY THE SAME AUTHOR.

Third Edition, printed in antique type, cloth extra, red edges, crown 8vo.,
price 5s.,
THE PRACTICAL POWER OF FAITH,
Illustrated in a Series of Discourses on Part of the 11th Chapter of the
Epistle to the Hebrews.

Thirteenth Edition, in crown 8vo., 2s. 6d.,
IS IT POSSIBLE TO MAKE THE BEST OF BOTH WORLDS?
A Book for Young Men.

Second Edition, in crown 8vo., price 2s., cloth,
SIR THOMAS FOWELL BUXTON, BART., A STUDY FOR YOUNG MEN.
THE WIFE; or, a Mirror for Maidenhood.   A Sketch.

In foolscap 8vo., price 2s. 6d., cloth lettered,
THE GREAT GORHAM CASE:
A History in Five Books, including Expositions of the Rival Baptismal
Theories.

In 8vo., price 1s. 6d., cloth limp,
EDUCATION.
Home Education.   Public Schools.   Secular Education.   Classical
Learning. Religious Education. Address to Boys. The School and
the Church. Modern Wants. Boarding Schools. Day Schools.
Development of the Religious Affections. Analogy between the
Boy's School-Life and the Man's World-Life. The *Spirit* of the
Moral Teacher, &c., &c.

Third Edition, 8vo., price 1s.,
RIGHTEOUSNESS EXALTETH A NATION.

In foolscap 8vo., price 3s. 6d., cloth,
TOWER CHURCH SERMONS.
Discourses preached in the Tower Church, Belvedere, Erith, Kent.
By the Rev. A. Monod, Paris; the Rev. Dr. Krummacher, Berlin;
the Rev. T. Binney, London. Edited by T. Binney.

*** This Volume contains Two Discourses by the Editor entitled respectively, "The Law our Schoolmaster;" and " Salvation by Fire,
and Salvation in Fulness."

In foolscap 8vo., price 4s. 6d., cloth,
FOUR DISCOURSES.
The Ultimate Design of the Christian Ministry.
The Christian Ministry not a Priesthood.
The Closet and the Church.
The Service of Song in the House of the Lord.

The above may be had in Three Parts, viz.: the first two Discourses in
one volume, 2s.; the third, 1s. 6d.; the fourth, 2s., cloth.

LONDON: JACKSON & WALFORD, ST. PAUL'S CHURCHYARD.

In post 8vo., price 7s. 6d., cloth,
PSYCHOLOGY AND THEOLOGY;
Or, Psychology applied to the Investigation of Questions relating to Religion, Natural Theology, and Revelation. By RICHARD ALLIOTT, LL.D.

"It is in every sense a first-class work."—*Homilist.*

In foolscap 8vo., price 5s., cloth antique, red edges,
THE CHRISTIAN HARP.
A Companion to "The Foreign Sacred Lyre." By JOHN SHEPPARD, Author of "Thoughts on Private Devotion," &c.

"Few volumes which Mr. Sheppard has published will be preferred to the one now before us. The light and pleasing play of fancy, the refined and delicate taste, the pure elevated tone of sentiment, and the chastened piety, which are so conspicuous in all his productions, give a peculiar charm to this collection of minor poems."—*Baptist Magazine.*

Also in foolscap 8vo., price 5s. 6d., cloth antique, red edges,
THE FOREIGN SACRED LYRE.
Metrical Versions of Religious Poetry, from the German, French, and Italian, together with the Original Pieces.

BY THE SAME AUTHOR.

I.

In foolscap 8vo., price 5s., cloth,
PRAYERS: CHIEFLY ADAPTED FOR TIMES AND OCCASIONS OF PERSONAL TRIAL.
"This volume bears the marks of a devout, earnest, practical, and highly cultivated mind. The train of thought, as well as the style of language, is fresh and striking."—*United Presbyterian Magazine.*

II.

Second Edition, in foolscap 8vo., price 4s., cloth,
THE RE-UNION AND RECOGNITION OF CHRISTIANS IN THE LIFE TO COME.
The Right Love of Creatures and of the Creator. Christian Conversation. In Three Essays.

III.

In 18mo., Illustrated with Twelve Wood Engravings, price 3s., cloth,
ON TREES, THEIR USES AND BIOGRAPHY.

IV.

In 18mo., price 2s. 6d., cloth,
ON DREAMS, IN THEIR MENTAL AND MORAL ASPECTS,
As affording auxiliary arguments for the Existence of Spirit, for a "Separate State," and for a Particular Providence. In Two Essays.

V.

Second Edition, in 18mo., price 5s., cloth,
AN AUTUMN DREAM:
Thoughts in Verse, on the Intermediate State of Happy Spirits. To which are appended, Collections, from various Authors, on the "Separate State," and on the Immateriality of Mind; with a Dissertation concerning the Mind of the Lower Animals.

VI.

In 8vo., price 2s., sewed,
A LECTURE ON THE ARGUMENTS FOR CHRISTIAN THEISM,
From Organized Life and Fossil Osteology. Containing Remarks on "Vestiges of the Natural History of Creation."

London: JACKSON & WALFORD, 18, St. Paul's Churchyard.

In foolscap 8vo., price 2s. 6d., boards,

JOHN HOWARD : A MEMOIR.

By HEPWORTH DIXON.   A cheap and revised edition, for general circulation.

"A work ably executed, and deserving of the wide circulation it has obtained."—*Examiner.*

In foolscap 8vo., price 1s. 6d., cloth limp,

ART : ITS SCOPE AND PURPOSE; OR, A BRIEF EXPOSITION OF ITS PRINCIPLES.

A Lecture delivered at a Mechanics' Institution (with subsequent additions).   By JOSIAH GILBERT.

"This is a very pleasant essay on Art, written with much feeling and eloquence, and enumerating some very important principles. We heartily recommend it to our readers."—*British Quarterly Review.*

"It is a lecture by an artist, not technical, all about oils and washes, but on the catholic subject of the province and powers of Art .... always enthusiastic and vigorous."—*Athenæum.*

Eleventh Edition, in royal 18mo., price 4s., cloth,

SELECT ENGLISH POETRY: DESIGNED FOR THE USE OF SCHOOLS AND YOUNG PERSONS IN GENERAL.

Edited by the late Dr. ALLEN.

" We can confidently recommend it for young persons in general, as calculated to promote the cultivation of poetical taste and an acquaintance with the different styles of many of our English poets."—*English Journal of Education.*

Twelfth Edition, with Vignette Title, in foolscap 8vo., price 5s., cloth,

THE CONTRIBUTIONS OF Q. Q.

By JANE TAYLOR.

"It is a work which cannot be too highly praised."—*Quarterly Review.*

"That clever little book."—*Times.*

Forty-fifth Edition, in 18mo., price 1s. 6d. cloth, lettered,

HYMNS FOR INFANT MINDS.

By ANN and JANE TAYLOR, authors of "Original Poems," "Rhymes for the Nursery," &c.

BY THE SAME AUTHORS.

New Stereotype Edition, price 2d. sewed, or 14s. per 100,

ORIGINAL HYMNS FOR SUNDAY SCHOOLS.

In square 18mo., price 6d. sewed,

A CHILD'S WALK THROUGH THE YEAR.

With Preface by Mrs. GILBERT.

"The book will form an excellent present for little folks just beginning to read."—*Patriot.*

In 8vo., with Portrait, price 12s. 6d. cloth,

MEMOIRS OF THE LIFE AND WRITINGS OF JOHN PYE SMITH, D.D., LL.D., &c.

By JOHN MEDWAY.

" His life constitutes a lecture, or an essay upon practical wisdom. We consider it a valuable addition to our biographical literature."—*Christian Witness.*

" We think he (the biographer) has produced one of the best of modern biographies."—*United Presbyterian Magazine.*

London: JACKSON & WALFORD, 18, St. Paul's Churchyard.

In post 8vo., price 2s. 6d., cloth limp,

THE APOCALYPSE OF SAINT JOHN:

A new translation, metrically arranged, with Scripture illustrations. By the Rev. JOHN H. GODWIN, Professor of New College, London.

"Let any one carefully read this valuable introduction of only six pages, and the five following books of translation, and we are persuaded that he will rise from the perusal with a clearer insight into the meaning and design of the divine book, and with a holier admiration of its historical predictions, relative to the advocates and the adversaries of the Christian Church down to the end of time."—*Evangelical Magazine.*

In foolscap 8vo., price 3s. cloth,

AUTOBIOGRAPHY OF THE REV. W. WALFORD,

Late Classical and Hebrew Tutor in the College at Homerton. Edited (with a Continuation) by JOHN STOUGHTON.

"This is a book singularly interesting, instructive, and affecting to the heart."—*Evangelical Magazine.*

"This is a most valuable piece of biography, particularly so to the psychologist, and all interested in the workings of a mind under the influence of disease."—*Winslow's Psychological Journal.*

In foolscap 8vo., price 2s. 6d. cloth,

CURÆ ROMANÆ: NOTES ON THE EPISTLE TO THE ROMANS.

With a Revised Translation. By W. WALFORD.

"We have never read a Commentary on the Epistle to the Romans in which we have found so much to approve and so little to which to object."—*British Quarterly Review.*

In foolscap 8vo., price 2s. 6d., sewed, a revised and cheaper Edition of

THE AGE AND CHRISTIANITY.

By R. VAUGHAN, D.D.

Second Edition, in 18mo., price 2s. cloth.

OBJECTIONS TO THE DOCTRINE OF ISRAEL'S FUTURE RE-STORATION TO PALESTINE, NATIONAL PRE-EMINENCE, &c.

With an Appendix on the Ten Tribes, and the Future Destinies of the World and the Church. By EDWARD SWAINE.

"We wish all writers on this subject would imitate the Christian spirit of the author of this volume. We have read it with pleasure and profit, although dissenting *in toto* from its conclusions."—*Quarterly Journal of Prophecy.*

IN THE PRESS.

In One large Volume, 8vo., a Second and Revised Edition of

FIRST LINES OF CHRISTIAN THEOLOGY.

By JOHN PYE SMITH, D.D., LL.D., F.R.S., F.G.S. Edited from the Author's MSS., with additional Notes and References, and Copious Indexes. By WILLIAM FARRER, LL.B., Secretary and Librarian of New College, London.

London: JACKSON & WALFORD, 18, St. Paul's Churchyard.

FOR GENERAL CIRCULATION.

In 18mo., price 3d., or 2s. 6d. per dozen,

SECRET PRAYER.

By the Rev. CHARLES STANFORD, author of "Power in Weakness:
Memorials of the Rev. William Rhodes," &c., &c.

"A tender and touching appeal."—*Freeman.*

BY THE SAME AUTHOR.

Fourth Edition, 18mo., price 6d., cloth limp,

FRIENDSHIP WITH GOD.

". . . Rich with consoling and ennobling sentiments."—*English Presbyterian
Messenger.*

Imperial 32mo., price 3d., or 2s. 6d. per dozen,

IMPUTED RIGHTEOUSNESS.

By the Rev. EDWARD STEANE, D.D.

BY THE SAME AUTHOR.

I.

Imperial 32mo., price 2d., or 14s. per 100,

THE GREAT TRANSACTION.

" A short, well-written tract, on an important subject. The text or motto is taken from
2 Chron. xxx. 8: 'Yield yourselves unto the Lord, and enter into His sanctuary;' and
with much force the writer applies the Old Testament saying to New Testament truth,
appealing earnestly and affectionately to the unconverted on the necessity of self-
surrender."— *Bible Readers' Journal.*

"We heartily recommend it to our readers for wide circulation."— *The Freeman.*

II.

Fifth Edition, 32mo., price 6d., cloth limp, gilt edges,

PRAYER THE CHRISTIAN'S HELP IN TROUBLE.

III.

Uniform with the above, price 6d.,

BEREAVED PARENTS COMFORTED UNDER THE LOSS OF PIOUS CHILDREN AND INFANTS.

Third and Cheaper Edition, in foolscap 8vo., with illuminated wrapper,
price 6d. sewed,

THE CHRISTIAN PHILANTHROPIST. A MEMORIAL OF JOHN HOWARD.

By Rev. JOHN STOUGHTON.

" One of the best outlines of a life we ever met with—crammed with facts; those facts
grouped intelligibly and effectively, and the impression a *whole* and striking one."—
Nonconformist.

In 18mo., price 4d., or 3s. 6d. per dozen,

A CATECHISM OF CHRISTIAN EVIDENCES, TRUTHS, AND DUTIES.

By Rev. W. WALFORD, author of "Curæ Romanæ," &c., &c.

"Clear, correct, very comprehensive, and adapted to be exceedingly useful."—*Christian
Witness.*

London: JACKSON & WALFORD, 18, St. Paul's Churchyard.